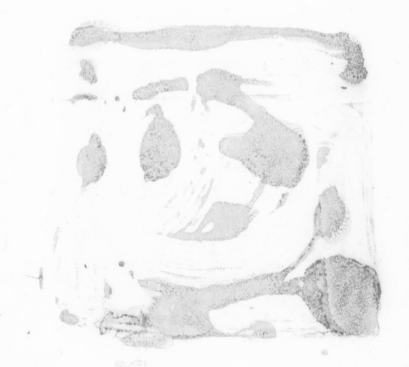

JACOB N. CARDOZO

ECONOMIC THOUGHT IN THE ANTEBELLUM SOUTH

No. 608 in
Columbia Studies in the Social Sciences
Edited by the Faculty of Political Science
of Columbia University

JACOB N. CARDOZO

ECONOMIC THOUGHT
IN THE ANTEBELLUM SOUTH

Melvin M. Leiman

1966

Columbia University Press

NEW YORK & LONDON

Melvin M. Leiman is Assistant Professor of Economics at Harpur College, State University of New York at Binghamton.

The Columbia Studies in the Social Sciences (formerly the Studies in History, Economics, and Public Law) is a series edited by the Faculty of Political Science of Columbia University for the purpose of making available scholarly studies produced within the Faculty

Copyright © 1966
Library of Congress Catalog Card Number: 66-27478
Printed in the United States of America

Acknowledgments

3/67 C+H 7.50

I WISH to acknowledge the encouragement and advice I received from Professor Joseph Dorfman at many stages of my research and writing. His monumental study, *The Economic Mind in American Civilization,* is a necessary starting point for all research in American economic thought. I also wish to thank Professors Robert Cross and Carter Goodrich for their many insightful suggestions. They helped me to clarify several obscurities and ambiguities.

A note of special thanks is due to Marian Maury for her thorough and skillful editing. The improved readability is largely a product of her patient efforts.

And I am most grateful to Harpur College for its generous financial assistance in making this study possible.

MELVIN M. LEIMAN

Binghamton, New York
July, 1966

Contents

ONE

Sources of Cardozo's Thought

J A C O B   N U Ñ E Z Cardozo, a Southern journalist-econo-mist who wrote from approximately 1817 to 1873, be-longs to that extensive group of able but neglected authors of the early American scene. Although overshadowed by their European contemporaries in reputation, volume of output, and refinement of writing, they revealed keen in-sights into the laws of political economy by skillfully ques-tioning many basic postulates of the classical political economy, such as the law of diminishing returns, the labor theory of value, the inverse wage-profit relationship, Mal-thusian population theory, differential rent theory, and Say's Law, against a unique American environment.

It is useful to examine briefly the general intellectual context of early American economic thought in order to evaluate Cardozo's contributions more accurately.

The European influence was paramount. By the 1820s,

editions of the works of Adam Smith, Ricardo, Malthus, Say, and others had been printed in the United States. European journals were read and commented on with considerable acumen by the new corps of American "social scientists."

Essentially two different streams of thought made their presence felt in America. Both developed out of, or in reaction to, a Smithian model; one started with Ricardo, the other with Lauderdale.[1] The former, with minor refinements, reached its most developed stage with the work of J. S. Mill. The latter benefited from critical refinements by Malthus. The Ricardo-Mill tradition, later enriched by Marshall's creative additions, became the dominant school of political economy. This group has been referred to as the classical school, and the Lauderdale-Malthus group has been called the anticlassical or anti-Ricardian group.[2] The main point of deviation of the anticlassicists from the classicists concerns their emphasis on aggregate demand, and the view that increases in saving and capital accumulation may be disadvantageous. A secondary distinction was their greater tendency to qualify or reject the labor theory of value.

Neither classical nor anticlassical thought should be viewed as a monolithic structure. Although broad lines of

[1] The Earl of Lauderdale (James Maitland), a Scottish lawyer, studied under John Millar, a Professor of Law at the University of Glasgow. He served in the House of Commons from 1780 to 1789 and subsequently in the House of Lords. A Tory after 1820, he had started his political career as an associate of Charles Fox, the liberal Whig leader. Lauderdale opposed virtually every reform measure introduced to the Parliament. See the *Dictionary of National Biography*, pp. 799–801, under "Maitland." Lauderdale's main work, *An Inquiry into the Nature and Origin of Public Wealth and into the Means and Causes of Its Increase*, first appeared in 1804. It was essentially a critique of Adam Smith's doctrines. A second edition was published in 1819.

[2] The inclusion of Malthus in the anticlassical grouping should not obscure the act that although pronounced differences existed between Malthus and the classicists, the latter were strongly Malthusian in terms of their

agreement did exist, there were also significant differences within the ranks of both groups. These internal differences, however, were considerably less than those between the two schools. The dividing line between the groups is neither distinct nor consistent; a common feature was their acceptance of the beneficence of private property and the wages-profit system.

American economic thought evolved from these two divergent intellectual strands in response to the unique experience confronting the United States. Important sectional influences—the agrarian nature of the Southern economy and the growing commercialism of the Northern economy—tended to result in the development of different patterns of economic thought.[3]

Early economic thought in the North revealed considerably more anti-Ricardian sentiment than in the South. The reason was related more to policy than to theoretical considerations. Because of its rapid development as a commercial and manufacturing area, the North had a sectional interest in maintaining a high protective tariff. This provided an inducement for rejecting Ricardo's free trade policies [4] and for questioning the analytical apparatus which lay behind these policies. The South, of course, felt an opposing sectional interest, which may help to explain why "A general tendency existed in the old South to accept at

---

"Law of Population." Moreover, Malthus' general acceptance of Ricardian rent theory and his partial acceptance of a variant of the labor theory of value indicate some prominent points of agreement with the classical tradition.

[3] Edwin R. A. Seligman, in "The Development of Economic Thought in America," *Economic Forum*, I, No. 4 (Fall, 1933), 347–48, stated that "Up to the Civil War, American economic theory was divided on almost geographical lines between the nationalist reaction in the North and the traditional doctrine of the South, where there was to be found the one point in common between a slave-holding society and the British capitalist economy-dependence on a foreign market."

[4] There was a small but vocal Northern group that supported free trade.

least the approach of classicism." [5] Cardozo's subtle questioning of the Ricardian analytical model, at the same time that he accepted most of its policy conclusions, sets him apart as a unique figure worthy of detailed study.

Jacob Cardozo's father, David, was one of six children of a London merchant, Aaron Cardozo, who immigrated to New York in 1752. The family was of Sephardic Jewish extraction. David went to South Carolina, fought with the American forces against the British during the Revolutionary War, and raised a family of five children, including Jacob Cardozo.[6]

Cardozo's formal schooling was terminated when he was twelve, and he worked as an apprentice in the mechanical trades and as a lumber clerk before becoming editor of the Charleston *Southern Patriot* on May 19, 1817. He became the owner on March 10, 1823, serving as editor and publisher until April 10, 1845. In 1842 Cardozo took on a partner, Martin Munro, to whom he had become indebted. A bitter dispute developed over monetary matters, in the course of which Cardozo lost ownership of the paper.[7] In his last issue of the newspaper, Cardozo stated that any editor who was not a true exponent of the public senti-

---

The most prominent members were Reverend John McVickar and Condy Raguet. See Joseph Dorfman, *The Economic Mind in American Civilization*, II, 516–22, 602–3.

[5] Michael O'Connor, *Origins of Academic Economics in the United States*, p. 40. Cardozo represents a partial exception to this statement.

[6] Biographical material is in the *Record of Wills* (Charleston County, South Carolina, 1834–1839), Book A, XL, pp. 272–76, cited by Abram Flora, "Jacob N. Cardozo, 1786–1873: South Carolina Economist" (unpublished master's thesis, University of South Carolina, 1949). Also see Barnett Elzas, *Jews of South Carolina* (Philadelphia, Lippincott, 1905), pp. 176–79.

[7] Cardozo claimed that Munro was not adequately performing his function as a business manager because he made deposits of bills he collected at irregular intervals. He claimed that he was wronged by Munro who "payed in no capital and took out half the profits." *Southern Patriot* (Charleston), January 3, 14, 1845. An arbitration award forced Cardozo to sell his interest for $5.00. *Miscellaneous Records* (Columbia, South Carolina, South Carolina Historical Commission, 1943), AAAAAA, p. 346, cited by Flora, p. 7.

ment would suffer financially; "slavery of the spirit . . .
wars with intellectual independence." [8]

By October 1, 1845 Cardozo had started another newspaper, the Charleston *Evening News*. In the fall of 1847 he
sold it to William Paxton but continued to occupy an editorial position under a series of owners until May 4, 1861.[9]
During the Civil War he wrote for papers in Mobile,
Charleston, and Atlanta.[10]

Charleston newspapers represented a considerable range
of the political spectrum, from those favoring nullification
and immediate secession to those with strong attachments
to the Union. Editorial debates were frequent and bitter.
A South Carolina historian described the Charleston *Mercury* as an "aggressive and able spokesman of the States
rights extremists." [11] It was the leading organ of the nulli-
ficationists in the early 1830s, and of the secessionists from
the late 1840s to the Civil War; it blamed the weaknesses
of the Southern economy on Northern exploitation of the
protective tariff. The influential Charleston *Courier* was a
voice of moderation. Like Cardozo's *Southern Patriot,* the
Courier, under the leadership of Richard Yeadon, emphasized the importance of banking and commercial conditions, absenteeism, depleted soils, and dependence on cotton instead of the tariff as the key to the South's economic
ills.

All three papers, of course, espoused the cause of free

[8] *Southern Patriot* (Charleston), April 10, 1845.

[9] Further details of this paper and its publisher may be found in William L. King, *The Newspaper Press of Charleston, South Carolina,* p. 81.

[10] Cardozo was co-associate editor of the Atlanta *Southern Confederacy*
during a short but productive period from January, 1863 to April, 1863.
He optimistically expected the war to end in a short time through joint
mediation and also misjudged the possibility of Louis Napoleon's interven-
ing on the side of the Confederacy to insure himself a supply of cotton. A
series of newspaper articles on the disturbed state of Confederate finances
was put into pamphlet form in Atlanta in 1863 under the title of *A Plan
of Financial Relief, Addressed to the Legislature of Georgia, and Confederate State Congress.*

[11] David D. Wallace, *South Carolina: A Short History, 1520–1948,* p. 480.

trade and defended slavery. The influence of Charleston newspapers extended beyond the local areas, since it was common practice for other newspapers—including Northern ones—to reprint their editorials. They were involved in local and national politics and frequently were used by political groups as trial forums for various political or economic policies. The coverage of local and national documents, proceedings, and treaties in the antebellum newspapers were as extensive as some of the best of their present-day counterparts.

Following the Civil War, in 1866, Cardozo published a nontechnical book, *Reminiscences of Charleston,* in which he mourned the passing of the low country planting class. To him, this class represented gentility, refinement, hospitality, and culture, while the relationship between slave and master was a "reciprocity of protection and obedience" beneficial to both. Cardozo was a regular contributor to the Savannah *Morning News* from 1866 until 1872, a year before his death at the age of 87.

There is some evidence to indicate that Cardozo was also involved in various kinds of commercial enterprise, although the exact nature and time of this involvement is difficult to ascertain.[12]

Cardozo is reputed to have been the father of Francis L. Cardozo, whose mother was of mixed Indian and Negro ancestry; he was a prominent figure in the South Carolina Reconstruction government.

Any attempt to assay the influence of a Sephardic Jewish heritage on Cardozo's thinking is necessarily speculative. On a simple level, Cardozo thought that the Jews were a

[12] In an undated letter from Cardozo to James R. Pringle, a government customs official for the port of Charleston, Cardozo refers to his importation of such disparate items as railroad iron, slate, spices, dried fruits, etc. This letter is in the South Carolina Historical Society. Pringle was also involved in Charleston politics during the nullification crisis of the early 1830s. He ran as a candidate for the mayor of Charleston under the Union Party in 1830.

"people essentially commercial," [13] and this may partially explain his early interest in business and economic subjects. Cardozo, as a member of the orthodox wing of a Charleston synagogue, Beth Elohim, participated in some of its activities,[14] although there is no evidence that he was involved, as were his father David and his uncle Isaac, in the country's first attempt at Reform Judaism.

Charleston was the most important Jewish community in the United States in the first quarter of the nineteenth century. In 1826, Charleston Jews numbered 1,200 out of a national total of 6,000. There was no Jewish "quarter"; Jews were involved in all areas of commercial and political life. One writer said, "The Jew was a man here." [15]

Supporters of the Southern "way of life" have described Charleston as a social and cultural center, where decorous manners reigned in the drawing rooms and gardens of the city's aristocrats. Yet, in Charleston, as in the rest of antebellum South Carolina, class lines were quite rigid. Education was elitist; little contact or sympathy was evident between rich and poor whites. There was a considerable gap between the slave-owning planters from the low country, who used their Charleston summer homes to escape malaria, and the subsistence up-country farmers. Political and economic life was controlled by the former with the acquiescence of the latter.

An active participant in the affairs of Charleston and of Southern intellectual life, Cardozo belonged to Charles-

[13] *Southern Patriot*, February 5, 1820. In this article, Cardozo rejected as unworkable a plan to establish a Jewish agricultural community in the State of New York.

[14] Cardozo was on a three-man committee of Charleston Israelites who drew up a resolution in which they urged the President of the United States to intercede in the Mortara Case. This case involved the abduction of a child of Italian Jewish parents by Roman Catholic authorities, on the grounds that the child had been secretly baptized by a nurse and was therefore a Christian by church standards. See *The Occident*, XVI (January, 1859), 500–2.

[15] Elzas, p. 150.

ton's debating group, the Philomathean Society, which included South Carolina's leading intellectual lights: Langdon Cheves, William Lowndes, John and Christopher Gadsen, Charles Snowden, and Charles Fraser.[16] In 1811 he delivered an address before this group entitled "An Oration on the Literary Character," which was printed in that year. Cardozo helped to organize the Chamber of Commerce in Charleston in 1823, which he claimed performed several valuable services: giving suggestions of developing agricultural resources, helping to extend commerce, and vindicating the principles of free trade.[17] In 1827–1828, he was on the committee which drew up the first Southern petition of Congress against the Tariff of "Abominations."

In 1828 Cardozo and other leading Southern intellectuals helped organize *The Southern Review*.[18] He also contributed to other leading Southern and Northern magazines such as the *Southern Quarterly Review* and *De Bow's Review* in the pre-Civil War period, and *Banker's Magazine* (of New York) and a revived *Southern Review* in the post-Civil War period. Cardozo's writings encompassed politics, economics, literature, and drama.

Cardozo acquired a considerable reputation as a sound thinker on political and economic subjects.[19] His voluminous works are found chiefly in newspapers, magazines,

[16] Susan S. Bennett, "The Cheves Family of South Carolina," *South Carolina Historical and Geneological Magazine*, XXXV (October, 1934), p. 130.

[17] Cardozo, *Reminiscences of Charleston*, pp. 23–24.

[18] This magazine lasted only four years, from February, 1828 to February, 1832. Elizabeth Bearden has ascertained authorship of the most of the articles through an intricate cross-checking system. The articles attributed to Cardozo were: "Political Economy—Rent," February, 1828, and "Modern Oratory," May, 1830. Leading contributors to the magazine included Stephen Elliot Sr., Hugh Legaré, Thomas Cooper, and Thomas Grimke. Elizabeth Bearden, "The Southern Review" (unpublished master's thesis, Columbia University, 1925).

[19] King, pp. 78–80. William G. Simms, "Early Writers of South Carolina," *XIX Century Magazine* (February, 1870), pp. 697–98. King and Simms ver-

and pamphlets, some of which are not easily accessible or identifiable. (Many are unsigned.) His only systematic economic treatise was a thin volume called *Notes on Political Economy*.[20]

Cardozo's writings reveal a blending of practical and theoretical aspects of the political economy. As a working journalist, he took a strong stand on the key issues of the day: the tariff, slavery, public land disposal, banking, nullification, internal improvements, the union movement, and socialism. His occupation provided continual inducement for relating economic theory to the historical process. The treatment of these problems is examined in their nineteenth-century historical setting, whose predominant characteristic was the agrarian nature of the Southern plantation-slave economy and the growing commercialism of the Northern economy.

Cardozo's theoretical writings will be considered for (1) their internal consistency, and (2) their relationship to his ideological preconceptions (chief of which was the view that the plantation system based on slave labor should be preserved and strengthened) and the social forces of his day.

An important key to Cardozo's system was a buoyant faith, justified by future history, in the ability of science to overcome diminishing yields. As a result, the basic conflict over distributive shares postulated by Ricardo does not exist in Cardozo's expansionary model of the American economic system. As Joseph Dorfman points out, Cardozo's emphasis on the cumulative effects of technological prog-

---

ify that Cardozo was an editor specializing in commercial and political subjects and thus provide justification for attributing unsigned editorials in the *Southern Patriot* and *Evening News* to him.

[20] Cardozo admitted that his reason for publishing the *Notes* was to counteract the influence of McVickar's *Outlines of Political Economy*, a Ricardian treatise. Cardozo, *Notes on Political Economy*, reprint edition (hereafter referred to as *Notes*), p. 111.

ress stamps him "as a significant prophet of the future of America." [21]

The social structure of the country underwent a momentous change in the period covered by Cardozo's writings. At the start, there existed a mixture of precapitalist and capitalist forms of production in the sense that the labor market included free labor, indentured servants, and slaves. A conflict within and between sections took place, paralleled by a rapid rate of economic development.[22] This development, however, was not spread evenly. The South, basing its economy on agriculture, continued to lag behind the North. Cardozo's home state of South Carolina increasingly found itself at a competitive disadvantage with the more fertile areas in the Southwest. Of deep concern to Cardozo was the fact that the Industrial Revolution never struck effective roots in the antebellum South. Charleston's position as a great trading center started to deteriorate after the turn of the nineteenth century. The volume and profitability of its commerce was declining.[23] Economic dependence on Northern business was increasing.[24] Cardozo was concerned with arresting this down-

[21] Dorfman, "Introduction to Cardozo," in Cardozo, *Notes*.

[22] The nature of this conflict is developed herein in Chapter Eight, on slavery.

[23] Alfred G. Smith, Jr. *Economic Readjustment of an Old Cotton State: South Carolina, 1820–1860*, p. 8. Also see John G. Van Deusen, *Economic Bases of Disunion in South Carolina*, pp. 184–85. Van Deusen attempted to count the notices of vessels advertised to sail from Charleston to foreign ports on the first of each month. He concluded that the commercial importance of Charleston relative to Northern ports declined significantly after 1819. David Wallace noted that in the decade 1820 to 1830 "the average annual duties collected [at Charleston] decreased by more than half." Wallace, p. 376.

[24] Examples of this dependence cited in a study of this period were: (1) Southern bonds for financing internal improvements were sold in the North. (2) Advances on Southern cotton were supplied by Northern banks. (3) Imports from Europe went through Northern merchants. (4) Northern ships brought supplies to Southern ports and carried away cotton exports. (5) Slaves were supplied by Northern slave traders. John G. Van Deusen. This general topic is examined herein in Chapter Eight.

ward drift and restoring Charleston to the ranks of an important commercial metropolis and gateway to the Carolina hinterlands. It is in the context of Cardozo's shift from an early nationalist position aimed at furthering the harmonious development of the entire nation's economic potential to his later, more sectional view focused on the safeguarding of Southern planting interests that his writings will be examined. A study of the economic thought of an antebellum Southern economist is necessarily intermeshed with an analysis of the Southern political economy.

TWO

Methodology

CARDOZO'S methodology was partially rooted in the abstract-deductive approach of the early classical school, and partially a product of the inductive type of analysis. It was probably inevitable that the former would become dominant in the early stages in the development of the science of political economy because of the lack of statistically verifiable data.

Cardozo appeared to be well aware of the limitations of the deductive model, without being wholly committed to the inductive approach. He admitted that statistical inquiries into the causes of national wealth were not capable of precise calculation without sufficient prior data accumulation.[1] He recognized the danger of drawing universal generalizations from limited observations.[2] He criticized

---

[1] Jacob Cardozo, "Political Economy—Rent," *Southern Review* (February, 1828), p. 193.

[2] *Ibid.* Cardozo rebuked those who would "construct systems of general

the type of situation in economic thought in which "discussions have arisen as to the causes of certain phenomena before the real character of the phenomena itself had been ascertained." [3] He lamented that investigations in the field of political economy were proceeding in a separated rather than an interconnected way. Unfortunately, he did not delineate his specific objections carefully enough. In the context of his writing, however, it appears that he believed that various schools of economic thought—the Physiocrats, Ricardo, Malthus—used inconsistent definitions of the phenomena they were examining and took a partial rather than total view of the economy; for example, in investigating the sources of wealth, the Physiocrats neglected the increasing productiveness of manufacturing, while Ricardo correspondingly neglected the effects of the increasing productiveness of agriculture. Cardozo thought this situation impeded an investigation of the leading principles of political economy.

He was interested in a dual effort: (1) to study and derive the general laws of political economy, and (2) to conduct empirical, statistical investigations of specific problems like supply-demand conditions in the cotton industry, the effects of tariffs on the economy, and comparative costs of production for slave and wage labor. Cardozo regarded these two levels of analysis as connected rather than separated.

In pursuit of the first objective, he critically examined the postulates of the Ricardian system.[4] These general laws were best studied in a "natural" society without

application from only one point of observation." In this discussion, he implicitly rejected the approach which criticized the Southern slave labor system for its alleged limited wealth-creating abilities by reference to the slave societies of antiquity.

[3] *Ibid.*

[4] The essential Ricardian notions were: (1) Exchange value is determined by the amount of labor embodied in a product. (2) Rent is a differential

monopolistic features or considerable inequality. He felt, for example, that the laws of profits, wages, and rent could be more successfully investigated in the United States than in Europe. With reference to these laws, Cardozo said:

> True theory in investigations of this nature is founded on a comprehensive examination of phenomena as they are presented in a natural state of the social system. . . . A country [e.g., the United States] whose institutions and laws have done less to derange the natural order of things than where a vicious social organization has resulted either from military violence or a selfish policy, will present the fairest field for analysis and speculation into the causes of wealth.[5]

The basic limitation of this approach is the fact that different social systems institutionalize different sets of "natural laws." Competitive private enterprise, monopolistic private enterprise, or a planned economy have different initial viewpoints concerning the essence of the "natural order." Therefore, even if there are some economic principles which are absolute and immutable (a possibility at least debatable), their total operating effect would be dissimilar under different social systems.

This type of study, by its very nature, is more deductive than inductive. In effect, the economist says, "If we assume a natural economy, a generalization which the United States approximates, we can deduce certain laws of distribution for this economy." The laws are a logical derivative of the generalizations.

In pursuit of the second objective, Cardozo found this deductive-abstract approach too restrictive. The inductive approach was more practical in economic investigations of

---

return dependent on relative fertility; it is a residual and not a component of price. (3) Profits and wages are inversely related. (4) Capital accumulation out of reduced consumption or expanded profits has the same beneficial effects. (5) Free trade based on the comparative advantage doctrine is mutually advantageous.

[5] Cardozo, *Notes*, Preface, p. iii.

actual situations. Cardozo's working methodology was a
basically deductive one to study the natural order and an
inductive one to study the aberrations from the natural
order. He used empirical studies to check the validity of
the deductive model.

Because business cycles and tariffs interfere with the
action of the natural economy, its effects should be studied
empirically. Cardozo employed that method which appeared most appropriate for dealing with a given problem.
He showed considerable intellectual ingenuity in shifting
between the inductive and deductive approaches. In static
terms, his empirical generalizations had considerable validity. In the last analysis, however, the validity of theory
depends on the adequacy of its assumptions and its effectiveness as a guide to action in dealing with critical problems. It is in this area that Cardozo's limitations are
evident.

In his pragmatic analysis, Cardozo was essentially concerned with collecting, integrating, and interpreting data
rather than with examining the total social process. Concern with the total social process necessarily involved dealing with the concept of total social change. Since Cardozo
desired to strengthen the security of the existing slave
property system, he was only willing to examine critically
that part of the social process which assumed the sanctity of
the given social system. He dealt with such changing economic variables as returns to the factors of production, foreign trade, and capital accumulation, within the confines
of the relatively static social system of slavery. Cardozo was
a spokesman for the conservative group that attempted to
contain the powerful forces of change.

Although Cardozo clearly supported the slave system,
the relationship between this support and his economic
analysis is less clear. The relationship is less evident regarding such theoretical aspects of political economy as

value and distribution theory, and more evident concerning the practical socioeconomic issues of the day such as tariff, banking, and slavery. Cardozo was in the difficult position of justifying the conclusions of the classical economists whose analysis attacked the British landed interests, while at the same time, championing the interests of the Southern agrarian society. Since the English political economy implicitly justified a policy aimed at reducing the power of the landed class, it posed a theoretical danger to the Southern plantation aristocracy. The English agrarian interests favored a tariff to protect their domestic market, while the Southern agrarian interests favored free trade to protect their foreign market. Cardozo's social commitments to the Southern way of life tended to affect at least the direction of his analytical efforts.

There is a strong analytical bent to all of Cardozo's works. In structure, his main economic treatise, *Notes on Political Economy,* is Ricardian [6] in that it deals principally with value, distribution, exchange, and taxation. The influence of the classical economists on Cardozo's methodology, organizational structure of economic questions, and policy implications is particularly evident in the chapters on value, distribution theory, and the tariff. Despite his disagreements with the theoretical underpinnings of Ricardian value and distribution theory, Cardozo heartily endorsed the economic policies of Ricardo. His rejection of specific aspects of Ricardian theory well fitted his effort to show that the interests of the agricultural classes were in harmony with those of the general public. The influence of the anticlassicists on Cardozo's methodology is most clearly revealed on two levels: a favorable orientation toward the landed class, and a willingness to deal with short-run situations in which imbalances develop between production and consumption. Cardozo spoke part of the

[6] Joseph Dorfman refers to Cardozo as the "Ricardian critic of Ricardo."

language of the classicists, but the social foundations of his thought came from Lauderdale and Malthus.

The content of Cardozo's analysis should not be considered as a mechanical reflection of his sympathies; nevertheless, those sympathies were important in influencing his analysis of both practical and theoretical questions on the political economy. An additional complication is the fact that Cardozo's socioeconomic thought reflected not only the influences of slavery and the plantation economy, but also the institutions he hoped would emerge—a commercial manufacturing economy with a considerable number of wage laborers. It is necessary to examine Cardozo's analytical apparatus as well as the social content of his views to obtain an over-all evaluation of his efforts.

In a comparison of American with ancient Greek civilization, Cardozo clearly grasped the notion that ideas came out of an historically conditioned setting:

To allege that the ancients knew not Political Economy and International Law is merely equivalent to saying that plunder and conquest, and not industry and commerce, constituted the principal sources of their subsistence. How could the laws of rent be deduced among a people fed on corn, distributed as an offering to appease the spirit of discontent, or as the price of popularity? What could be known of the level of profit, the benefits of interchange and reciprocity in trade with the rules of humanized warfare in such a period.[7]

Cardozo believed that the dominant economic doctrine prevailing in a country or section would reflect the economic potential of that country as affected by its relative factor supplies of land, labor, and capital, perhaps because

Dorfman, *The Economic Mind in American Civilization*, II, 551.

[7] *Southern Patriot*, September 13, 1827. In an earlier article, Cardozo added that although there was a "conflict between opposite interests in every community," the introduction of commerce in our society had reduced the conflict between the people and their rulers. *Ibid.*, March 24, 1821.

people's ideas are subtly influenced by their socioeconomic environment. Although a short supply of natural resources and land relative to the size of the population contributed to high rents and low wages in Europe, the reverse situation prevailed in the United States. To illustrate his view that institutions and general conditions influence man's ideas, Cardozo said, "Theories in fact, in almost all cases, may be traced to some bias or prepossession, resulting from the position of those who devise them." [8] Physiocratic and Ricardian doctrines were seen as the logical product of the environmental conditions in the countries in which they were dominant. Those ideas take root which are in harmony with the objective conditions in a particular country.

Cardozo viewed the growth of economic theory as a reaction to key social problems, preceded by a considerable amount of suffering and/or clash of interests between classes or groups. He said, "We may trace almost every truth of the science [of political economy] to its source in some public disorder or abuse of the time." [9] Material suffering stimulates intellectual activity which eventually provides greater insight into the economic "laws" of society. Cardozo claimed that the development of economic thought in early nineteenth-century England was intimately connected with an attempt to deal with the problems created by the Poor Laws and the Corn Laws:

The comprehensive examinations . . . into the policy of the British system of Poor Laws and restriction on the import of corn, were intimately connected with the extreme pressure of

[8] Cardozo, "Political Economy—Rent," p. 199. Cardozo said, "It is not difficult of comprehension why the agricultural [Physiocrat] system has found the greatest favor in countries where nature has been bountiful in fertile territory and why on those sections where . . . she has given superior facilities for manufacturers and commerce the [Ricardian] system by which they are best promoted, should be preferred."

[9] Ibid., p. 195. An example presented by Cardozo was that the widespread

the former [Poor Laws] on the payers of the rates and the latter [Corn Laws], on all classes except landlords.[10]

Cardozo attempted to demonstrate that Ricardo's propositions were functionally related to the particular conditions existing in England and on the Continent, such as a high population-to-land ratio, and did not possess the universality ascribed to them by the Ricardian school.

Since the problems faced by the United States were considerably different, Cardozo said, "We ought not to be implicitly guided by the results of investigations pursued by European writers . . . without an examination of the circumstances on which their systems have been framed." [11]

He pointed out that the theories of political economy which had developed out of European conditions were inadequate to deal with the realities of the American scene. This insight indicates Cardozo's recognition of the need for changing economic theory to reflect these realities.

---

suffering associated with the South Sea Bubble break led to a clearer discussion of the economics of issuing paper money.

[10] *Ibid.*, p. 196.

[11] Cardozo, *Notes*, Preface, p. iv. This reference is to the Physiocrats and Mercantilists, as well as to the Ricardian school.

THREE

Value Theory

CARDOZO'S writings on value theory are basically in the anticlassical tradition of Lauderdale and Malthus.[1] They represent a reaction to the doctrines of the classical economists, particularly Ricardo.

The former group accepted some form of the labor theory of value. Ricardo, for example, embraced an "embodied" labor theory of value while he rejected the "labor command" version, both of which had been presented as alternatives (under different conditions) by Adam Smith. Although acknowledging several qualifications of the labor theory, Ricardo nevertheless held that the exchange value of a commodity was controlled "by the total quantity of labor necessary in various forms from first to last, to produce and bring it to market . . . their value depending

---

[1] A perceptive, recent study of this tradition, including its points of tangency and conflict with Ricardian analysis, is Morton Paglin, *Malthus & Lauderdale: The Anti-Ricardian Tradition.*

not on the rate of profit, nor on the rate of wages, nor on the rent." [2]

Since anti-Ricardianism was a critical strand of Cardozo's value theory, a brief summary of its main line of development is pertinent.

While agreeing that labor was a source of value, Lauderdale rejected the classical labor theory of value as a measure of value, for the following reasons:

(1) The value of labor, rather than being fixed, differs at different times and places. Lauderdale said:

No commodity can possess fixed and intrinsic value. . . . As nothing can be a real measure of magnitude and quantity, which is subject to variations in its own dimensions so nothing can be a real measure of the value of other commodities which is constantly varying in its own value. . . . Labour is the thing most subject to variations in its value.[3]

The quest for an absolute measure of value was fruitless. Lauderdale gave several examples to show that wages vary both within and between countries, depending on the relative factor supply and demand conditions. In addition, if the productive powers of labor are improving, the value is clearly variable rather than fixed. Lauderdale criticized Smith for his inconsistency in maintaining that labor "never varies in its own value," [4] at the same time that he claimed that the division of labor improved the productive powers of labor.

(2) Value can only be expressed by the comparison of two commodities. Therefore, no one commodity can be a measure of value of another commodity. This position is acceptable only if labor is not considered to be a commod-

[2] David Ricardo, *Principles of Political Economy and Taxation*, pp. 37, 46.

[3] Earl of Lauderdale, pp. 12, 25. See also *ibid.*, pp. 11, 19, 35.

[4] The reference is to Adam Smith, *An Inquiry Into the Wealth of Nations*, p. 33.

ity. In order for a commodity to have value, according to Lauderdale, it must possess utility and scarcity. He concluded that the degree of value which every commodity possessed depended solely on the forces of demand and supply, and that land, labor, and capital were all sources of wealth:

We cannot express value, or a variation of value, without a comparison of two commodities, and every variation in the expression of value, must depend upon some alteration in the proportion betwixt the quantity of and demand for, one or other of the commodities compared.[5]

Malthus' important contribution was to show the relationship between costs and supply-demand analysis. He rejected Ricardo's idea that:

It is the cost of production which must ultimately regulate the prices of commodities, and not, as has often been said, the proportion between the supply and demand.[6]

Malthus took this position:

The cost of production only influences the prices of commodities, as it influences their supply compared with the demand. . . . It follows that the relation of the supply to the demand is

[5] Lauderdale, p. 19. See also *ibid.*, pp. 13, 15, 16, 36.

[6] Ricardo, p. 260. There has been some disagreement concerning the role attributed to supply and demand in Ricardo's analysis. Ronald Meek, *Studies in the Labor Theory of Value* (London, Lawrence and Wishart, 1956), p. 122, says, "All that Ricardo maintained was that it was not enough to say ONLY that supply and demand regulated value. That was simply 'saying nothing.' A theory of value, in his opinion, had to make some determinate statement about the level at which the forces of supply and demand fixed prices in the 'normal' case." A considerable debate has taken place concerning Ricardo's ultimate position on the labor theory of value. Stigler has suggested that Ricardo became progressively less satisfied with his original embodied labor theory of value, and in fact claimed that Ricardo ended up with a cost of production value theory. See George Stigler, "Ricardo and the 93% Labor Theory of Value," *American Economic Review*, June, 1958, pp. 357–67. Sraffa, however, claims that Ricardo never abandoned a real labor-cost value theory. He points out that in the last edition of his *Principles*, Ricardo kept the chapter on value essentially intact. See Pierro Sraffa (ed.), *Works and Correspondence of David Ricardo*

the dominant principle in the determination of prices, whether market or natural, and that the cost of production can do nothing but in subordination to it, that is, merely as it affects the ordinary relation which the supply bears to the demand.[7]

Malthus emphasized the importance of profits as a prerequisite for offering a supply; exchange value was determined by supply and demand market forces, and under ordinary conditions equaled the cost of production. Induced by expectations of profits, the payment of wages, rent and capital, which were precisely set by supply and demand conditions, were the creators of exchange value. The measure of value, as distinct from the cause of value, was viewed as the amount of labor a commodity would command in exchange. Malthus said:

The labour worked up in a commodity is the principal *cause* of its value. . . . It is not a measure of it. The labour which a commodity will command is *not* the *cause* of its value, but . . . the measure of it.[8]

In other words, labor is the creator of value, but the best measure of the value of a product is the amount of labor it can command (purchase) in the form of another product.

Although Ricardo's "labor embodied" theory of value was useful for examining the relative shares of labor and capital, Lauderdale's supply-demand value theory or Malthus' "labor command" theory of value was better equipped for dealing with the problems of inadequate demand, sustained capital accumulation, and the determination of a given commodity and factor price structure. The respective approaches of the two groups reflect their concern with different economic questions. Unlike the anticlassicists, "Ricardo was not primarily interested in the

(Cambridge, England, University Press, 1951–55), I, xi. A useful comparison of these two views is found in Morton Paglin, pp. 169–79.

[7] Thomas Malthus, *Principles of Political Economy*, pp. 72–73.

[8] *Ibid.*, p. 83.

determination of a given structure of prices, but rather in the relative trend of natural prices as between raw produce and manufactured commodities [and the relative trend in wages, profits, and rent]." [9]

Although Daniel Raymond, an early American follower of the Lauderdale-Malthus tradition, agreed that prices were determined by supply and demand,[10] he rejected Lauderdale's idea that land, labor, and capital were all original sources of wealth. Raymond drew a distinction between the source and the cause of wealth; he described land as the only source or "fountain" of wealth, and labor as the only cause or "creator" of wealth.[11] He related the failure of previous economists to draw a distinction between the source and the cause of wealth to their prior failure to distinguish between public and private wealth.[12] Since the income from private property enables the individual to procure the needs and amenities of life, this property is both a source and a cause of wealth to an individual. But, for the nation as a whole, only labor can be regarded as the cause of wealth because a nation cannot obtain the wherewithal to support the entire citizenry without the use of labor. Raymond regarded capital as neither a source nor a cause of wealth but merely as an instrument which increased man's capacity to create wealth:

Capital is not the agent in the performance of these mighty works [a water wheel, steam engine or ship]; but merely the instrument in the hands of man.[13]

This train of thought is contrary to that of Lauderdale, who viewed capital as both a source and a cause of wealth

[9] Leo Rogin, *The Meaning and Validity of Economic Theory* (New York, Harper, 1956), pp. 123-24.

[10] Daniel Raymond, *Elements of Political Economy*, I, 183. An earlier edition of this work (1820), entitled *Thoughts on Political Economy*, was the first comprehensive American treatise on political economy.

[11] *Ibid.*, I, 97-102.   [12] *Ibid.*, I, 94-95.   [13] *Ibid.*, I, 101.

when it replaced labor in performing some task. Raymond simultaneously held to a modified labor theory of value in the sense that labor was viewed as the sole creator of value, and to a supply-demand theory of value, but he did not raise the question of their possible irreconcilability.

Lauderdale indirectly related value theory to the public-private wealth distinction, insofar as he showed that individual riches possess utility and scarcity, which underlie demand and supply respectively and which, in turn, determine value. He took the position that a rise in private riches presupposes a fall in public wealth, and vice versa.[14] This position stems from his definition of these terms. Public wealth was defined as the supply of desired commodities, whereas individual riches was viewed as the money value of commodities.[15] Consequently, the latter would be increased by scarcity and diminished by abundance. In the short run, when only market or short-run equilibrium is achieved, Lauderdale's conclusions may be correct: a fall in production can mean an increase in private riches under proper elasticity assumptions (i.e., an inelastic demand). In the long run, however, when com-

[14] Lauderdale, p. 49. Ernest Teilhac in *Pioneers in American Economic Thought*, E. A. J. Johnson, trans., p. 9, criticized the imprecision of Lauderdale's definition although he acknowledged the important conceptual contribution made by Lauderdale in differentiating national and private wealth. He said, "If Lauderdale had really considered the nation as a unit, he would never have supposed that the mass of individual wealth could possibly be increased through scarcity of such a commodity as water. The sum of individual wealth would remain the same because the total wealth of the rest of the community would decrease in exactly the same proportion as the wealth of the monopolists of the water springs would increase." This point was also made by Raymond, I, 178–80. The only case in which individual and public wealth can be simultaneously increased, according to Lauderdale, is when both supply and demand are simultaneously increased. Lauderdale, pp. 99–100.

[15] The precise definition of public wealth given by Lauderdale is that it consists of "all that man desires as useful and delightful to him." Individual riches are defined as "all that man desires as useful or delightful to him which exists in a degree of scarcity." Lauderdale, pp. 57–58.

petitive equilibrium is attained, public wealth and private riches are identical.

Although Raymond commended Lauderdale for drawing a distinction between public and private wealth, he rejected Lauderdale's approach. Lauderdale's distinction is based on the degree of scarcity; he views private wealth as being increased by scarcity and public wealth as being increased by abundance. According to Raymond, goods acquire value through the process of exchange rather than through scarcity. Consequently, individual wealth would be at a high level if the value of property (lands, goods, money, and stock) held by the individual could be exchanged for a considerable quantity of the necessities and comforts of life.[16] A valid evaluation of public wealth necessarily demands the use of another criterion. A nation must be viewed as a unity that does not possess property for purposes of exchange. Raymond defines public wealth as "the capacity for acquiring the necessities and comforts of life" for all its citizens.[17] This capacity depends primarily on the industrious habits of the people. Secondarily, it is affected by a wide variety of other factors such as geographical and climatic conditions, denseness of population, the degree of equality in the distribution of property, the state of the industrial arts, monopolistic advantages in commerce and manufacturing, and the quality of government.[18]

Cardozo was very critical of both Raymond's and Lauderdale's approach on this issue:

Both have lost their way . . . by confounding value in use with value in exchange. In denying that there can be any pri-

---

[16] Raymond, I, 36.   [17] Ibid., I, 47.

[18] Ibid., I, 48–53. There is an ethical connotation to Raymond's concept of national wealth. He regards a smaller nation with a more equitable distribution of wealth as being wealthier than a large country producing a greater absolute level of output, but having property more unequally dis-

vate wealth without exchange value, they omitted some of the most essential elements of wealth—namely, all that is produced to be consumed, and not to be exchanged.[19]

Although almost all goods produced today, except those consumed by the farmer out of his own production, enter the process of exchange in which a money value is determined, these goods possessed more than minimal significance during the period of Cardozo's writings.

Cardozo dealt with the distinction in a more general way: "There is a more effectual addition to the real wealth of a country from the cheapness of all commodities than from the increase of revenue of one or a few of its inhabitants." [20] This indicates that he did not equate an increase of profit with an increase of public wealth. He also criticized Ricardo for "neglecting to distinguish a partial from a general increase of wealth, or making the benefit of one class of society to the correspondent injury of some other the criterion of a general augmentation of riches." [21]

Cardozo rejected the labor theory of value on these grounds: (1) the value of labor was itself variable; [22] (2) the theory neglected demand as an element in the de-

---

tributed. Raymond said: "If the whole territory, and all the property of a country are engrossed by a few, while a much greater number are sunk into a state of hopeless poverty and wretchedness, it matters not how great the sum total of individual wealth may be, provided the nation is to be considered as a *unity* composed of all its citizens, it can never be said to enjoy a high degree of national wealth. . . . National wealth prevails to a much greater degree in New England than in Virginia, not because the territory is more extensive or the land more fertile for in these respects Virginia has the advantage, but because property in New England is more equally divided." *Ibid.*, I, 52, 54.

[19] *Southern Patriot,* February 7, 1821.

[20] Cardozo, *Notes,* p. 113.

[21] *Ibid.*, p. 13. Cardozo's discussion of the relationship between savings-expenditure analysis and the public-private wealth distinction will be taken up in the business cycles chapter.

[22] Cardozo criticized Ricardo, claiming that he "views labor erroneously when he considers it as not subject to the same laws that regulate the increase and the prices of commodities in general." *Ibid.*, p. 69.

termination of value; and (3) the theory gave a disproportionate weight to labor as a creator or determiner of value.

Cardozo attributed an important wealth-creating role to
the forces of nature, with these "forces" interpreted in the
broadest sense. Its pervasive effects were evident in commerce and manufacturing as well as in agriculture. He
claimed that Smith and the Physiocrats overlooked the influence of nature in making commerce and manufacturing
productive, while Ricardo made the same error regarding
agriculture. With particular reference to the latter, he
said, "All theories of Political Economy that do not admit
the agency of Nature concurrently with the labour and ingenuity of Man in the creation of value must necessarily
lead to erroneous conclusions." [23]

In contrast to Ricardo, Cardozo claimed that natural
agents have some value in their natural state, and in combination with man "possess the power of adding to value"
if sufficient demand exists for their services. Therefore,
they constitute "as much as labor among the elements of
value." [24] He rejected Ricardo's view that "natural agents,
though they add greatly to *value in use,* never add exchangeable value." [25]

Cardozo's notions on value theory have greater kinship
with those of Lauderdale than of Raymond. Unlike the
latter, he did not draw a distinction between land as the
only source of value, and labor as the only cause of value.
Cardozo and Lauderdale think of labor as only one element of value; both think of capital as an additional part
of value. Cardozo states that there is "an intimate connection between labor and capital in all stages of social improvement . . . [t]here is no period in which capital does

[23] *Ibid.,* p. 5. He added, "Nature concurs with Man in each of the arts
of life, either conferring or giving additional value to objects of use and
exchange." *Ibid.,* p. 6.
[24] *Ibid.,* pp. 8–9.
[25] Ricardo, p. 190. Ricardo criticized Say for a position that was akin to
Cardozo's.

not constitute one of its ingredients." [26] He rejects the classical view, supported by Raymond, of capital as simply "jellied labor." "The notion that capital is nothing but accumulated labor is," according to Cardozo, "as erroneous as the idea that labor is the sole element and only regulator of value." [27] Land, labor, and capital are component elements of value.

Cardozo's position was that the value of labor, as well as the value of commodities, was determined by market supply and demand conditions. He said, "There can be no variation in prices unless the due proportion has been altered between demand and supply." [28]

The recognition of this interdependence, and his sympathy with the anticlassical emphasis on demand are seen in these statements:

Mere quantity without demand can determine nothing in relation to exchangeable value. . . . Supply produces demand, as well as demand supply. . . . However it is more usual for the demand to be in advance of the supply of food and raw materials than the converse.[29]

Cardozo, like Malthus, regarded the acquisition of profits as the critical condition of supply:

It is a law or principle of ultimate operation that the market price of a commodity must yield the fair and average rate of profit on capital or the supply must cease. This is a condition of supply but not a regulator of price. This is the center around which the market price oscillates, and it is properly called the natural price. In this sense cost and natural price are identical. But this is not the price which is immediately and at all times under the influence of the law of demand and supply.[30]

[26] *Evening News* (Charleston), April 14, 1849. Cardozo, *Notes*, p. 7.
[27] *Ibid.*, p. 8.
[28] *Ibid.*, p. 84. See also *ibid.*, pp. 22, 33, and Cardozo, "Political Economy —Rent," pp. 216–17.
[29] Cardozo, *Notes*, p. 32; "Political Economy—Rent," pp. 201–2. For a similar view, see Lauderdale, pp. 97–98.
[30] *Southern Patriot*, September 20, 1837.

In other words, if demand and supply conditions do not yield a price which covers cost and a normal profit, further supply will not be forthcoming.

Ricardo's error in dealing with value theory, according to Cardozo, stems from regarding price and exchange value as equivalent under all conditions. This is based on Ricardo's assumption of an unchanging value of money.

In drawing a distinction between value and riches, Ricardo held that anything which diminishes the use of labor, such as machinery, has the effect of decreasing exchange value and increasing riches by augmenting the supply of commodities.[31]

Cardozo held that:

Value and price differ, however, when demand is properly proportioned to supply, or when produce is distributed exactly according to the wants of consumers, or, which is the same thing, price is, under such circumstances, in an inverse proportion to quantity.[32]

Although an increase in the output of commodities results in falling prices, if it is matched by a rising demand, total exchangeable value will likewise rise. Relative value, however, remains constant. Thus, price and exchange value were viewed as identical only when the normal proportions between demand and supply were upset. The following examples presented by Cardozo illustrate this point:

Case 1. Suppose that in one period 1,000 hats exchange for 1,000 shoes, and that similar technological advancements in both sectors result in an exchange of 1,200 hats for 1,200 shoes in the subsequent period (the same number of workers having turned out more in the second time

[31] He stated his position: "By constantly increasing the facility of production, we constantly diminish the value of some of the commodities before produced, though by the same means we not only add to the national riches, but also to the power of future production." Ricardo, p. 183.

[32] Cardozo, *Notes*, p. 64. See also p. 13.

period). Ricardo would claim that the value of both items had fallen. Cardozo differed:

The exchangeable value of both shoes and hats will have increased, for each commodity exchanges for a greater quantity of the other. . . . It is their price only which will have been reduced [due to an increase in supply relative to the demand]. . . . Their relative value continues as before, but their value when exchanged for each other has varied—it has increased.[33]

Case 2. Assume the same initial situation. Subsequent technological developments result in an exchange of 1,200 hats for 1,000 shoes. Ricardo's explanation would be that the value of hats had fallen and the value of shoes had remained the same. Cardozo's explanation again differed:

The exchangeable value of the hats and their price had fallen, if the demand continues as before for both commodities, [this element was ignored by Ricardo] for in exchanging hats for shoes a greater quantity of the former must be parted with to obtain the same quantity as before of the latter. . . . The price and exchangeable value of shoes will have risen.[34]

In this case, Cardozo makes the artificial assumption that a rise in price and exchange value of one commodity must be accompanied by a proportional fall in price and value of the other commodity for which it is exchanged. He concludes by stating, "Price and exchangeable value are identical when demand and supply are not in exact or natural proportion to each other."[35] Here Case 2 as opposed to Case 1 applies.

[33] *Ibid.*, p. 65. Porter, in an otherwise critical review of Cardozo's *Notes*, agreed that an increase in exchange from 1 stocking = 1 cloth to 2 stockings = 2 cloths (as a result of rising productivity) meant that the total of exchange value had doubled, but denied Cardozo's claim that Ricardo had confused price and exchange value. He said that the "real price of an article must be the same as its exchange value." Jonathan Porter, "Cardozo's 'Notes on Political Economy,'" *North American Review*, XXIV (January, 1827), 180.

[34] Cardozo, *Notes*, pp. 65–66.   [35] *Ibid.*, p. 66.

Cardozo appears to be using relative and exchange values in a sense different from Ricardo's. To the latter, they are the same: the value of a unit of one commodity in terms of the other. To Cardozo, this is an accurate definition of relative, but not of exchange, value. Exchange value refers to the total value of a commodity which exchanges for the total value of another commodity. If, for example, the quantity of both products increases by a similar amount, prices will fall. Although relative value remains the same (since one unit of commodity A exchanges for the same amount of commodity B), exchange value, seen as the total amount of value of commodity A which exchanges for the total amount or value of commodity B, rises.

Whereas Ricardo views exchange value and wealth as differnt, they are essentially the same to Cardozo. There is nothing in Cardozo's classification that is intrinsically superior to Ricardo's, but it does have the merit of focusing on the immediate determinants of price. He understood that changes in demand could complement or offset the effects of supply changes; thus, a falling demand was viewed as intensifying the effect of a rising supply on the price level.

Cardozo was critical of Ricardo's rejection of Smith's labor command theory of value.[36] Ricardo's reasoning was as follows: Rising productivity has the effect of increasing output per worker. The exchange value of each unit falls because less labor time is needed for its production. The producers will not gain, however, because they will have to part with a greater amount in order to purchase a day's labor in the form of another product; conversely, the

[36] The particular sentence by Smith, cited as erroneous by Ricardo and correct by Cardozo, was, "A man must be rich or poor according to the quantity of labor which he can afford to purchase," Ricardo, p. 186. Adam Smith, p. 30. Cardozo, *Notes*, p. 70.

riches of those buying the commodities involved will rise.
No additional workers will be employed, says Ricardo. An
essential assumption in the Ricardian model is that increased output can be achieved without increased labor.
Cardozo criticized Ricardo's statement that "A certain
quantity of clothes and provisions will maintain and employ the same number of men, and will therefore procure
the same quantity of work to be done, whether they be
produced by the labor of 100 or 200 men." [37] He claimed:

It is obvious that without the 200 men the same quantity of
work will not be done or such a quantity of clothes and provisions provided as will maintain and employ the 200. Neither
the power nor the inducement to provide clothes and provisions for 200 men could possibly, under such circumstances,
exist.[38]

Abandonment of the assumption that increased labor is
not a prerequisite for increased output would tend to
make the embodied labor theory of value less valid. In this
situation, the increase in the worker's productivity does
not lower the unit exchange value of the worker's product,
because the labor time does not fall; more of the product
does not have to be given up to buy a day's labor.

In Cardozo's model, an expansion in the commodities
market implies an expansion in the labor market, and vice
versa. The same laws of demand and supply are operative
in both sectors. Cardozo wrote:

[Ricardo] views labor erroneously when he considers it as not
subject to the same laws that regulate the increase and the
prices of commodities in general. It is obvious that without
this condition of a constant and equal augmentation in the
supply of labor with capital, and a proportionate fall of its
price [in money terms] with the price of productions generally,

[37] Ricardo, p. 186, cited by Cardozo in *Notes*, p. 70.
[38] Cardozo, *Notes*, p. 70.

that both the power and the will to accumulate would cease on the part of producers.[39]

Lowering of wages was considered necessary to give owners of capital sufficient incentive to expand the output of commodities. The continued expansion of output had a twofold function of providing maintenance for the laborers and a rising population, and of providing employment.

Cardozo's insistence on a constant ratio between labor and capital in the process of economic development is clearly wrong, but his claim that supply-and-demand conditions determine the price of labor as well as the price of commodities provides a better explanation of market prices than does Ricardo's combination of the wages fund, the law of population, and the embodied labor theory of value. The relationship between the price of labor and the price of commodities is an interdependent one:

The price of labour does not, however, regulate the prices of commodities more than the prices of these do the price of labour. They have a mutual influence and fall in regular and equal proportion [this refers to Cardozo's ideas that in the process of economic development the prices of factors and products fall].[40]

The strength of Cardozo's approach, in common with the anti-Ricardian tradition, was in constructing a short-run rather than a long-run model. In his later writings, Cardozo indicated an awareness of the distinction between the short- and long-run levels of analysis:

Among the rudiments of political economy is the distinction between value as governed temporarily or immediately by demand as compared with supply, and permanently or ultimately by the costs of production. . . . If the price of a commodity falls below cost of production it ceases to be produced at all, or if produced, only in such quantity as the demand will take

[39] Ibid., p. 69.   [40] Ibid., p. 71.

off at remunerative prices. In this way all commodities, unless subject to monopoly, are under the influences of demand and supply in their present or immediate, and the cost of production in their ultimate effects as the condition of supply.[41]

Value theory was not an area in which Cardozo made an original contribution. He was more successful in attacking the classical system than in constructing an adequate replacement.

[41] *Southern Confederacy* (Atlanta), March 18, 1863.

FOUR

Distribution Theory

RENT

CARDOZO'S contributions to rent theory are most fruitfully viewed as a reaction to the Ricardian-Malthusian models. Although the differential rent doctrine was essentially accepted both by Ricardo and Malthus, the social implications of their respective versions were different: Ricardo claimed and Malthus denied that the interests of the landlord were at variance with those of the rest of society.[1]

Ricardo's rent formulation had incorporated earlier contributions of Malthus regarding population and the law of diminishing returns. However, as the Corn Laws and the status of agriculture in a society undergoing industrialization became the strategic variable for Malthus, he

---

[1] It should not be thought that Ricardo favored a radical solution, such as land nationalization for harmonizing interests between classes. He continued to favor private property at the same time that he attacked the Corn Laws favored by the landed interests.

shifted away from his earlier position. He emphasized the importance of technology in agriculture, labeled "permanent improvements," and the possibility of creating increasing returns in that sector. Although Malthus never specifically repudiated his earlier population doctrines, he accorded them less importance in his later work, *Principles of Political Economy*. He accused Ricardo of understating the importance of technological developments:

Mr. Ricardo has never laid any *stress* upon the influence of permanent improvements in agriculture on the profits of stock, although it is one of the most important considerations in the whole compass of Political Economy. . . . Soil of poor quality . . . might by continued improvements in agriculture, admit of the employment of a vast mass of capital for hundreds of years, with little or with no fall of profits. . . . Powerful and certain as this cause is [i.e., cultivation of inferior soils on the basis of diminishing returns as population increases], in its final operation, so much so as to overwhelm every other; yet in the actual state of the world, its natural progress is not only extremely slow, but is . . . frequently counteracted and overcome by other causes.[2]

The basic idea of Ricardo's rent theory is that as poorer and poorer soils are used, the increased cost of cultivation leads to rising rent on the more fertile lands. Ricardo held that rent was equal to the difference between the value, or physical yield, of the output on a given tract of land and that on the least fertile land in use, assuming the employment of equal quantities of capital inputs on each tract. The equilibrium price was the cost of production, or normal profit plus wages, on the no-rent, marginal land. The

[2] Malthus, cited in Paglin, pp. 82–83, from the first edition of *Principles of Political Economy* (London, John Murray, 1820), pp. 331–32. On the basis of the above quotations, Paglin concludes "Malthus of the *Principles* has pushed the population doctrine and diminishing returns into the background. . . . [He] rejected the classical implications of his own theories of population and rent." *Ibid.,* p 82.

demand for subsistence by a rising population determined the margin of production. Rent was thus a surplus return to the owners of the fertile lands. Ricardo's assumption of the validity of the law of diminishing returns as applied to agriculture was of decisive importance in his differential rent theory model. The possibility of agricultural improvements, although acknowledged, was a factor of secondary importance.

Malthus justifiably accused Ricardo of slighting the long-run effects of land improvements and concentrating on short-run factors. Ricardo maintained that land improvements had the immediate effect of lowering rents since they reduced the labor time needed for production. He implicitly assumed an inelastic demand for food and emphasized the effects of improvements in reducing costs; actually, they may increase the sale of total output and thus increase total rents. Malthus held that agricultural improvements were the main source of rising rents.[3]

Ricardo was critical of Malthus' claim that "The cause of the high price of the necessaries of life above the cost of production [i.e., rents] is to be found in their abundance rather than their scarcity." [4] What Malthus had in mind was the notion that price would be high relative to the cost of production if fertile lands were employed to keep costs low. The sharp contrast with Ricardo can be seen in the latter's statement, "When land is most abundant, when

[3] Malthus (reprint, 2nd ed.), p. 196. Malthus says, "I should further say, that not only have improvements in agriculture never lowered rents, but that they have been hitherto, and may be expected to be in the future, the *main* source of the increase of rents." Malthus gives other causes for rising rents: (1) accumulation of capital, (2) increase of population, (3) rising price of agricultural products as a result of increased demand. *Ibid.*, pp. 157–73. It should be noted that Ricardo did not view agricultural improvements as being contrary to the landlord's long-run interests. He said that "As they give a great stimulus to population, and at the same time enable us to cultivate poorer lands with less labour, they are ultimately of immense advantage to the landlords. A period however must elapse, during which they are positively injurious to him." Ricardo, p. 43.

[4] Malthus, p. 275.

most productive and most fertile, it yields no rent." [5] Un-like Ricardo, Malthus and Cardozo appeared to be aware of both the cost-reducing and output-expanding effects of technological improvements.

In criticizing Malthus' views on the relationship of relative scarcity and rent, Ricardo dealt with a combination of micro- and macro-elements:

[The land's] increased fertility renders it capable of paying at some future time an augmented rent . . . [but] it is one thing to be able to bear a high rent, and another thing actually to pay it. . . . Whatever the nature of the land may be, high rent must depend on the high price of the produce; but given the high price, rent must be high in proportion to abundance and not to scarcity.[6]

In other words, although rent rises only when a general condition of scarcity of fertile land prevails, from the standpoint of the individual producer the gain will be greatest if he has an abundant output. Fertile land has greater power to yield rent, but generalized scarcity must exist in order to realize this rent. In response, Malthus claimed that Ricardo's statement, "Given the high price, rent must be high in proportion to abundance," was "begging the whole of the question. The price can not be given." [7]

Cardozo's critique drew from both of these sources. Philosophically, he was closer to the more dynamic Malthusian approach, although he did not share all of its methods of policy conclusions. The main part of his criticism was directed against the Ricardian school. Cardozo questioned the validity of Ricardo's assumptions as well as his logic. He was the first American economist systematically to attack Ricardian rent theory.[8]

Unlike Ricardo, Cardozo posited that the probability of

[5] Ricardo, p. 35.   [6] Ricardo, pp. 276-77.   [7] Malthus, p. 145.
[8] Raymond, whose writings preceded Cardozo's, took a position which

increasing returns was just as great in agriculture as in manufacturing. Technology distributed its cumulative benefits to all sectors of human activity:

In agriculture the inventive powers of producers will be as efficacious from the same cause as in manufacturing. . . . There is no just ground for the conclusion that improvements in cultivation are necessarily partial and not progressive like manufactures.[9]

Although Cardozo did not deny the possibility of diminishing returns, he did deny its necessity even in the case of inferior soils:

The cultivation of soils naturally inferior . . . is not *necessarily* followed by a less return compared with the expenditure. . . . But in the regular progress of wealth and population there is always room for the employment of fresh capital on the land with increasing profit, because with every addition to the quantity and consequent fall of price of produce . . . the demand for it is extended. The increased return is the fund which pays not only increased profit, but increased wages.[10]

The optimism of Cardozo's expansive model reflected the unique conditions of the American environment in the early nineteenth century. The combination of limitless fertile land and technology was able to overcome the problem of diminishing yields. This approach was effectively criticized by Fletcher: "None of the early American economists point out that intensive cultivation might show in-

on the whole was critical of Ricardian theory. Distribution theory, however, was not of primary importance to him. Consequently, this part of his analysis was undeveloped. References to Ricardian rent theory can be found in his *Elements of Political Economy*, I, 187–90; II, 111. Like Cardozo, Raymond foresaw the possibility of increasing returns in agriculture. See John R. Turner, *The Ricardian Rent Theory in Early American Economics*, pp. 28–31, and Hugh M. Fletcher, "History of Economic Theory in the United States, 1820 to 1866," (unpublished doctoral dissertation, University of Illinois, 1926), p. 35.
[9] Cardozo, *Notes*, p. 36; Cardozo, "Political Economy—Rent," p. 211.
[10] Cardozo, *Notes*, pp. 15–16. Cardozo's assumption of high price elasticities (as in the above quotation) was quite common in his writings.

creasing returns up to a point after which the phenomena
of decreasing returns would commence to appear." [11]

Cardozo rejected the Ricardian view that the landlord
reaped a double gain as the growth of population caused
the cultivation of inferior land. Specifically, Ricardo had
said:

Since the same cause, the difficulty of production, raises the exchangeable value of raw produce, and raises also the proportion
of raw produce paid to the landlord for rent, it is obvious that
the landlord is doubly benefitted by difficulty of production.
First, he obtains a greater share, and, secondly, the commodity
in which he is paid is of greater value.[12]

Although Ricardo's analysis was couched primarily in
"real" terms, he claimed that the landlord was the recipi-
ent of both higher money rent and higher corn rent.

Cardozo based his criticism on the distinction between
these types of rent:

The *money* rent of the landlord is of course plainly distinguish-
able from his *corn* rent—but they must, under all circumstances, rise and fall in an inverse ratio. His money rent is governed by the proportion which the demand bears to the supply
of raw produce—his corn rent by the absolute quantity of raw
produce. What he gains in the one way he loses in the other.[13]

Cardozo's insistence that corn rent and money rent have
to vary in an inverse relation is clearly wrong. If an increase in supply is accompanied by rising demand, both
corn and money rent will rise, and this will also occur if
supply rises or falls but demand is relatively price-elastic.
Cardozo's claim was that the idea of the landlord doubly
benefiting from the sale of a rising quantity at an increased
price was inconceivable. This flaw in Cardozo's analysis
was more than matched by Ricardo's inadequate treatment
of the distinction between a real and a money level of

[11] Fletcher, p. 261.　　[12] Ricardo, p. 45.　　[13] Cardozo, *Notes*, p. 23.

analysis. (This shortcoming is further developed below, in the section on wages and profits.) The strength of Cardozo's approach was in recognizing that supply-demand conditions in the product market were the key element in determining the distribution of income (output). He correctly pointed out that the landlord's share would rise if demand rose more than supply or if supply fell more than demand.

Cardozo criticized Ricardo's position that relative fertility determined the origin, rise, and inequality of rent. Ricardo had said:

It is only, then, because land it not unlimited in quantity and uniform in quality, and because, in the progress of population, land of an inferior quality, or less advantageously situated, is called into cultivation, that rent is ever paid for the use of it. . . . With every step in the progress of population, which shall oblige a country to have recourse to land of a worse quality, to enable it to raise its supply of food, rent, on all more fertile land, will rise.[14]

Cardozo claimed that relative fertility explained only the inequality of rent, or the fact that different grades of land yielded different rents:

Relative fertility can only account for the *inequality* of rent, it can neither explain its *origin* nor its increase. . . . Lands of *different* degrees of fertility will yield *different* rents. Relative fertility will therefore account for relative rent, and nothing more.[15]

Cardozo found the origin of rent in the natural properties of land which allow it to produce a surplus above expenses:

---

[14] Ricardo, p. 35. Ricardo also noted that applying more capital to land already in cultivation was commonly resorted to as a temporary alternative to using poorer land.

[15] Cardozo, *Notes*, p. 21.

The rent of land has its origin in natural fertility [referred to by Smith and Ricardo as the 'original and indestructible powers of the soil'] . . . by which it is made to yield a surplus above the profits of the capital and the wages of labor employed in its cultivation.[16]

Absolute fertility, rather than relative fertility, accounted for the origin of rent.

Cardozo questioned the validity of Ricardo's view that rent does not arise until a scarcity of fertile land develops:

It is not true that land exists anywhere in such boundless quantity as to be without price or value when available for profit to a cultivator. . . . We consider rent, therefore, to commence from the moment land is taken into cultivation. . . . Whenever or wherever land is cultivated, whether it be more or less fertile, near or distant to markets, it pays rent, and it seems neither agreeable to fact nor just theory, to say that rent does not commence before the natural power of the soil to produce food begins to diminish. . . . Its *amount* will be regulated by the surplus which it will yield after the replacement of the capital of the cultivator with the *average* rate of profits and wages.[17]

Cardozo claimed that Ricardo's differential rent theory, based on relative fertilities, was inconsistent with his view of rent as compensation for the "original and indestructible powers of the soil," this compensation being based on absolute fertilities:

This definition is, however, essentially different from the other, and confounds that Rent 'which is paid for the use of the original and indestructible powers of the soil,' with that paid in consequence of the advance in the price of raw produce from restrictions on the trade in corn, and the monopoly which in some countries is connected with the possession of land.[18]

---

[16] *Ibid.*, pp. 29–30.   [17] *Ibid.*, pp. 31, 33–34.
[18] Cardozo, *Notes*, pp. 19–20. Cardozo also concluded that Malthus' rent formulation was inconsistent.

Cardozo noted that the answer to the question, "When does rent begin?" would be different depending on the definition used. According to that definition based on the "original and indestructible powers," rent should logically commence when those powers are put in cultivation. As a differential return, however, it would begin only when land of decreasing fertility is placed in cultivation. Hence, claimed Cardozo, Ricardo's definitions were internally inconsistent.

The rise in rent, in Cardozo's view, was dependent on monopolistic conditions, which restricted the supply, and technological improvements, which increased the productive powers of the soil. He also implied that rising demand for the agricultural output was a prerequisite for rent increases, since "The natural powers of the soil may not be fully called forth from the want of adequate demand." [19] Cardozo criticized both Ricardo's (and Sismondi's) contention that rent is always a monopoly return as well as Malthus' claim that rent is never due to monopoly. He drew a critical distinction between "natural" rent and monopoly rent. The former represented the price paid for the natural fertility of the land in a thoroughly competitive market. The latter arises from infringements with the workings of the competitive market, e.g., monopolies, unequal distribution of land ownership, and laws restricting the alienation of land. Cardozo commented on the situation that exists when free competition prevails in the purchase and sale of land:

Rent . . . is the interest on a capital invested in its purchase, or laid out in its improvement. . . . Land, when acquired by purchase, with the same facility and on the same principles as capital in general, will obey its laws. Its rate in these circumstances must be regulated by the general rate of interest at the

[19] Cardozo, "Political Economy—Rent," p. 201.

time for the tenant will never pay the landlord more than this, when, by borrowing money at this rate, he is enabled to become a proprietor himself, and derive the usual rate of profit in agriculture. . . . The sum given annually for the use of its [the land's] 'original and indestructible powers', cannot be considered as connected with monopoly of any kind. This is . . . the *natural* rent of land. . . . The price of food raised on such land, the price of the land itself, and its rent, will all be at fair competition rates—which we may call the natural price and rent of land.[20]

Monopoly rent, on the other hand, arises through its influence on demand-supply conditions, and is due to society's institutional arrangements of land distribution and property laws rather than to laws of nature. Cardozo said:

All that portion of price and rent obtained above what would have been obtained if land had been subject in its rent and price to the principles of unrestrained competition, may be denominated monopoly rent and monopoly price. . . . The augmentation of rent arises, under all circumstances, from whatever cause prevents the supply of food from being proportioned to the demand.[21]

Cardozo astutely noted that landlords prefer receiving rents from rising prices rather than from decreasing production costs, since the latter necessitates capital investment in the land. The suggestion is that landlords with monopolistic powers can realize returns because of their influence over prices.

Cardozo emphasized that certain noneconomic factors, such as purchasing land for political power as opposed to commercial purposes, may prevent prices from falling to

[20] *Ibid.*, pp. 204–5. Cardozo, *Notes*, pp. 27, 36.
[21] *Ibid.*, pp. 25, 27, 28. Jonathan Porter questioned Cardozo's view that legal restrictions on land alienation tended to push rents beyond the "natural" level. He claimed that these restrictions kept rents lower by tending to keep land in the hands of those who might not make the most profitable use of it. Porter, "Cardozo's 'Notes,' " pp. 177–78.

their competitive level and thus may lead to rent in excess of the natural level. Whereas Ricardo related rises of rent to a law of nature, Cardozo related it primarily, although not exclusively, to the way social institutions affected demand and supply. The existence of a monopoly return from agriculture was not, in Cardozo's view, a necessary result. With reference to the United States, Cardozo said:

Where more natural arrangements prevail, there is no surplus for rent [i.e., monopoly rent] in the sense of this term as it is generally understood. The proprietor of land in a new and fertile country . . . derives . . . an amount in addition to the profit on the capital employed in cultivation, in proportion to his investment in the purchase of the land itself.[22]

Although Cardozo acknowledged the existence of monopoly rent in Europe, he appears to have believed that its appearance would be indefinitely delayed in land-rich America.

Cardozo also claimed that monopolistic conditions as applied to land had the effect of transferring income from wages and profits to rent. He attempted to demonstrate that the appearance of monopoly rent in Ricardo's model followed from his erroneous acceptance of the labor theory of value:

Mr. Ricardo, thus setting out from the principle, that labour is the sole element and regulator of value, and taking for granted that the level of profit between Agriculture and other employments is still maintained, notwithstanding the increase of expense in raising raw produce, was bound to conclude, *assuming population at the same time to augment,* that there was a proportional advance in the price of the products of the land, which made an addition to Rent. . . . Thus, when labour is made the sole constituent and regulator of value, it is impossible to avoid the conclusion that, as a greater quantity of it,

[22] Cardozo, *Notes,* p. 38.

or which is the same thing, an increased sum in wages, is made necessary to an augmentation of raw produce, which leads, finally to an advance of rent, the balance of advantage must be on the side of Agriculture compared with other employments. Rent will, on such a system, be higher than it ought naturally to be, and every addition to it, must be at the expense of the other classes of society.[23]

Ricardo's view that agricultural prices depended on the cost of production on the highest cost no-rent land was based on an acceptance of the labor theory of value. Cardozo, on the other hand, claimed that given a certain demand, prices were a function of the cost of production on the most efficient land:

The price, generally, of the products of the soil, like the price of articles produced by machinery, will be governed, in the absence of all unnatural excitements [e.g., high demand conditions in wartime] by the expense of raising that portion which is produced at the least cost.[24]

Cardozo's position is thus much closer to the modern theory of pricing in competitive market structures.

Cardozo correctly pointed out that the profit equilibrium assumption, accepted by Ricardo, was inconsistent with his rent theory, in which diminishing returns were accompanied by greater profitability in agriculture. If population increased and diminishing returns prevailed in agriculture, as Ricardo assumed, profits in agriculture and manufacturing would be different. He stated this inconsistency:

It is impossible, however, to admit that profits will *continue on a level*, on the supposition that raw produce is, *from the nature*

[23] *Ibid.*, p. 9.

[24] Cardozo, "Political Economy—Rent," p. 211. This is similar to Smith's statement that "the most fertile mine, too, regulates the price of coals at all the other mines in the neighborhood." Adam Smith, p. 167. This sentence was criticized by Ricardo, who claimed that "It is always the least fertile mine which regulates the price of coal." Ricardo, p. 222.

of things, raised at a comparatively greater expense than that which is manufactured, *whilst the population at the same time increases.* If we suppose population to come to a stop, profits will fall to a level; but if the condition of an increase of population be an additional expense in raising food to support it, without a proportionate return in its quantity, the level of profit between different employment is necessarily destroyed.[25]

Cardozo rejected the relationship, postulated by Ricardo, between the increased cost of production as inferior land was brought into cultivation, and rising prices. Whereas Ricardo viewed the major causal arrow as pointing from the former to the latter, Cardozo claimed that an opposite relationship prevailed in the real world. The prospects of profits were the strategic variable for Cardozo. Land which is unprofitable to cultivate under one state of demand and prices may become profitable when these variables change. If demand-supply conditions are such that prices and profits are high, the additional expense of cultivating inferior land will become a worth-while venture. He said, "The high price *precedes,* and never can *follow* extension of cultivation. It is never the *effect,* but invariably the *cause* of additional expenditure." [26] The attention that Cardozo called to this relationship between prices and expenses was one of his most significant contributions to rent theory. He stated the alleged inconsistency of the Ricardian school:

They make the rise of raw produce to *follow* from difficulty of production, and yet they state that the demand for additional produce *precedes,* as it must, the cultivation of inferior land, which is, in fact, saying that the increase of price is both *cause* and *effect.* The price of raw produce rises, say they, *because* the cost of obtaining an additional quantity is increased,

[25] Cardozo, *Notes,* pp. 10–11.
[26] Cardozo, "Political Economy—Rent," p. 210. A favorable reference to Cardozo's approach can be found in Fletcher, p. 43.

and yet this additional quantity is produced *in consequence* of the demand augmenting and the price rising. This is making the increase of the price the effect of additional demand, and, also, the effect of additional expediture.[27]

In other words, Ricardo appears to take two contradictory positions: (1) The increased difficulty of production causes prices to rise. (2) Rising population causes demand and prices to rise, which induces the cultivation of additional inferior land at higher cost.

Cardozo claimed that Ricardo's assumption of a rising population, with consequent increased demand for food and decreasing returns, is unrealistic. The fall in profits under these conditions would "proportionally" (it is difficult to know whether Cardozo used this word to connote an exact or rough equality) decrease the wages-fund maintaining the workers. Population would subsequently decline. Consequently, Ricardo's rent theory, dependent on a rising population for extending the margin of cultivation, was based on a false premise.

Cardozo connected a rising population with the increased output made possible by technological developments:

The increase of population, therefore, depends on the extent of the improvements in agriculture, and inferior land is laid down in tillage exactly in proportion as these improvements extend. This is the reverse of the new theory [i.e., Ricardian] which connects the augmentation of population and produce with the increased difficulty instead of the increased facility of production.[28]

The only time that rent could be expected to rise as inferior land was cultivated on the basis of diminishing returns would be when prices had been previously forced up. This, in turn, would depend on the state of demand

---

[27] Cardozo, *Notes*, pp. 24–25.   [28] *Ibid.*, p. 35.

and supply in the product market. In strikingly modern terms, he said, "The landlord obtains in all cases a rent in proportion to the price at which raw produce sells in the market—that price depends again on the proportion between the demand and the supply of such produce." [29]

The Ricardian notion of the necessity for bringing successively inferior land under cultivation was unacceptable to Cardozo: "It is not susceptible of evidence, admitting there are many qualities of land, that man must necessarily go from the best to the worst of these, to obtain increased supplies from the soil." [30]

Like Ricardo, Cardozo concluded that rent would be higher on the more fertile rather than less fertile lands. Profits, however, would tend toward an average level. Rents would be "in proportion to the surplus it [the land] can be made to yield after the deduction of all the expenses of cultivation, including of course, average profits and wages." [31] If the average level of profit could not be attained with a particular piece of land, it would remain uncultivated. The variation in rents in accordance with the productiveness of the land enabled all cultivators to

[29] *Ibid.*, p. 22. With the use of supply-demand analysis, Porter arrived at the anti-Ricardian position that the cultivation of poorer lands did not result in rising rents. He said, "Cultivation of less fertile lands will, in some measure, keep the price of rents and produce down because they furnish a partial supply and thus make demand less intense." Porter, p. 171. The discussion of this point by a fellow Southern economist, George Tucker, reveals the influence of Cardozo. In his criticism of Ricardian rent theory, Tucker claimed that Ricardo had mixed up cause and effect. He said, "Raw produce does not rise [in price] because inferior soils are cultivated, but they are cultivated because raw produce has risen and the effect of their cultivation is to lessen or arrest the rise rather than to produce it." George Tucker, *The Laws of Wages, Profits and Rent, Investigated*, pp. 35-36. Tucker added, as an illustration of Ricardo's illogical reasoning, "That when the rise of raw produce is inferred from the greater expense of labor required in its production, the same rise of raw produce should be said to cause the rise in the price of labor, which is the same thing as saying that the fall of labor causes the rise of labor."

[30] Cardozo, "Political Economy—Rent," p. 212.

[31] Cardozo, *Notes*, p. 34.

obtain the same rate of profit in Cardozo's model. The precise difference between rent and profits was left unclear. Instead of rent on the fertile land varying as poorer land was used, Cardozo thought that poorer land would merely bring in less rent:

It is not to effect a level of profit in agriculture, by the rise of rent on the better lands, that this difference [between returns from soils of different fertilities] is caused, but by the fall of rent on the poor soils, to enable them to be cultivated with the existing and average rate of profit. . . . It is by beginning at the highest degree of productiveness and falling in rent for the inferior soils, at every step in the descent and rising in the rent on the better tracts, if they yield higher returns than the general and average rate of profit, that that law [of rent] is to be truly deduced. . . . It is to enable the cultivator of No. 2 [i.e., land less fertile than No. 1] to obtain the same rate of profit with the cultivator of No. 1, that the rent on No. 2 falls, in proportion to its more limited powers, and from no other cause.[32]

Cardozo employed a Ricardian type model to explain this approach with greater precision:

Suppose land Nos. 1, 2 and 3 to yield, with the employment of an equal quantity of capital and labour, 100, 90, and 80 quarters of corn respectively, and suppose 60 quarters to be the net return on each quality, the surplus on no. 1, which would constitute rent would be 40 quarters, on no. 2, 30 quarters, and on no. 3, 20 quarters. These portions would exactly measure the originally productive power of these different qualities of land. Now, as the population increased, so as to make a resort to no. 2 necessary, the increase of skill and science in Agriculture that had taken place, would permit capital to be employed on No. 2 with increased returns [on the extensive margin]. Whether it were employed on No. 2 or No. 1, would make no difference as to profit—the capital applied to No. 2 would be

[32] Cardozo, "Political Economy—Rent," pp. 207, 209.

equally productive with that applied to No. 1, with proportionally less rent. No. 2 is resorted to, however, because land is of limited extent, and constant additions to the quantity of raw produce cannot be made on the same surface [suggesting diminishing returns on the intensive margin]. No. 2 would not then be cultivated unless it could be made as productive and profitable with the same outlay as No. 1, and unless the landlord consented to receive a relatively less rent than the owners of No. 1, in the ratio of the difference in their productive powers.[33]

In a review of Henry Carey's *The Past, Present and Future,* Cardozo also rejected the anti-Ricardian idea that it is the least fertile soils that are used first. Cardozo's analysis contains several dynamic elements, such as the importance of the time period for recouping one's investment as a factor in decision-making:

The question here is whether the land first taken into cultivation does not yield a larger relative return for the capital and labor expended, than land more productive, but requiring a larger outlay. The settler in the West who chooses a comparatively poor piece of soil in a healthy situation [capable of yielding some return], in preference to a richer parcel of bottom land nearer to a market, does it on the principle that his outlay being small and his return quick, it is more for his interest to give to the former $1.25 per acre, than for the latter the same or perhaps a less price. *Time* is a necessary element in his calculation. The return would be relatively greater if at the end of the first year his land produced 10 bushels of wheat to the acre, the whole outlay being $1000, than if the richer land costing the same price, produced at the end of 2 years 20 bushels to the acre, the outlay being proportionally larger. It is then the quickness or slowness of the return, in proportion to the capital expenditures on land that determines the practical question, whether land more or less naturally productive, or more or less distant from markets, should be earlier or later taken

[33] Cardozo, *Notes,* pp. 34-35.

into cultivation. . . . It is not therefore the relative fertility of land alone, but the relative expenditures including the time it would take to clear and bring into cultivation the naturally richer soils, which impels a new settler to choose his location.[34]

Cardozo concluded that the decision would and should be based on the self-interest of the parties.

The dynamic nature of Cardozo's theory stands in marked contrast to the static rent models of Ricardo. The basic conflict over distributive shares postulated by Ricardo does not exist in Cardozo's expansionary model of the American economic system. The economy of Cardozo's universe bears a close relationship to the American conditions of that period: widespread land ownership and large supply of fertile land.[35] It is in this dynamic historical context that rent emerges for Cardozo. It is unreasonable, however, to agree with Fletcher's comment that "American dissenters [in the pre-Civil War period] merely reflect the influence of the superficial aspects of the circumstances under which they wrote." [36] Cardozo's stress on the crucial role of technology reflected more than temporary phenomena; it cut to the heart of the American condition. The irony of his analysis is that it was least appropriate for describing conditions in Cardozo's state of South Carolina, with the possible exception of some progressive planters.[37] The declining fertility of the soil in this region of the Old South made Cardozo's optimistic rent models less than fully justified.

Cardozo also dealt more effectively with the important reciprocal relationship between economic development

---

[34] *Evening News*, January 6, 1848.

[35] It is worth noting, however, that widespread land ownership was less characteristic of Cardozo's home state of South Carolina than of the western areas of the country.

[36] Fletcher, p. 89.

[37] An account of the nature and limits of agricultural reform measures in South Carolina and other Southern states in the antebellum period can be found in Eugene Genovese, "Limits of Agrarian Reform in the South" (unpublished doctoral dissertation, Columbia University, 1960).

and the distribution of income than either Ricardo or Malthus.

WAGES AND PROFITS

Cardozo's writings on wages and profits are consistent with, and to a large extent derived from, his rent theory:

There can be no addition, in the first instance, to raw products unless the productive powers of the soil are increased. The additional produce is brought within the reach of a greater number of consumers from the fall of its price. The number of consumers is increased in proportion to the addition made to the means of subsistence on the principle that as quantity augments, price is reduced and consumption enlarged. The labourers, in the ratio of their increase, are compelled to receive less wages [Cardozo has in mind money wages], which enables the capitalist with the same money amount, to employ an additional number of labourers. . . . Wages do not encroach on profits nor profits on wages. All that is necessary to the final results is, that science and skill should be able to overcome the difficulty of production on land of decreasing fertility.[38]

Although it is not clear that Cardozo understood Ricardo's framework, he criticized the inverse wage-profit relationship that Ricardo postulated. In his essentially static model, Ricardo was concerned with the problem of proportion: what share of a given output at any particular time would go to labor and capital respectively. The logical conclusion of this type of approach was that wages would rise only if profits declined, and vice versa. A characteristic statement of this position was that, "Profits depend on high or low wages. . . . A rise of wages would not raise the profit of commodities, but would invariably lower profits." [39]

[38] Cardozo, *Notes*, pp. 40–41.
[39] Ricardo, pp. 71, 76. See also *ibid.*, pp. 80–81. Ricardo admitted that it

Cardozo's more dynamic model dealt with the total amounts going to labor and capital. From this perspective, he could argue with equal logic that wages and profits would simultaneously rise in an economy characterized by the progressive employment of technological improvements.

Central to Cardozo's approach is the distinction between a money and real level of analysis. He said that the process of economic development was accompanied by falling money wages, rising real wages, and rising real profits (defined as the quantity of produce for which money returns on an investment will exchange):

In the progress of society money wages fall, in a natural state of things, and real wages rise. Real wages rise because the price of necessaries falls [Cardozo assumes that increasing returns may prevail], and the labourer's command of them is increased. Money wages fall, because the labourer, from the rise of his real wages, is induced to marry and multiply, by which the number of labourers is increased in the market. But real wages will rise in higher proportion than money wages fall [i.e., prices of goods would decline more rapidly than money wages]. . . . Money profits do not fall in the progress of society, for although the prices of all commodities decline, their quantity increases in an equal proportion [Cardozo appears to be assuming a situation of unitary price elasticity], and the capitalist receives as large a money amount as before the decline. Real profits rise, for they depend on the amount of the returns *in produce,* compared with the amount of the expenditure, and as the quantity of productions in the progress of society is multiplied, the real gains of the capitalist must increase.[40]

These views are in marked contrast to Ricardo's. He claimed that money wages would increase in the process of

---

was possible for profits in particular sectors to rise although wages were rising. He insisted, however, that the general rate of profits would fall as wages increased.

[40] Cardozo, *Notes,* p. 40.

economic development because the rising price of necessities, due to cultivation of inferior soils, outweighed the fact that the supply of laborers would augment more rapidly than the demand for their services. The proximate cause of the falling profits was the rising money wages, but the underlying cause was the increased cost and prices of food cultivation as inferior land was used to feed a rising population. Although this tendency could be temporarily checked by technology, Ricardo saw the repeal of the Corn Law as the only permanent cure. Such a step would bring him closer to Cardozo's universe of discourse. Under these conditions, profits would rise, money wages would fall, and the rapid rate of capital accumulation would permit a rise in real wages.

Cardozo criticized the Ricardian school:

[They] never view the increased *quantity* of labour necessary to an augmentation of produce in connection with a fall in its *price,* or conceive the possibility of such a reduction of money wages as will enable the capitalist to employ an additional number of labourers . . . to obtain an augmentation of produce, without a proportional increase of expenditure.[41]

Cardozo, in other words, assumed the existence of a very price-responsive, wage-flexible, market mechanism. A fall in the price of commodities was expected to elicit a proportional or more than proportional increased demand for the commodities, and a derived demand for labor, whose money wage would adjust quickly to falling costs and prices. Cardozo was especially optimistic over the economic effects of employing machinery. He said, "Every invention that reduces the price of labor has the effect of giving employment to an additional quantity." [42]

[41] *Ibid.,* p. 42.
[42] *Ibid.,* p. 57. Cardozo took the extreme view that "the labourers themselves are fully as much interested in improvements in machinery as the masters themselves."

Technology was as critical a strategic factor for Cardozo as repeal of the Corn Laws was for Ricardo. They were the keys to cumulative economic development in their respective models. For Cardozo, technology had a highly desirable multilevel effect, resulting in increased output and lower prices of agricultural and manufactured goods, which encouraged a rising population and subsequent increased employment at lower money wages. The reduced outlay on money wages and the increased returns from the sale of an increasing output provided the capitalist with a continuous source of savings for capital accumulation. Real wages and profits in this model continually move in an upward direction. Diminishing returns is rejected even as a remote possibility. Cardozo stated:

If the capitalist regularly augments the difference between his outlay and his returns, he proportionally enlarges the sphere for the employment of the whole of what he saves from his necessary expenditures, not only with undiminished but constantly increasing revenue. . . . It is obvious that without this condition of a constant and equal augmentation in the supply of labor with capital, and a proportionate fall of its price with the price of production generally, that both the power and will to accumulate would cease on the part of producers. The power to accumulate is founded on the reduced [money] wages of labour; for it is by savings in these that capital is made available for an increase of population, and it is by the consequent addition to the number of working producers that productions are multiplied and profits still further augmented.[43]

Cardozo had an unshakable faith in the continued existence of unlimited investment opportunities. A profitable market for products and labor could be indefinitely extended. He specifically rejected Malthus' contention that

[43] *Ibid.*, pp. 60, 69.

the abundance of accumulated capital will eventually cause the profit rate to fall. A rising population was viewed as a favorable sign on several grounds: (1) It supplied labor for production. (2) It was a source of market demand for the commodities produced. (3) By reducing money wages, it provided an inducement to the capitalist to engage in profit-motivated economic activity.

Cardozo commented on the last point when he wrote:

> The capitalist has every interest in that excess of population, which while it tasks the labourer to the utmost of his bodily energies from the pressure of want, keeps down his money wages to the lowest possible limit. . . . In the ordinary state of things, the sacrifices of the labourer will very nearly determine the gains of the landlord and capitalist.[44]

On first reading, this paragraph appears to contradict Cardozo's contention that wages and profits do not encroach on each other, but in actuality, there is no contradiction. A decline of money wages, in Cardozo's view, was a critical step in initiating the process of capital accumulation. He remained optimistic that in the long run real wages and profits would advance together. Although he stressed that "What is gained by the labourer, is not *necessarily* lost to the capitalist, and vice versa," [45] it equally follows that what is gained (or lost) by the laborers is not necessarily gained (or lost) by the capitalist. The underlying principle is that "profits as well as wages depend on the great law of demand and supply." [46] If population is excessive relative to the demand for labor, wages may be low, while profits may, at the same time, be either low or high. "It is competition [i.e., supply-demand market forces] that must determine the share that falls to each class under every condition of things, whether rent be paid or not." [47]

[44] Cardozo, "Political Economy—Rent," p. 215.
[45] *Ibid.*, pp. 216–17.   [46] *Ibid.*, p. 216.   [47] *Ibid.*, p. 216.

In this discussion, Cardozo accepted a distinction drawn by Malthus between the regulation and the limitation of profits. The former was determined by the state of the market demand and supply. The limiting principle, however, was concerned with the boundaries of profitability, and, in reference to this, Cardozo said that profits "cannot exceed the natural or acquired powers of the soil." [48] In other words, the fertility of land sets the limits to the rate of profit, but does not regulate or determine its exact level at any given time. That is performed by demand and supply. Cardozo's emphasis on demand as a determinant of the returns to the factors of production places his writings in sharp contrast to those of the classical school:

It is demand, therefore, that raises wages, it is demand, therefore, that raises profits and we may add, that raises rent, notwithstanding the necessity of employing more labour in cultivation, and paying for that labour at a higher price.[49]

In rejecting Ricardo's inverse wage-profit relationship, Cardozo developed the concept of an adjustable standard of living. Ricardo based his profit theory on the view that rising food prices led to rising money wages that enabled the real wages to remain constant. He assumed an inflexible standard of living in his analytical model, although in his general discussion he asserted the possibility of changes in the conventional subsistence minimum. Cardozo more realistically claimed that rising prices may result in a depression of real wages. Money wages do not necessarily rise when the prices of food increase. This is a key concept, because, if true, the events forecast by the Ricardian model—

[48] *Ibid.*, p. 216. Cardozo did not give any exact reference to Malthus on this point. Discussion can be found in Malthus, p. 271. Malthus' wording is couched in more marginal terms. He says that profits are limited by "the productiveness or unproductiveness of the last capitals employed upon the land."

[49] *Ibid.*, p. 214.

falling profits, slackened capital accumulation, etc.—would not necessarily materialize. Even assuming the validity of the Ricardian labor theory of value, a transfer from profits to wages in a market of rising prices would therefore take place only if the living standards of the people had reached the irreducible minimum. Only in this situation would money wages have to rise when prices increased.

There is a different scale of comfort for the working population in the same country, at periods not very far separated, and it cannot be conceded, that habit is so connected with a certain and invariable standard of necessaries for the labourer, that the rate at which he is recompensed in money, must be necessarily raised as the rate of his reward in commodities in general is lowered. . . . The labourer must receive fewer commodities when they exist in relative scarcity, and a smaller sum in wages, if there are a greater number seeking employment than there is demand for the products of capital and industry. . . . There is never any transfer, as insisted on by the new school [Ricardo] of profits to wages, as the difficulty of procuring the subsistence of the labourer increases, unless the working portion of the population can submit to no further reduction in the quantity or quality of their food and no increase of physical exertion.[50]

Cardozo claimed that, in the absence of unusual market disturbances, it was rational to expect that "as a greater share fell to the lot of the labourer, a larger quantity would be assigned to the capitalist. . . . Profits and [real] wages advance inevitably in the regular process of society."[51]

In a later newspaper article, Cardozo expressed the same point more specifically:

[50] Ibid., pp. 215, 217. Tucker, a Southern contemporary of Cardozo, also criticized Ricardo for his assumption of a fixed standard of subsistence. The increased demand for food as population rises may, according to Tucker, cause prices to rise and real wages to fall (i.e., a poorer diet may be used). Tucker, pp. 35, 36, 156.
[51] Cardozo, "Political Economy—Rent," p. 217; Cardozo, Notes, p. 50.

The proportion received by the capitalist, whether his capital
is in land, money, or commodities, diminishes with the progress
of society, but as the quantity of commodities constantly increases, all classes receive a greater share of those commodities.[52]

Cardozo apparently was the earliest American economist
to take the position that the relative share of capital falls in
the course of economic development although its absolute
amount rises, while labor gains both relatively and absolutely. Later, Henry Carey, the leading American economist of the pre-Civil War period, also embraced this optimistic position. Although Carey did quote on occasion
from Cardozo's editorials in the *Southern Patriot* and *Evening News*, there is no mention in his works of Cardozo's
major effort, *Notes on Political Economy*. However, the
similarity of their views on this issue is remarkably—one
might almost say suspiciously—close. Carey said:

The proposition in regard to the distribution of wealth that
we may have submitted to the reader, is, that, with every increase of production the labourer takes an increased proportion
of the product, leaving to the capitalist a *diminishing proportion,* but that with this diminution of proportion there is a
constant increase in the quantity allotted to him and that consequently the wages of the labourer and the profits of the capitalist increase with the augmentation of capital and improvement in the quality of labour.[53]

Cardozo examined the British experience during and
following the Napoleonic Wars against the expectations of
his distribution model; he questioned whether the presence of war prosperity or postwar gluts altered the validity
of his thesis that money wages and prices fall while real
wages and profits rise in the course of economic growth.
During the war, money wages, profits, and prices rose.

[52] *Southern Patriot,* January 11, 1838.
[53] Henry Carey, *Principles of Political Economy,* II, 310.

Cardozo attempted to explain this phenomenon as a product of the unusual wartime conditions. A labor shortage developed because of the high war-induced demand for labor relative to its supply, and the resulting high level of money wages and profits created a high level of effective demand which caused the prices of commodities to rise.

Cardozo described the market as one which "advanced money wages in a higher proportion than it depressed real wages." [54] Although awkwardly expressed, it is clear in context that he was explaining that money wages rose less than prices, thus causing real wages to fall. In greater detail, Cardozo said:

The high wages of labour, as well as the high profits of capital, kept up also the price of raw produce, for the labourer and capitalist had an increasing money amount to devote to the purchase of the necessaries of life. The supply of raw products was augmented, but it was not increased in proportion to the additional wants or additional demand of the increasing population. The demand was always therefore in advance of the supply of necessaries, which augmented their price. . . . Although that portion of the cultivator's expense, consisting of wages, increased with other parts of his outlay, still the quantity of produce obtained far exceed this increase of expenditure [i.e., real profits increased].[55]

Cardozo also insisted that the Poor Laws kept wages lower in this wartime period:

The wages of labour . . . were prevented from rising to the height they would have reached from the effect of the legal assessment for the relief of the poor. The labourers, from an unnatural competition among themselves, were thence precluded from receiving as large a recompense as they were entitled to, from the increased demand among employers.[56]

[54] Cardozo, *Notes*, p. 45.   [55] *Ibid.*, pp. 45, 46.   [56] *Ibid.*, p. 46.

Cardozo's precise meaning is unclear. A reasonable interpretation is that capital provides employment for labor, and to the extent that the capitalists pay charity, they have less funds (circulating capital) to employ labor. Hence the supply of labor for existing jobs is higher than it would otherwise be. In the absence of the Poor Laws, wages would have risen to a higher level. Cardozo's conclusion was that his general views on the relationship of wages, profits, and prices were valid under normal conditions, but in a period of wartime or market gluts a more complex level of analysis was required, e.g., abandoning Say's Law of Markets.

Ricardo attempted to apply his wage-profit doctrines to the foreign trade sector. Like Cardozo, he stressed the mutual benefits of free trade, but unlike Cardozo, Ricardo claimed that the extension of foreign trade would not increase the value of the goods in the country. Ricardo also maintained it would not raise profits unless the necessities consumed by the workers could be obtained at a lower price:

No extension of foreign trade will immediately increase the amount of value in a country. . . . As the value of all foreign goods is measured by the quantity of the produce of our land and labour which is given in exchange for them, we should have no greater value if . . . we obtained double the quantity of foreign goods in exchange for a given quantity of ours.[57]

This type of approach indicates, as Cardozo pointed out, Ricardo's prior acceptance of the labor theory of value. The reason he can say that the lesser or greater quantity of goods imported will not affect their value is that the value has been set by the amount of labor time involved in the production of a commodity. In these terms, a given amount of labor time can purchase any amount of im-

[57] Ricardo, p. 77.

ported products without changing their value. In Ricardo's scheme, trade or technological developments are thought of as affecting the prices of goods, not profits or wages:

The ratio of profit can never be increased but by a fall in wages, and . . . there can be no permanent fall of wages but in consequence of a fall of the necessaries on which wages are expended. If, therefore, by the extension of foreign trade or by improvements in machinery, the food and necessaries of the labourer can be brought to market at a reduced price, profits will rise. . . . If the commodities obtained by a cheaper rate, by the extension of foreign commerce, or by the improvements of machinery, be exclusively the commodities consumed by the rich, no alteration will take place in the rate of profits.[58]

Cardozo astutely noted the absurd implications of Ricardo's approach, namely that profits would be lower in luxury goods industries (producers and importers) than in those producing necessity goods. This would upset the profit equilibrium assumption and erase the incentive of the manufacturers of luxury goods to increase their output.

Another level on which Cardozo rejected Ricardo's view that trade expansion does not increase the value of commodities was the distinction drawn between the profitability of a producer's and a merchant's economic activities. Cardozo, unlike Ricardo, claimed that the profit principle operated differently for the merchant and manufacturer:

Although, as commodities increase in quantity . . . the profits of their producers continue always on the same money value [based on an assumption of unitary elasticity], this is not true of the profits of the merchant. . . . The merchant's gains are always received as well as estimated in money, and, although his real profit is in proportion . . . the quantity of both money

---

[58] Ibid., p. 80, cited by Cardozo in Notes, pp. 109–10.

and real profit is always equal in his case, unless some disturbance of prices has occurred. But, in the case of the *producer* his money and his real profit are always unequal, if no such disturbance of price has taken place.[59]

Cardozo claimed that the merchant had to receive a greater return from a larger than from a smaller quantity in order to maintain a profit rate comparable to that of the producer. He illustrated this principle with a hypothetical example:

Suppose a manufacturer was to produce this year 1000 yards and to obtain one dollar per yard for it, should he the next year augment the quantity 25 per cent he must submit to a reduction of price in this proportion—he must accept [a price] of 80 cents per yard when its quantity is increased in the above ratio. . . . This is the situation of the *producer;* but the case is different with regard to the merchant. . . . He must receive a larger money amount for a greater than a smaller quantity of commodities, or his profits will be below the general level. Thus if we suppose him to export 1000 yards of cloth when its price is one dollar per yard, and to derive 25 per cent profit [i.e., the same return as the producer], he must sell the commodity he imports for $1250; but when he invests this amount in the purchase of cloth, the quantity having proportionally increased to 1250 yards [i.e., the merchant's exports are assumed to increase by the same amount as manufacturer's output], he must obtain $1562.50 [i.e., a 25 per cent return on $1250], for the goods he imports in return; for as the gain of the manufacturer of cloth is 25 per cent when its quantity . . . has increased in this ratio, the possession of the above sum is necessary by the trader in this article to put him on the same footing in regard to profit.[60]

Ricardo's profit equilibrium assumption is obviously inconsistent with his view that the gains of the merchant will

[59] Cardozo, *Notes*, pp. 105–6.
[60] *Ibid.*, pp. 106–7. In an early newspaper article Cardozo said that "The

not be affected by the quantity of foreign goods obtained in trade. Ricardo's case rested on the labor theory of value and the idea that classes could gain only at the expense of other classes, and this was based on a relatively static set of conditions.

Not restricted by these assumptions, Cardozo could state, "It is by increasing the mass of commodities that the general rate of profit is augmented and from no other cause." [61] Cardozo says that profits and wages do not directly depend on each other. Demand and supply in the labor and commodities market determine wages and profits. Under normal conditions, they influence each other but do not definitely determine each other as in the strict Ricardian formulation.

In a later discussion of the determination of the rate of interest and the rate of profit in the long and short run, Cardozo's analysis has several modern elements:

The rate of interest is influenced temporarily by demand as compared with the supply of money, but permanently and in the long-run by the rate of profit, as this [i.e., the rate of profit] is governed by the demand as compared with the supply of capital.[62]

Perhaps Cardozo's most effective discussion of profits proceeded on a macro-level of analysis: He related the problem of maintaining a continuity of profits with that of sustaining a balance between general production and general consumption. (This will be taken up in close detail in the chapter on business cycles.)

Cardozo drew a distinction between the individual and

---

merchants of each country sell their productions for more than they cost, and the whole profit which each country gains is in proportion to the whole capital invested." *Southern Patriot,* July 17, 1819.

[61] Cardozo, *Notes,* p. 109. Cardozo did not appear to be fully aware of the assumptions under which Ricardo was operating—a long-run static model. Hence his criticism often did not directly confront Ricardo's presentation.

[62] Atlanta *Southern Confederacy,* March 18, 1863.

social profitability of the type of investment (such as railroads) that is now referred to as social overhead. He said that if the rate of profit on railroad investments was less than the general profit rate, those investments should be undertaken nevertheless. Other elements besides the rate of dividends on railroad securities should be taken into account in computing total profitability. The savings in time, the increased ease of communication, and reduced cost of consumer goods through the construction of railroads, should be counted as part of the social profit. Pecuniary losses to the railroad proprietors may be compensated by pecuniary gains to society in general. Cardozo presented the issue in this way:

If by connecting two points which observation and convenience suggest as commercial and natural thoroughfares there is considerable saving of time . . . this is certainly to be viewed as a constituent of profit, and not to be omitted in a consideration of the pecuniary advantages to society in general, from an outlay that produces this result. . . . The reduction in the cost of articles of daily consumption from the rapidity of intercourse by Railroad, in which the proprietors of Rail Road stock participate, in proportion to their expenditure, with the rest of the community . . . must be taken into any estimate of mere profit and loss.[63]

Cardozo also appears to have been aware of the external economies created by a developed railroad network. He pointed to the gains reaped by other sectors of the economy, claiming that the owners of railroad stock were rent, wage, and profit receivers from commerce and agriculture, and these incomes would rise as the result of a better transportation system:

The proprietors of Rail Road stock generally are, we must suppose, also the receivers of rents, of the wages of labour, or of the profits drawn from commerce, internal and external, in its

[63] *Southern Patriot,* May 26, 1840.

various spheres and occupations. The more rapid transportation of staples of commerce and the products for immediate consumption, the augmented expenditure for travelling must tend to enlarge the rents of landlords, the wages of labour and the gains of trade in a far greater ratio than . . . the loss of revenues on a portion of the general investment in such public works.[64]

(The social implications of this approach will be discussed in Chapter Nine, Social Philosophy.)

[64] *Ibid.* Also see Guy S. Callender, "The Early Transportation and Banking Enterprises of the States in Relation to the Growth of Corporations," in Lambie and Clemence, ed., *Economic Change in America*, pp. 555–56.

FIVE

The Tariff Issue

CARDOZO wrote during a period in which the economic keynote of the country was expansion. The financial system reflected this trend. He closely examined developments of the tariff, banking, and credit structures, since these influenced the manner in which the burgeoning commercial system operated.

The large majority of Southern thinkers, including Cardozo, reflected the interests of an agrarian section in championing the cause of free trade. Their writings on the tariff question reveal the key intellectual influence of the early classical economists. Smith and Ricardo, for example, stressed the mutually advantageous increase in efficiency resulting from free trade. Their rationale was that countries would be able to make more effective use of their resources if they employed them in those operations in which they had a natural or acquired advantage. Cardozo's position was unusual in that he was one of the few early American economists who favored free trade while rejecting Ricardian distribution theory.[1]

A brief historical description of the tariff issue is a useful backdrop for examining Cardozo's contributions. The period of embargo and war restrictions from 1808 to 1815 gave a vigorous stimulus to the growth of manufactures in many sections of the United States by cutting off importations of foreign goods. It was an effective substitute for a protective tariff. There was comparatively slight opposition to the tariff of 1816 due to the existence of a large public debt. The average rate of duties was about 20 to 25 percent.[2]

The South was split on this tariff, but reached near-unanimity in its opposition to succeeding protective tariff legislation.[3] The crisis of 1819 marked the main beginning of the protectionist movement; previous to that period, tariff duties were not widely regarded as protection per se. The attempt to introduce a tariff bill in 1820 failed by one vote but was carried successfully in 1824 by a com-

---

[1] Turner, p. 19, says, "On the whole, protectionists have contested the Ricardian rent doctrine, while free traders have accepted it." George Tucker is another exception. He rejected Ricardian distribution theory, although on grounds different from Cardozo's, while adhering in the main to a free-trade position. George Tucker, *The Laws of Wages, Profits and Rent Investigated*, esp. Chapter IX.

[2] This brief historical account leans heavily on Frank W. Taussig's *The Tariff History of the United States*.

Although Taussig's general position was that protective tariffs had little direct influence in promoting the introduction and growth of manufacturing in the United States, he leaned to the view that the tariff of 1816 may have performed the limited service of sustaining some of the manufacturing industries in the difficult development from agriculture to manufacturing in the 1816 to 1819 period. Taussig, Chapter 1, particularly pp. 33–35.

With specific reference to South Carolina, a recent writer stated, "The tariff had not seemed to be a particularly heavy burden on the South Carolina economy before 1820." Alfred G. Smith, Jr., p. 14.

[3] The Congressional voting pattern of the Southerners on the successive tariffs reveals the change: 1816: 23 for, 34 against; 1824: 14 for, 54 against. Of the 14 favorable votes, 13 were from Tennessee and Kentucky. Davis R.

bination of middle and western states—the stronghold of protectionism in that period. A clash of sectional interests manifested itself at the time, as indicated by strong Southern opposition and divided opposition from New England; the older commercial interests were antitariff and the rising manufacturing interests were protariff.

The tariff of 1828 was the high peak for tariff protection in the pre-Civil War period. The nominal rate was $33\frac{1}{3}$ percent, but a complicated system of minimum valuations, under which products costing between a minimum and a maximum price were charged a duty as if they cost the maximum price, made the actual rate considerably higher. This "Tariff of Abominations," as it was called, contained a motley mixture of high duties on both imported manufactured goods and raw materials.[4] Cardozo took an active public position on this issue. He drew up a memorial in 1827 in Charleston on the tariff problem, "The Memorial of the Chamber of Commerce and Citizens of Charleston against the Tariff on Woolen Goods Proposed at the Second Session of the Nineteenth Congress," which was

Dewey, *Financial History of the United States*, pp. 163, 175. Important conflicts also existed within several Southern states. A study of South Carolina tariff history, for example, indicated that the coastal areas (controlled mainly by the commercial interests of Charleston), the back country (representing the small-scale independent white farmer), and the interior cotton plantation area (based on slave labor) often held conflicting positions on the tariff issue. See John L. Conger, "South Carolina and the Early Tariffs," *Mississippi Valley Historical Review*, March, 1919, pp. 415–33.

[4] According to the standard interpretation, passage of this bill was part of a plan, hatched by Jackson's supporters, which miscarried. They hoped that the high tariffs on raw materials would split the protariff Northern states by setting New England against the western and middle states. For details, see Taussig, pp. 88–89, and Dewey, pp. 177–80.

A recent questioning of this view stressing the critical role played by Van Buren—at that time the Senator from New York—has been advanced by Robert V. Remini. See his "Martin Van Buren and the Tariff of Abominations," *American Historical Review*, July 1958, pp. 903–17. He claims that Van Buren tried to engineer the passage of this tariff in response to pressure from his New York constituents and to widen the support for Jackson in the West and North.

adopted unanimously by the citizens of Charleston at a Public Meeting.[5]

The Tariff Act of 1832 passed with the partial support of the South; it was supported by Virginia and North Carolina and opposed by South Carolina and Georgia.[6] By and large, this reduced the protective duty schedule to the earlier 1824 position. Although this measure was acceptable to many Southerners including Cardozo, the States Rights group in South Carolina rejected it and precipitated the nullification crisis. After the passage of the nullification ordinance in South Carolina, the Clay-sponsored Compromise Tariff of 1833, providing for a gradual reduction of the tariff to 20 percent over a ten-year period ending in 1842, was passed. Except for a brief period of high tariff protection during the Whig administration of Harrison and Tyler between 1842 and 1846, rates gradually declined in the remaining pre-Civil War years. In the period of great industrial prosperity following 1846, the tariff question became a subsidiary issue,[7] while slavery became the key national question.

Cardozo's antitariff writings were presented in a more statesmanlike and less sectional manner than those of other Southern critics. During the early nullification crisis, he took the view that the breakup of the Union was a greater

[5] Although Cardozo is not listed as the official author of the document, the following sources attribute authorship to him: (1) obituary notice in the Charleston *News and Courier*, September 2, 1873; (2) an article by William King in the same paper the following day also mentioning Cardozo's having authored the petition; (3) Cardozo's own reference to his authorship in *Reminiscences of Charleston*.

[6] Dewey, p. 185. Statistics on Congressional voting by geographical sections are presented. Also see Van Deusen, p. 21. He points out that some of the representatives from South Carolina—Drayton, Blair, and Mitchell—supported the tariff of 1832. "They did not approve the bill but voted for it because they thought it contained a partial reduction of duties."

[7] The decline in importance of the tariff issue is indicated by the fact that Cardozo wrote no articles on this question between April, 1846, and June, 1854, although he wrote continuously during the long interval.

evil than that posed by the tariff. He said, "We should consider it a lesser evil to have this system of protection, with all of its attendant losses and prospective risks, to a separation of the States." [8] He criticized those Southerners who exaggerated the adverse effects of the tariff, and stressed the national rather than sectional loss caused by the tariff. Even in the 1850s, when his sectional views hardened, Cardozo continued to view the tariff as only a minor cause of Southern economic weaknesses, and as an issue on which compromise was both acceptable and desirable.

Cardozo presented these arguments in favor of free trade:

(1) It enabled a country to obtain a more profitable use of its factor supplies. He took the position that profitability was greatest in the agricultural sector where the South's factor supplies gave it the greatest productive powers:

Nature has herself pointed out that agriculture should be the leading pursuit of our country because we possess boundless and fertile lands that are cultivated with little labor and expense of capital. Agriculture must therefore yield the largest return for our industry and capital. . . . it is simply because we have not as large a capital as Great Britain is able to invest in manufacturing, that we are obliged to employ a less capital to the cultivation of land.[9]

Free trade was thus seen as resulting in the most efficient allocation of a society's resources.

(2) It would be a stimulant to industry, commerce, and peace, and therefore would further the national interest.[10]

[8] Cardozo, *The Tariff: Its True Character and Effects Practically Illustrated* (hereafter referred to as *The Tariff*), p. 50.
[9] *Southern Patriot*, May 26, 1819. Cardozo also claimed that labor would be directed toward agriculture because of its comparatively higher value in that sector. *Ibid.*, May 27, 1819.
[10] *Ibid.*, May 2, 1818.

(3) The benefits of free trade are reciprocal. He held that the exportation of agricultural products by the United States and manufactured goods by England provided subsistence for an increasing population in England, which would increase the demand for food and raw materials from the United States. In turn this would provide a further stimulus to the development of our agricultural resources and increase the wealth of both countries. He said, "All nations share pretty equally in the advantages of trade, in proportion to their skill, capital and enterprise." [11]

(4) Free trade was viewed as the grand remedy for trade stagnation. By creating new wants, Cardozo thought that it would restore a balance between expanding production and lagging consumption.[12]

(5) It increases the effectiveness of international lending-borrowing operations by setting up a mutually beneficial chain of credit.[13]

Cardozo took the position that tariffs imposed for war preparedness were a valid exception to the doctrine of free trade.[14] Retaliatory tariffs, under certain conditions, were also viewed as a permissible exception. They were considered in the acceptable category if employed as a brief defensive measure, aimed at inducing another country to remove its trade restrictions. Cardozo justified the defensive use of countervailing regulations against British trade with the United States, since England was preventing American ships from engaging in direct trade with the West Indies.[15] However, he rejected the notion that a nation automatically benefited from imposing a counter tariff. He

[11] *Ibid.*, July 17, 1819; August 6, 1819.   [12] *Ibid.*, May 30, 1829.
[13] *Ibid.*, April 22, 1818; August 18, 1819.
[14] *Ibid.*, April 14, 15, 1818; July 8, 1842. In the latter article, he also recognized navigation laws for protecting a merchant marine as a justified exception.
[15] *Ibid.*, April 15, 1818; September 7, 1819; August 15, September 6, 1821;

called our retaliation against the British Corn Laws "retaliation with a vengeance." [16]

In a later article, Cardozo indicated that he was willing
to widen the range of reasons which would temporarily
justify the imposition of tariffs. During a period in which a
very unfavorable American balance of trade had resulted
in an excessive drain of specie, Cardozo favored temporarily increasing the import duty on luxuries (from France in
particular) to halt this drain. Indicating his acceptance of
the expediency of imposing commercial restrictions, Cardozo said:

The trade operates at particular intervals as an inconvenient
drain on our stock of precious metals. . . . To increase the
duties therefore on such luxuries as wine, silks and laces, etc.
would constitute such a restriction on a particular class of imports as would be consistent with commercial reciprocity while
it would operate as a tax on that branch of consumption that
would tend to an equalization of the duties on imports and
assist to keep the coin of the country in a state of repose.[17]

He also claimed that this tax on luxuries reduced the necessity for a direct tax on such things as houses, land, and
capital. Although Cardozo did not stand for an unqualified
adoption of the principles of free trade, he felt that retaliatory regulations were a doubtful expediency because they
frequently led to commercial wars and market instability.

January 30, 1822. Cardozo labeled as "inexpedient and improper" a petition
by citizens of Charleston calling for removal of American restrictions on
trade with the West Indies (American counter-restrictions prohibited British ships from carrying United States produce for purposes of consumption
in the West Indies) on the grounds that our representatives were negotiat-
ing with Britain for removal of their restrictions on American trade with
the West Indies. *Ibid.*, January 11, 1822. Also, Cardozo, *Reminiscences of
Charleston*, pp. 25–26.

[16] *Southern Patriot*, September 15, 1828; June 12, 1820. He pointed out
that England imposed a low tariff on our largest export product of cotton,
and a higher tariff on some of our minor exports.

[17] *Ibid.*, March 6, 1841.

Cardozo's views on the Corn Laws were similar to Ricardo's. He advocated their repeal as the only remedy for England's postwar economic problems.[18] He thought that such a policy would increase the sale of grains to England, thereby raising foreign income and consequently augmenting the sales of English manufactures and thus increasing the wages fund for the employment of labor. In other words, repealing the Corn Laws would have the effect of increasing employment and decreasing the price of food.

The interaction of the British Corn Laws and American tariffs had the effect of producing disequilibrating conditions in the cotton market. According to Cardozo, the Corn Laws caused American production to shift from foodstuffs to cotton and thus augmented the domestic supply of cotton, while the American tariff on foreign manufactured goods tended to reduce foreign demand for our raw cotton.[19] Cardozo also stated that by excluding American grain from England, the Corn Laws aided in the forging of a political alliance between the Western and Eastern sections aimed at excluding the manufactured goods of Europe. He predicted that the repeal of the Corn Laws would weaken the protariff position of the Northwest. It is possible that the repeal did have the effect of postponing the alliance between the West and the East.

Like Ricardo, Cardozo viewed the Corn Laws as a tax on the commercial and manufacturing classes for the benefit of the landed monopolists, which had the effect of weakening England's competitive position relative to the Continental countries. Cardozo said that these restrictions

. . . encumber the channels of trade and become . . . inseparably interwoven with the habits, the interests and the privileges of its various classes. . . . Commercial restrictions become

[18] *Ibid.*, June 17, 1820.   [19] *Ibid.*, March 7, 1821.

after a lapse of time so interlocked that they are consolidated into one whole, no material part of which can be removed without discordance and injury.[20]

He insisted that British wealth had been attained in spite of her restrictive Corn Laws:

Her regulations have, perhaps, rather accompanied than preceded, or probably did not long precede, her progress in this department of industry [i.e., manufacturing]. It is certain, however, that her limited territory and compact population would have early favored independently of her regulations the establishment of manufacture.[21]

His criticism of the Corn Laws was that they directed more capital into the relatively less productive agricultural sector and progressively increased the cost of production.

Cardozo rejected the idea of many tariff proponents that the gains made by Britain from free trade with the United States were greater than those reaped by the United States. The critics of free trade had pointed to the considerable difference between the high price at which England sold manufactured goods to the United States and the low price at which England bought raw cotton from the United States. Cardozo claimed that England received only "the fair and ordinary profit of manufacturing countries, and falls far short of profits on capital in agricultural states with fertile territory." [22] If Britain made a higher total profit from international trade than did the United States, it was because more capital was employed in manufacturing than in agriculture. The higher price of manufactured goods reflected the greater amount of labor and capital

[20] *Ibid.*, June 5, 1821; December 11, 1839. See also November 8, 1839.
[21] *Ibid.*, August 20, 1819.
[22] *Ibid.*, August 12, 1819. Cardozo appears to have accepted Smith's concept of the hierarchy of employments of capital. He said, "The interest of the employment of an equal amount of capital will be more considerable in agriculture than in manufacturing because the fertility of nature here cooperates with industry."

that was needed in manufacturing.[23] Cardozo concluded
that Britain was not benefiting at the expense of the
United States, and that free trade "distributes her benefits
with a nearly equal hand to all." [24]

Cardozo's statesmanlike approach to the tariff question
is illustrated by his opposition to the drastic reduction advocated by many of his fellow Southerners. Although he
had opposed the setting up of tariffs, Cardozo felt that once
it had been established, sudden repeal would have injurious effects on the economy:

We would oppose and did oppose, by every means in our
power, its [the tariff's] establishment among us. But after it was
established measurably—after millions of capital have been invested and thousands of persons live by it who would lose the
means of subsistence by its abandonment—the question becomes one in which policy, if not justice, becomes blended with
principle. . . . If certain branches of Southern industry had
been fostered by law, we would be as much the enemy of its
sudden repeal or abandonment as we are now opposed to the
infliction of a similar evil on the Northern states . . . . [T]he
proposition made by McDuffie [of reducing duties across

[23] A reason why the price of manufactured goods is higher than the price
of raw produce, according to Cardozo, is that "Manufacturing commodities
contain . . . a certain quantity of capital which has been already expended," e.g., buildings, machines, etc. Part of the price goes toward the
replacement of this capital. *Ibid.*, September 11, 1820.

[24] *Ibid.*, June 12, 1819. Cardozo said that the ratio of the cost of production of rude to that of manufactured cotton was the same as the ratio of
the price of rude to the price of manufactured cotton; and that the ratio
of the quantity of labor and capital used to produce rude to that used to
produce manufactured cotton was the same as the ratio of the price of rude
to the price of manufactured cotton; i.e.:

$$\frac{\text{Quantity of labor} + \text{capital producing raw cotton}}{\text{Quantity of labor} + \text{capital producing manufactured cotton}} =$$

$$\frac{\text{Cost of producing raw cotton}}{\text{Cost of producing manufactured cotton}} = \frac{\text{Price of rude cotton}}{\text{Price of manufactured cotton}}$$

Unfortunately, Cardozo did not present any empirical evidence to sub-
stantiate his thesis.

the board from an average of 25% to 12½%] . . . would be the means of prostrating every manufacturing establishment in the country.[25]

Consequently, he favored a gradual change after careful investigation had indicated the least painful way of bringing it about. Cardozo held that the rapid change from excessive tariff rates to very moderate rates led to a lack of confidence, which was one of the factors producing marked instability in the money market.[26]

Cordozo viewed the Tariff Acts as "more an abuse than a usurpation of power," [27] and held that American prosperity existed in spite of the tariff regulations and would be greater with their repeal. He cautioned his fellow Southerners against intemperance on the tariff question.

A major reason for Cardozo's general opposition to tariffs was that they created a misallocation of the nation's capital and forced the birth of manufacturing before society was ready for such a step. He stressed the importance of the gradual development of manufacturing to avoid the disorder following legislative interference. In the early period of tariff legislation, Cardozo stated that the United States did not possess the prerequisites for the development of manufacturing, such as dense population, abundance of capital, limited supply of land, and cumulative technological improvements. As an advocate of gradual balanced development, Cardozo said:

If the circumstances of the commercial world have prepared us to become manufacturers this will be accomplished as it ought

[25] *Ibid.*, August 17, 1832. The proper method of procedure was to "Enquire how restraints may be got rid of with the least convulsion and the smallest injury to the interests of the parties likely to be affected by the repeal." George McDuffie was an important figure in South Carolina politics, serving at various times as Senator, Congressman, and Governor.

[26] *Ibid.*, January 18, 1842.

[27] *Ibid.*, February 3, 1831. This position foreshadowed his opposition to the nullification movement in South Carolina in the following year.

to be, gradually, with the least disturbance, or without the violence that follows legislative interference. The shifting of capital from a less to a more profitable employment may surely be left to the instinct of individual sagacity.[28]

Cardozo reacted strongly to a variety of protariff arguments:

(1) Tariffs foster the development of manufacturing, create a better balance between agriculture and manufactures, and facilitate the growth of the domestic economy. Cardozo held that we could not retain the foreign market for our exports while developing domestic manufacturing with the aid of a tariff, since the domestic market could not expand as rapidly as British imports from the United States declined. He estimated that it would take twenty years for the United States to reach the stage where it could annually absorb as much raw materials in domestic manufacturing as the British purchased from us. Moreover, the higher profits of the industries protected by the tariff would be squeezed out by the entrance of new competitors, and the higher prices caused by the tariff would tend to decrease consumer demand and employment. He said, "The consumption of one class of producers is measured and limited by the consumption of another class of producers who respectively exchange the fruits of their industry." [29] Consequently, tariffs would not help the formation of a better balanced economy or encourage economic growth.

[28] *Ibid.*, August 31, 1819. See also August 9, 1819. Earlier articles by Tucker had stressed the importance of a dense population for the development of manufacturing. George Tucker, "On the Future Density of the United States," *The Portfolio* (October, 1814), p. 394, and "On Density of Population," *The Portfolio* (August, 1815), pp. 166–67. They were later reprinted in his collection, *Essays on Various Subjects of Tastes, Morals, and National Policy* (Georgetown, D.C., Milligan, 1823). Tucker's main point was that a dense population provided the necessary labor supply for turning out manufactured goods and a sufficient market to purchase them.

[29] *Southern Patriot*, June 12, 1821. See also May 26, 1819; July 24, 1828 for a general discussion of this point.

(2) Tariffs can be used to help maintain a balance in international payments,[30] while free trade was a cause of overimportation and loss of specie.[31] A scheme aimed at equalizing the value of our imports and exports with a specific country was valueless, according to Cardozo, because of the multilateral nature of foreign trade. Excessive credit, rather than free trade, was, in his view, the source of overimportation and specie losses. Cardozo felt that the attempt to adjust tariffs in an effort to control imports was impractical, since the circumstances affecting imports were constantly changing.

(3) Calhoun argued that the rise in tariff rates tends to be cumulative as it causes increases in the money supply and costs of production, thereby making the previous level of protection inadequate. Cardozo rejected this theory. He presented historical evidence to show that the tariff and money supply were independent phenomena rather than causally related.[32] His explanation for the cumulative increase in the tariff is that the rate of protection was found to be inadequate because of the superior productivity of producers in the older countries.

(4) Reduction of the tariff will be associated with economic distress. The line of reasoning, as expressed by an American manufacturer, was that tariff repeal would increase the value of imports and create an adverse balance of trade. The resulting exodus of gold would reduce bank

[30] *Ibid.*, July 13, 1842; *Evening News,* October 12, 1854.

[31] *Ibid.*, July 28, 1854.

[32] Cardozo indicated that in 1816 the tariff was increased while the money supply declined. In the 1824–1828 period, the tariff was increased while the money supply remained stable. During the 1828–1833 period, the rise in the tariff was accompanied by an increase in the money supply. He added in explanation, "Every increase of the tariff gives the domestic manufacturer a temporary benefit, which of course ceases as soon as the foreign manufacturer can task his skill to counteract the protection and the smuggler his ingenuity to evade the payment of the increased duty." Concerning Calhoun, Cardozo said, "Our differences from him regards rather his analysis of causes, than his general conclusions." Obviously, both opposed the tariff. *Southern Patriot,* February 20, 1840.

reserves and lead to economic distress. Cardozo claimed that this erroneous notion was due to a confusion of nominal and real exchange rates. He said that a country whose currency has depreciated has an unfavorable nominal rate of exchange. Gold, in this case, would be exported because it is profitable to do so; a profit could be made by merchants on the difference in value between our own currency and foreign currency, since specie will purchase greater value, in the form of commodities, in a country where prices have not risen. If, however, a country's currency has not depreciated (i.e., when it is in balance with the general value of foreign currencies) even though it has an import balance, the country will only have a deferred debt, the extent of which will be indicated by the exchange rate. This unfavorable real rate of exchange, caused by the temporary excess of imports, tends to stimulate the exportation of commodities and to correct the unfavorable exchange rate.

Cardozo said, "The effect of an unfavorable real exchange is to stimulate the exportation of commodities. . . . The effect of an unfavorable nominal exchange is to lead to an export of coin." [33] What Cardozo appears to have in mind is that if a currency is not sound, as would occur if there were overissuing of bank notes, an export of gold is certain to result, and the ensuing unfavorable rate of exchange may be longer than a temporary phenomenon. If the currency is sound, the export of gold is a possible but not a necessary consequence, and if that occurs, it will be a short-run measure soon replaced by an export of commodities. Therefore, Cardozo concluded that the repeal of tariff restrictions would stimulate rather than retard economic activity. He acknowledged that tariff repeal might have the temporary effect of driving up the prices of our

[33] *Evening News*, March 4, 1846.

exports until its supply was augmented; i.e., the lag of supply behind the rising demand, induced by the tariff repeal, would cause prices to rise. In a similar vein, he held that protective tariffs would decrease the foreigners' demand for Southern cotton but would not permanently reduce the price of cotton.[34] Cardozo viewed gold movements between countries as essential for maintaining exchange and commodity price stability. His position went somewhat beyond the classical framework; he held that a country could export gold to a country with whom it had a favorable trade balance if the exchange value of gold was high relative to the value of currency. In other words, if the price of commodities is high, it may be profitable to export gold as a commodity. Thus, gold exports, in Cardozo's model, are not necessarily undertaken in discharge of debt.[35]

Cardozo also rejected Henry Carey's notion that the depreciation of American railroad investments was due to free trade. Carey's line of reasoning was that free trade stimulated excessive importation, particularly iron for railroad development, and caused an adverse balance of trade, loss of gold, and depreciation of railroad investments. Cardozo said that the cause of the depreciation of railroad stocks was that the railroad promoters "borrowed at home and abroad huge sums . . . more rapidly than the annual income realized could cover the current expenses and interest on the sums they borrowed." [36] This led to a loss of public confidence and subsequent depreciation. In other words, Cardozo took the position that speculative investments rather than free trade were the cause of depreciation.

Cardozo looked upon the tariff as adversely affecting the interests of all sections and classes, with the exception of a

[34] Cardozo, *The Tariff*, p. 25. [35] *Southern Patriot*, July 17, 1819.
[36] *Evening News*, December 31, 1855.

few Northern manufacturers, through the misdirection of resources from their natural use. The benefits derived by the domestic manufacturer of import-competing goods stemmed, in Cardozo's opinion, from a double source.[37] (1) He can sell at a higher price and buy raw materials from domestic sources at lower prices. (2) The domestic producers of raw materials are under pressure to lower their prices to induce the foreigner to continue his purchases despite his declining sales to the United States, whereas the tariff reduces the competitive pressure on the domestic manufacturer, enabling him to increase his prices. Cardozo thought that the gains made by the domestic manufacturer would be more than offset by the losses of other classes.

Cardozo seemingly was considering the public-private wealth distinction when he said, "That the ruin of some branches of manufacturing may follow unlimited freedom of importation is possible, but that an injury can fall generally on the capital and industry of the country importing freely is inconceivable." [38] He viewed the loss created by the tariff on several levels:

(1) By increasing the price of imports, it tends to diminish domestic consumption. This effect of the tariff is felt by all sections, including the North.

(2) The value of exports produced in the tariff-imposing country tends to fall, due to declining export prices and the fact that the decreased value of imports tends to lead to a decline in the value of exports, since countries acquire purchasing power mainly through selling to other coun-

[37] *Southern Patriot,* April 29, 1820; March 20, 1821.

[38] *Ibid.,* August 16, 1821. Generally, free trade advocates held that a harmony of individual and national interests existed or could be brought into existence by a high level of competition, while protectionists tended to draw a distinction between these interests. Adam Smith, p. 423. Raymond, I, 220. In this latter citation, Raymond said that the question of free trade should not be decided on the narrow grounds of private interest, but upon the "more expanded and noble principles of public interests."

tries. Export prices fall because of the pressure to maintain sales to the foreigner. Cardozo assumed that the decreased foreign demand for American agricultural products would not be compensated for by an increased domestic demand. This loss caused by the tariff in its effects on our productive efforts was mainly absorbed by the South.[39] He doesn't deal with the point that, insofar as the price of raw materials exported by the United States declines, the tendency for a tariff to result in an increase in the price of foreign manufactured goods imported by the tariff-imposing country may be partially overcome. Whether prices rise at all depends upon the degree of the comparative disadvantage and the price flexibility of the raw materials under the downward pressure of the market.

(3) The higher profits in the protected manufacturing industries results in an unproductive diversion of capital from agriculture to manufacturing. Eventually profits must settle at a new equilibrium level as the increase of capital in manufacturing brings about a gradual decrease in the price and profits in manufacturing, while the reverse effect occurs in agriculture.[40] Like Ricardo, Cardozo thought that tariffs only conferred a temporary advantage as capital and labor shifted from the nonprotected to the protected sector. Eventually the forces of competition would adjust the individual profits to the general rate.[41]

Cardozo pointed to the existence of a common bond of interest between North and South. He thought that it would be likely that the South would purchase many products which did not require much capital from the North rather than from England. He said:

[39] Ibid., July 23, 1828.
[40] Cardozo added that "Whether they [prices of domestic manufactured goods] will fall as low as in those countries from which we now export them, will depend on the degree of our skill, the extent of our capital, and the low price of our labor in manufacturing compared to those countries." Ibid., August 6, 1819.
[41] Cardozo, Notes, p. 80.

Excluding iron, and the cotton and woolen manufacturing, the great mass of the articles made by hand in the United States, and with the aid of little capital, can not be imported with the charges of transportation from Europe added to their value, so low as they can be supplied in the United States.[42]

In addition to pointing out the injurious effect of the tariff for the Northern states in causing higher consumer good prices, Cardozo held that the domestic market for Northern products, such as corn, flour, hay, bacon, and whiskey in the Southern states would contract as a result of the tariff. Cardozo claimed that about forty percent of Southern income was spent on articles produced in the North and West. The value of these articles purchased by the South was considerably greater than of those it imported from foreign countries. In stressing the importance of an interdependent trade nexus between the North, South, and Europe, he said:

It is obvious that on the preservation of the European markets for the Southern staples, depends the Southern market for the Northern and Western commodities. With the loss of one must perish the other. If Southern industry is deprived or curtailed of its fair remuneration, by the policy of prohibition, Northern and Western labor must suffer in a nearly equal proportion. . . . As the tax on imports leaves a diminished value in the pockets of the Southern payers of the import, so must a less value fall, in the nature of things, to Northern and Western producers of commodities for Southern consumption.[43]

Cardozo also pointed out that the Southern market enabled the North, in part, to pay for its imports of European merchandise and to provide employment for an estimated four to five million people in the North, particularly farmers and shippers. With a tariff in operation, the

[42] Cardozo, *The Tariff*, p. 16.
[43] *Ibid.*, p. 15. See also *Southern Patriot*, August 5, 19, 20, 21, 1828; June 25, 1831.

South would sell less to England, buy less from the North and West, thus causing economic losses and unemployment in those areas; it would then be forced to direct its capital to other sectors where its productivity was low. Cardozo appears to have had a rudimentary model of the export multiplier and import propensities. He attempted to trace the cumulative effects of a tariff on the various sections: A tariff could be expected to reduce Southern exports causing a fall in its income; consequently the demand by the South for Northern and Western commodities would decline. Employment in these sections would fall, thereby decreasing their ability to purchase imports.

Cardozo rejected the notion held by many Southerners that a tariff was a benefit to the Northern states to the extent that it hurt the Southern states. Although Cardozo believed that the tariff put an unequal and unjust burden on the South, he berated Southern writers, particularly McDuffie, for exaggerating the losses incurred by the South. He said that there were circumstances under which the imposition of the tariff might not create actual impoverishment in the cotton-growing states; furthermore, it was impossible to foresee accurately a timetable of harmful effects. He thought of the tariff as more of an eventual, long-run check on the prosperity of the South, the true effects of which could only be understood in reference to many other circumstances.[44] Among the effects with which he was concerned were the portion of Southern income which went into the purchase of dutiable imports, and the level of demand of Northern manufacturers for Southern cotton.

Cardozo attempted to demonstrate that the protective tariff system, as a national rather than sectional burden, "injures the prosperity and lessens the resources of the

[44] *Ibid.,* June 14, 20, 1831. In the latter article, he stated that the South had "far more to lose due to tariffs than other sections of the country."

Southern states in no higher proportion than their relative income." [45] Although Cardozo was in accord with the free trade conclusions of McDuffie, he often accused him of "errors of doctrine," particularly the notion that the major burden of the tariff was borne by the Southern cotton producer. McDuffie started with the idea that in a series of years the value of a country's imports and exports must approximately balance. He then deduced that since the value of exports from the Southern region was a trifle more than half of the total American exports, the value of imports consumed by the South would be approximately the same percentage of total imports except that the tariff reduced the purchasing power needed to buy this amount of imports. This argument has been referred to as the "forty-bale theory," because McDuffie claimed that the cotton exporter had to provide forty percent more cotton for imported goods protected by the tariff.

The fallacy of this approach, as Cardozo indicated, was that not all of the planters' income was spent on purchasing dutiable imports; a large part of the wealthier cotton exporters' income was spent on the purchase of domestic products, land, and slaves, all duty-free. In reality, they paid duties only on the portion of the total imports which they actually consumed. Cardozo held that since "each class is obviously and inevitably consumers for the productions of the other," [46] the tariff was a potential burden on the producers and consumers in the North and South, as well as England.

[45] Cardozo, *The Tariff*, p. 44. Cardozo added, however, that he thought that a continuation of the tariff would result in the "most pernicious inequality" for the South. Flora said that this pamphlet "seemed to have had as its chief object the discrediting of the McDuffie argument." McDuffie was an ardent nullificationist. Cardozo's attack on his tariff doctrines was therefore indirectly aimed against his nullification stand. Abram C. Flora, Jr., "Jacob N. Cardozo, 1786–1873: South Carolina Economist," p. 83.

[46] *Southern Patriot*, May 27, 1831.

Cardozo said that all classes or sections that used the taxed manufacturing commodities absorbed part of the tariff. His position was that the incidence of the tariff depended on the effect that it had on the prices of raw materials and manufactured items, which in turn depended on demand-supply market conditions at the time the duty was imposed. Cardozo acknowledged the possibility of cases in which the entire tariff burden would be borne by either the producer or consumer; conditions of excess supply relative to consumption tend to throw the major burden on the producers, while cases of relative scarcity tends to shift the burden to the consumers. For example, conditions of a low domestic supply of manufactured goods with the same or rising demand, cause price increases which force the consumer to pay the duty. If, however, there is a high domestic supply of manufactured goods or a declining foreign demand, prices will fall and split the burden between the producer and consumer. Cardozo said, "The burden of the duty will, in such cases, be divided between the producer and consumer in that proportion which competition between the foreign manufacturer and importer will adjust." [47]

With specific reference to the American cotton market, Cardozo claimed that the tariff burden would not necessarily fall on the Southern producer if demand conditions were such that the British manufacturer continued to buy the same amount of raw cotton from the United States:

Whether the American producer suffers at all, the extent of that suffering depends on circumstances extrinsic to the system of duties. . . . The tendency of that system [tariffs] is to diminish demand for our staple products. . . . We dispute that the extent of that diminution is always in proportion to the amount of duty imposed or that the duty necessarily and im-

[47] *Ibid.*, February 4, 1842. See also *ibid.*, July 13, 1842.

mediately falls on the American producer in the diminished price of his staple.[48]

Cardozo denied McDuffie's contention that commercial restrictions would initially cause an inflow of gold by reducing our imports and creating an unfavorable balance of trade. McDuffie held that the subsequent increased supply of money would increase the prices of goods (with the exception of our export crops) and depreciate the currency, thereby making gold profitable to export and cotton unprofitable to export. Although Cardozo agreed that commercial disturbances brought about a redistribution of gold stocks, he claimed that it did not necessarily create a favorable balance of trade and importation of gold, since declining imports could be offset by declining exports. He regarded McDuffie's view on the original influx of gold as contrary to fact, and held that if there was a later exportation of gold, it was an indication that the price of export staples had risen. Here he contradicted McDuffie's claim. In drawing a distinction between short-run and long-run pricing effects, Cardozo held that the price of cotton might or might not increase when a tariff was in effect. He said that the price of cotton exports in the home market was regulated by their price in the foreign market

. . . as regards price permanently and in the long run. But derangements of a temporary nature will occur which run counter to the general laws of trade. . . . Our staples of exportation may temporarily increase or decrease in price from a debasement or enhancement in the value of money quite independently of their value in foreign markets. McDuffie wishes to make it appear that the growers of these staples receive no equivalent in an increase of their money prices, while they have to pay an advance on all articles enhanced in their money prices by our commercial restrictions.[49]

[48] *Ibid.*, May 31, 1831.
[49] *Ibid.*, July 7, 1832. See also July 1, 12, 1832.

His more moderate approach was shown by his implied criticism of McDuffie: "The evils of the Protecting system are bad enough without overstating them." [50]

Cardozo also differentiated between necessities and luxuries in terms of the incidence of the tariff, and claimed that a high tax on the former fell on the consumer while a high tax on the latter fell mainly on the producer. He felt that the incidence of the tariff could be affected by the existence of monopoly power, in that a reduction of the tariff might not benefit the consumer because the monopolist is often able to prevent a price decline.

Cardozo's analytical technique can be examined in closer detail by presenting his attempt to measure the direct and indirect loss to the public as a result of the tariff of 1828. He divided the total sum paid for protection into these categories: (1) Duties paid to the government on goods imported from the foreigner. (2) The amount paid to the American manufacturer for the higher priced domestic goods which competed with the foreign imports. The former portion was estimated by obtaining, in the first step, the average annual value of imports for which duties were paid. To do this, Cardozo deducted the following items from the total value of imports: (1) The part of the import value which was re-exported. (2) The value of the imports which came in free of duty. (3) The value of imports for which there were no substitutes in the United States.

The resulting average annual value of imports requiring the payment of duties was multiplied by the average tariff rate to obtain the total duty paid to the government as a result of the tariff.[51] Cardozo estimated the portion paid

[50] *Ibid.*, August 18, 1832. The practical ramifications of the dispute with McDuffie are not precisely clear. Cardozo's keen rebuttal of McDuffie's argument had the probable effect of weakening disunionist sentiment in South Carolina.

[51] Cardozo took 25% as the average excess of price due to the tariff, since

to the American manufacturer for his higher priced substitutes for the foreign imports. He computed the total annual expenditures on the protected commodity (i.e., the value of the imported goods on which the duties are paid plus the value of domestic import-competing goods) by multiplying the expenditure per person on the protected commodity by the number of persons buying the commodity.[52] From the total annual expenditures on protected commodities, he subtracted the average annual value of imports on which duties were paid to the government. This gave the annual amount paid to American manufacturers of those domestic goods which compete with foreign imports. To obtain the bounty paid to American manufacturers as a result of the tariff, one need only multiply this figure by the percent of average excess of the price of domestic protected goods over foreign imports. Cardozo defined the real rate of protection to the American manufacturer as:

the difference between the selling price in our market of the domestic fabric and the selling price of a similar foreign article of equal quality, taking into view also the difference if any, between the price of the raw material to the foreigner and American manufacturer respectively.[53]

Cardozo's remarkably detailed analysis seemingly overlooked the price reactions of the foreign exporters when tariffs were raised in the United States, which could vitiate the results under certain elasticity conditions. If the United States demand is price-elastic, for example, the for-

this was the percentage difference between the revenue tariff of 1816 and the protective tariff of 1828. Cardozo, *The Tariff*, p. 5.

[52] Cardozo assumed that individuals spent about a fourth of their income on protected commodities, and that somewhat more than half of the population were nonpurchasers of these commodities (particularly cotton and woolen manufactured items) since they produced them in the household.

[53] *Southern Patriot*, August 18, 1832.

eigner may have to lower the prices of his exports to maintain his sales. The more price-elastic the demand, the
greater is the likelihood that the incidence of the tariff will
not be shifted to the American buyer.[54]

Cardozo viewed the sum benefit of protection as fairly
evenly split between the government, in the form of duties
on protected commodities, and the American manufacturer, in the form of higher prices on import-competing
goods.[55]

Cardozo was aware of the relationship of the tariff to
other social questions of the day. Although he felt that the
tariff weakened the security of the slave system, he regarded the growth of Southern manufacturing as a way of
overcoming the effects of the tariff. The most vigorous
antitariffites in the South in general were least in favor of
developing Southern manufacturing.[56] Cardozo, in contrast, implicitly viewed the tariff as a symbol but not a
cause of the economic backwardness of the Southern economy.

[54] This type of analysis assumes something other than pure competition
among the exporters, since lowering the prices of export goods in competitive conditions reduces their profit below the market level and stimulates
a shift of capital to a higher profitability sector.

[55] Cardozo calculated the annual burden on those consuming protected
commodities as $2.50 per person, which amounted to a bounty of $1.25 per
person to the American manufacturer and the government. Cardozo, *The
Tariff*, pp. 8–9.

[56] Robert R. Russel, *Economic Aspects of Southern Sectionalism, 1840–
1861*, pp. 154–55.

SIX

Banking

CARDOZO'S views on banking problems, which altered at several critical junctures partly in response to changing historical conditions, reflected the continuous American debate over the relative virtues and defects of centralized and decentralized banking, and the proper amount of government control over banking activities. There were four distinct stages in Cardozo's thinking on money and banking issues. They are outlined below, and then examined in juxtaposition to the historical conditions.

Stage 1. In the earliest phase, Cardozo championed a national bank, the Second Bank of the United States, and claimed that it provided a unified currency with considerable control over the note-issuing ability of the local banks. Cardozo, at this point, did not fully accept the principles of laissez-faire as applied to banking.[1] He favored the free-

---

[1] The term "laissez-faire," as applied to practically all banking operations, is used here to connote an absence of statutory restrictions on the

dom of banks to lend funds placed on deposit, including their own capital, but advocated restrictions on the banks' power to issue their own "money" in the form of bank notes. Cardozo emphasized that operation of the banking system, according to the principles of laissez-faire, would bring about so many fluctuations in property values, income, prices of labor, and products, that interference would become necessary.[2] This phase lasted roughly from 1818 to shortly after the onset of the crisis of 1837.

Stage 2. In this next period, Cardozo favored a separation of government and banking. He abandoned his pronational bank position because he felt that the leaders of the system had used their concentrated control and profit-making ability in such a way as to foster business cycles. Cardozo was not yet a full advocate of laissez-faire banking operations, but, as before, he favored allowing competition in deposit and discount operations while controlling the note-issuing ability of the banks. This phase continued from mid-1837 to the latter part of 1847.

Stage 3. This was Cardozo's free-banking period. As a full-fledged advocate of laissez-faire in banking, he no longer separated deposit-discount operations from note-issuing. He thought that competition should be allowed to prevail in both. In this period, he stressed the primary role of the public, rather than of the banking system, in causing expansion and contraction of credit and economic activity. Accepting the selfish nature of man, he thought

---

issuance of either bank notes or bank deposits dealings, and a reliance on free competition in the money market. In its most extreme form, acceptance of the term also excludes the requirement of specie convertibility, a position rarely advocated except by the early anti-bullionist school. Cardozo approached this viewpoint for a brief period in the late 1840s.

[2] It is interesting to note that Adam Smith relaxed some of his laissez-faire principles in the area of banking. He favored prohibiting the issuing of bank notes under £5 denominations, although he recognized that this step would be a violation of natural law. He said, "But those exertions of the natural liberty of a few individuals which might endanger the security

that thoroughgoing competition was a more effective technique of safeguarding the public interest than concentrating control. This phase of his thought lasted from 1847 to roughly 1853–1854.

Stage 4. By this last period, Cardozo realized that centralized and decentralized banking could lead to abuses of the general public. He observed that in the absence of controls, banks engaged in speculative abuses, such as creating a scarcity of money, which hurt legitimate business ventures. Cardozo then took the position that the law must clearly define the legitimate and nonlegitimate areas of banking, and after this had been done, laissez-faire principles should be allowed to operate. Thus, uncontrolled, profit-motivated banking could prevail in the designated legitimate areas. He continued to adhere to this modified laissez-faire position, advocating such measures as rigid legislative control over bank management operations, including note-issuing.

1818–1837

In the earliest period of embryonic capitalism when nonmarket elements were an important feature of economic life, Cardozo stressed the stabilizing benefits of controlled banking and the ruinous effects of uncontrolled competition in banking. He viewed the significant benefits of a national bank [3] in this manner:

---

of the whole society are, and ought to be, restrained by the laws of all governments." Adam Smith, p. 308.

[3] The bank referred to is the Second Bank of the United States, whose charter ran from 1816 to 1836. Twenty percent of the bank's capital was held by the Federal government, while the remainder was in private hands. The power to appoint bank directors was proportionate to the respective shareholdings. It served as a depository for government funds and operated partly as a private profit concern and partly as a regulator of the monetary

(1) The use of notes of the Bank of the United States had the advantageous effect of giving greater uniformity and stability to the value of the currency, which facilitated exchange between the different sections of the country.[4] Exchange equilibrium could be maintained by allowing overdrawings by one section at one time to be equalized by overdrawings of other sections at other times. Cardozo thought that this would help to keep up the value of Southern staples.

(2) By efficiently checking the extravagant issues of paper money by the local banks, the mass of depreciated money was reduced and speculation curbed.[5]

(3) Property values were kept at a more stable level as a result of operations of the Bank of the United States [6] (i.e., price and exchange rate stability would tend to make property values more stable).

(4) Cardozo thought of the Bank of the United States as "the great balance-wheel of our monetary system," [7] although his precise meaning of this phrase was unclear.

Cardozo's discussion of the relative merits of the national bank is most effectively examined in the context of those conditions which shaped the Southern point of view. The disorderly state of financial conditions during and after the War of 1812 created considerable support in all sections for rechartering the national bank. Calhoun was one of the leaders in setting up the Second Bank of the

system. Bray Hammond declares, "Its establishment in 1816 derived from the extreme fiscal needs of the federal government, the disorder of an unregulated currency, and the promotional ambitions of businessmen." Bray Hammond, "Jackson, Biddle, and the Banks of the United States," *Journal of Economic History* (May, 1947), p. 1.

[4] *Southern Patriot*, September 2, 1819; December 5, 1826. In the first article, Cardozo disagreed with Hezekiah Niles' contention that the Bank of the United States was an abominable institution run by speculative and power-seeking tyrants. He claimed that the bank's regulations were reasonable. Niles published the influential protectionist newspaper, *Niles' Weekly Register*.

[5] *Ibid.*, November 18, 1818; August 30, 1821.

[6] *Ibid.*, December 5, 1826.   [7] *Ibid.*, April 15, 1836.

United States in 1816, and Cheves, another South Carolinian, became its president in 1819. Cheves' conservative policies restored the bank to a sound condition after the loose expansionist policy under William Jones had almost bankrupted it. The sharp reduction in bank credit and the reduction in dividends to the stockholders, however, created considerable anti-bank sentiment. Private and state banks, in particular, resented the regulation of their credit-creating activities by the Bank of the United States. Hammond described the process by which the Bank acquired control:

The government's receipts arose principally from taxes paid by importers to customs collectors. These tax payments were in bank notes . . . mostly those of private banks; the B.U.S. [Bank of the United States] received these notes on deposit from the customs collectors and, becoming thereby creditor of the private banks that issued them, presented them to the latter for payment. . . . The pressure of the central bank upon the private banks [Hammond uses the term to include state banks] was constant, and its effect was to restrict their lending and their issue of notes. . . . Its regulatory powers were dependent on the private banks' falling currently into debt to it.[8]

An account of the relationship between the Bank of the United States and a specific state bank was provided by Van Deusen:

The officers of the Charleston Branch of the United States Bank attempted to hamper the state in its contest with the federal government by compelling the Bank of South Carolina to suspend specie payment and thus affect public credit. For this purpose they insisted that the Bank of South Carolina pay its notes either in specie or in notes of the United States Bank payable in Charleston. This policy . . . provoked angry protests.[9]

[8] Hammond, "Jackson, Biddle, and the Banks of the United States," p. 2.
[9] Van Deusen, p. 151. Van Deusen mentioned that the mutual opposition of the Bank of the United States and South Carolina politicians to Jackson

Cardozo defended several of these unpopular practices of the Bank of the United States. He supported the action of the national bank in demanding specie payments from the banks in Charleston on a debt balance owed to the former.[10] In an elaborate analysis of cotton-market financing, Cardozo explained that a previous period of high prices in the cotton market brought on commodity price speculation, trade fluctuations, and a specie shortage for the national bank which obliged the bank to demand the payment of due claims in specie. The insecure financial position of some state banks was due to their overtrading and not to the demands of the Bank of the United States for the redemption in specie of balances owed to it by the state banks. He held that it was inordinate credit and speculation, rather than the actions of the Bank of the United States, that were responsible for the 1819 depression.[11] He also supported the bank's practice of not redeeming its notes in places other than where they were issued, and claimed that it was impossible for the Bank of the United States to provide a currency of equal and uniform value for all parts of the country as long as the local banks refused to make prompt payment for their notes.[12]

During this early period, when his pro-bank leanings were strongest, Cardozo was less than favorably disposed to state banks. He attacked the proposal of the South Carolina State Comptroller to tax the shares of the stock of the national bank held in South Carolina, because this would

---

may have somewhat lessened their conflict with each other. *Ibid.*, pp. 151–52.

[10] *Southern Patriot,* December 4, 1818.

[11] *Ibid.,* September 11, November 20, 1819. In this latter article, Cardozo described the actions of the Bank of the United States as one of "accommodation and forbearance." A perceptive recent study of the 1819 crisis is Murray N. Rothbard, *The Panic of 1819: Reactions and Policies.* Favorable reference to Cardozo's editorials on banking can be found on pp. 63–64.

[12] *Southern Patriot,* September 28, 1819; April 29, 1829. Cardozo held that the slowness of the state banks in redeeming their notes kept prices artifically high. *Ibid.,* June 24, 1819.

repel capital from the state. Although many State officials
were apparently irked by the ability of the national bank
to control their credit issues, Cardozo held, "The Branch
Bank [of the United States] of this city has been of
the most salutary benefit, not only to the commerce of
this city, but to the agricultural interests of the State at
large." [13]

Cardozo also rejected the idea of giving the states a monopoly position in banking, on the grounds that there
would be insufficient checks on their operations.[14] Cardozo said that thorough legislative control over the state
banks was desirable, since they were a "public establishment and not a private concern." [15] Possible mismanagement of the bank's financial facilities therefore required
careful supervision of its activities.

Cardozo's approval of the Bank of the United States in
the 1820s stemmed from its deliberate policy of restraining
monetary expansion within reasonable limits by exercising
control over state bank-note issuing. Although Cardozo
recognized that an easy credit policy would facilitate terri-
torial expansion, he saw this benefit as being outweighed
by the speculation and instability fostered by such a monetary policy.

Cardozo and Jackson both favored a hard-money policy,
but in a somewhat different sense. Jackson was literally in
favor of a metallic currency while Cardozo favored a mixed
convertible currency operated in a carefully controlled
manner. Unlike Cardozo in this pro-bank stage of his
banking views, however, Jackson attacked the Bank of the
United States on the grounds that it concentrated power

[13] *Ibid.*, December 4, 1826. Cardozo favored bringing the Bank of the
State of South Carolina under closer public scrutiny, e.g., requiring annual
published statements of its capital, rotation of bank directors, etc. *Ibid.*,
November 26, 1818.

[14] *Ibid.*, December 11, 1822.

[15] *Ibid.*, November 23, 1819; November 27-29; December 11, 1820.

and privilege, both economic and political, in the hands of
a financial oligarchy. Jackson also held that the Bank of
the United States pursued inflationary measures and did
not provide a uniform currency. Although disagreeing
with Jackson at the time, Cardozo later accepted the
former point. The South as a whole was intensely anti-
bank, as evidenced by its Congressional voting pattern on
rechartering the bank.[16]

Cardozo was sympathetic with Biddle's efforts to renew
the bank charter during the 1832–1834 period. He attacked
the Jackson administration for withdrawing government
deposits from the Bank of the United States, claiming that
this was instrumental in creating economic distress.

Cardozo, at this time, held that the bank was "not only
constitutional, but essentially necessary to carry on the
business of the country safely and preserve the currency in
a wholesome condition." [17] He thought it was of particular importance in carrying on foreign exchange transactions,[18] and moreover denied that the bank had monopolistic powers since "rival institutions hold it in check by a
counteracting influence." [19] When the bank adopted a
more inflationary policy, which culminated in the crisis of
1837, Cardozo withdrew his support.

[16] Jean Wilburn, "Support of the Second United States Bank" (unpublished doctoral dissertation, Columbia University, 1964), pp. 7–23. She
points out that Louisiana was an exception to the Southern voting pattern.
It completely supported votes for rechartering the Second Bank of the
United States.

[17] *Southern Patriot*, September 26, 1833. Cardozo minimized the importance of Biddle's tactics of subsidizing the publication and distribution of
articles with a pro-bank viewpoint, although he acknowledged that they
damaged the public reputation of the bank. *Ibid.*, October 1, 1833.

[18] Cardozo defended Biddle against Raguet's charge that the foreign exchange dealings of the bank had caused monetary disorders. He attempted
to show that some disturbances in the foreign exchange market may be
due to changes in the commodities market rather than faulty bank actions.
Ibid., May 6, 1829. Cardozo considerably altered his views on this topic in
the following period.

[19] *Ibid.*, March 13, 1834.

Cardozo stressed the danger that an excessive number of banks would issue an excessive amount of bank notes, resulting in speculation, price fluctuations, changes of property ownership ("revolutions of property"), an exodus of gold, and other undersirable effects. He said that "the ruin of credit and sacrifice of property rapidly overtake those who have been seduced to borrow. . . . [T]he number of these [banking] institutions ought to be abridged. . . . Competition in the case of banks may be carried to an extreme; it is in this respect worse than monopoly." [20]

Cardozo objected to the principle of regulating the money supply by the interest of the banks and the wants of the borrowers, because the banks cannot adequately distinguish between two types of borrowers—speculators and legitimate businessmen. He was favorably disposed toward the earning of the "fruits of regular industry and sober enterprise," [21] but was suspicious of get-rich-quick speculative schemes.

In this early period, Cardozo's views on banking theory reflected a mixture of the "currency" and "banking" schools of thought. Whereas the former favored basing the amount of paper currency on the size of the specie holdings, the latter preferred basing it on the "needs of trade." [22]

The "currency" school developed out of the bullionist doctrine during the 1820s in England, which favored the convertibility requirement in order to prevent the over-issuing of bank notes. Although adherents to the "cur-

---

[20] *Ibid.*, November 12, 1818; cf. November 24, 1819.

[21] *Ibid.*, September 22, 1819.

[22] Two useful sources of information on early American banking theories are Harry E. Miller, *Banking Theories in the United States before 1860,* and Lloyd W. Mints, *A History of Banking Theory in Great Britain and the United States,* pp. 61–73. A thorough account of the early English controversy between the "currency" and "banking" schools can be found in Jacob Viner, *Studies in the Theory of International Trade,* pp. 218–89.

rency" principle claimed that the exportation of specie prevented a permanent overexpansion of bank notes, they held that the possibility of short-run excessive note issuing justified the imposition of legal restrictions to prevent adverse exchanges and financial crises. Since they did not view bank deposits as part of the currency, they wanted fluctuations in the amount of bank notes to correspond with changes in the supply of specie. The inflation or deflation following the importation or exportation of gold was thought of as correcting the foreign exchanges. Operating the monetary system, according to the "currency" principle, created an inelastic currency through restrictions on the issuing of paper money, and tended to result in considerable internal instability, partially balanced by external stability.

Those sympathetic to the "banking" principle held that excessive issuance would be impossible if bank notes were issued in response to the needs of the trading community and were convertible into specie on demand. Both schools agreed that currency should be convertible into specie in order to maintain relative stability of value. The position of the "banking" school was thus more in favor of regulation than the anti-bullionists—who were against the convertibility requirement on the grounds that it prevented banks from meeting the proper needs of the business community—but favored less legislative control than adherents of the "currency" school. They rejected an alleged distinction between bank deposits and bank notes, and held that laws controlling bank credit operations were impossible and undesirable. One member of the "banking" school said that "errors and extravagances of credit are unfortunately beyond the pale of legislation." [23]

[23] John Fullarton, *On the Regulation of Currencies* (2nd ed., 1845), p. 195, cited by Viner, p. 234. The English Bank Act of 1844 set maximum limits on note-issuing in accord with the "currency" principle. It was not

A majority of the nineteenth-century writers believed that the gold standard was the ideal norm for achieving money of stable value. Cardozo, too, felt that it was desirable to have specie backing for the paper currency in order to keep its value stable. If excessive paper money was issued, its value would fall, and people would be induced to convert it into specie. This would decrease the supply of money and eventually increase its value relative to specie. Paper money should not be prohibited, but Cardozo thought that since only gold had intrinsic value, it should be representative of an actual deposit of specie. A further development of the "banking" principle, referred to as the "real bills" doctrine, added the widely held view that a properly elastic currency could be achieved and over-issuing prevented, if banks issued notes in discounting only real commercial paper (i.e., bonafide, self-liquidating paper which arose from actual transactions).

Since Cardozo reacted strongly to several of Adam Smith's pronouncements on money and banking issues, a brief review of the latter's views [24] is appropriate.

Smith took the position, to be followed by the English bullionists, that the convertibility requirement prevented the excessive issuing of bank notes. He held that the value of paper money could not be greater than the value of the specie it replaces, since the excess (the amount greater than needed for business transactions) would be converted into specie and exported in exchange for productive goods. Smith said that bank paper money "can never exceed the quantity which the circulation of the country can easily absorb and employ," and advocated that banks discount only real bills of exchange. In drawing a distinction between "chimerical projectors" and "sober and frugal debt-

---

effective in preventing monetary disturbances, and government intervention was resorted to in periods of crisis.

[24] The following summary comes from Adam Smith, Book 2, Chapter 2.

ors," Smith implicitly rejected the idea that banks should supply paper to meet all business "needs." Unlike Cardozo, he did not, however, stress the pernicious aspects attending the use of paper money. By substituting paper money for part of the specie, Smith claimed that the banks were increasing the commerce and industry of a country. They were able to convert dead stock into productive capital although at the same time increasing the insecurity of commercial life. According to Miller:

. . . the theory that convertibility of bank notes is a complete guarantee against their being issued in excess received no great support in this country. As in England the most common objection was that convertibility does, indeed, prevent a permanent excess of currency, but that it can not prevent temporary over-issue.[25]

Cardozo's views on these topics are somewhat unclear. He regarded the issuing of paper money—bank notes—as "taxation in disguise." [26] When paper money was issued in excess of that needed to circulate the production of goods, gold would be exported in proportion to the amount of the excess, and the exchange value of the goods would settle at a value lower than it was previous to the money issuing.[27] Then the country issuing paper money would experience a decline in the value of its exports (relative to imports) which was exactly proportional to the amount of the paper-money issue. Cardozo appears to have taken the position that the increased issue of paper money

[25] Miller, p. 60. He also added that "this excess, even though short-lived, may be considerable." *Ibid.*, p. 100.

[26] Cardozo, *Notes*, p 80. Also, *Southern Patriot*, October 26, 1819.

[27] Cardozo, *Notes*, p. 80. Both Smith and Cardozo had the notion that a certain amount of money was necessary to circulate the annual output of society. Whereas Smith thought the excess money in the form of gold would be sent abroad because that would be more profitable than its remaining idle at home, Cardozo attributed the gold exodus following the issue of paper money to the development of an adverse balance of payments.

necessarily hurt our sales to foreigners, even though some of the sales on the domestic market would increase. The decreased value of exports would then necessitate an exportation of gold to pay off the debt.

Unlike Smith, Cardozo held that it was possible to introduce an amount of paper money which exceeded the value of the specie that it replaced. He said, "Dr. Smith's views on the subject of money in general, and paper money in particular, have assisted in giving an extensive and lasting influence to error in this branch of Political Economy." [28] The view that the output in any given period would be less if paper money were employed as an instrument of circulation differed from Smith's idea that the substitution of bank notes for specie, if issued in a moderate way, had several beneficial economic effects.

According to Cardozo, the origin of Smith's error lay in his implicit assumption that an equal rise in the price of all commodities takes place when paper money is substituted for gold. The rise in price resulting from an issue of paper money was considered as a partial one rather than general. Cardozo said, "The rise is only in certain articles for which the demand will have increased, accompanied by an equivalent fall in the prices of other articles which will have experienced in the same degree, diminished demand." [29] Clearly he was assuming the restrictive case of a constant total demand in which the suggestion was made that the increase in demand for some goods following the issuance of paper money would be accompanied by a decline in demand for other goods, particularly in a country's export products.

Cardozo's line of reasoning in this case was not particu-

[28] *Ibid.*, p. 83.
[29] *Ibid.*, p. 84. In an earlier period, Cardozo had taken a more traditional position in favor of the quantity theory of money At this time, he had said, "An increase of currency is invariably attended with a general increase of prices." *Southern Patriot*, December 22, 1818.

larly convincing. He claimed that the country issuing paper money would develop a deficit in the balance of payments as a result of the decreased demand for its exports by the foreign producer of specie. The increased use of paper money was regarded as equivalent to a decreased demand for gold, creating a declining income in the specie-producing country and a subsequent declining demand by this country for the exports of the paper-issuing country.[30] Even if it is granted that the issuance of paper money does not result in a general price rise, it does not necessarily follow that the export sector will be the one experiencing a selective price rise. Suppose, more realistically, that neither country is a specie producer. Then there is no evidence that the income in the non–paper-issuing country will fall when the other country substitutes paper for specie. Furthermore, even assuming a given level of total demand, there is no automatic reason for the country issuing paper money to develop a trade deficit. This would depend on several exogenous factors as well as production and cost conditions in the various sectors of the economy. Cardozo's position was tantamount to making a possible situation into a necessary one.

In rejecting the quantity theory of money, a position generally taken by the banking school, Cardozo was on stronger ground. He argued that a change in the quantity of money affected price only insofar as it changed the proportion between the supply and demand of commodities. Cardozo's view that the increased quantity of money might have differential effects on the various sectors of the economy and consequently precipitate a movement of capital and labor from the less profitable to the more profitable sector was an example of his keen insight into the workings of the economy. His insistence, however, that the export

[30] Cardozo, *Notes*, pp. 85–86. Miller, p. 52, refers to the above-stated approach of Cardozo as a "specious argument."

sector necessarily contracted and that the value of total production would fall is clearly wrong. Conditions may be such that the domestic market expands more than the export market contracts, so that the value of total output rises.

Cardozo, in a later article, expanded his views on the quantity theory of money:

> The currency is both cause and effect in its connection with price. . . . Prices must sustain the circulation as well as stimulate its increase. If the banks were to make large emissions of paper, there being nothing in present values to sustain such an emission, it would be thrown back upon them, to be converted into specie, almost as rapidly as the emission was made. . . . Bank issues beyond the accustomed wants of circulation can not sustain prices. . . . Prices do not depend on the popular wish or want of money, nor on banks, nor on political changes, but on foreign markets and on purchasing power of the people.[31]

Cardozo thus appears to be saying that the demand for the output of commodities is the cause of both increased money for transaction purposes and increased prices. An increased money supply does not raise prices unless there is a demand for the use of this money. Cardozo held that, in the main, currency adjusted to the demands of commerce rather than vice versa.

Cardozo was among the first writers to deal with the concept of elasticity related to banking operations.[32] He

---

[31] *Southern Patriot,* November 13, 1840; September 24, 1844. Cardozo suggested in the former article that in a period of rising production, rising prices follow from a rising money supply while in a period of falling production, falling prices precede a decline in the money supply. In the latter article, Cardozo favorably cites Tooke, a prominent spokesman of the banking school, for the view that speculative price rises precede an increase in the money supply.

[32] Miller says that Erich Bollman had the first such reference. He also favorably cites Raguet and Cardozo. The reference to the latter, however, was a magazine article published in 1850 whereas Cardozo had dealt with this subject in several earlier newspaper articles. Miller, pp. 72–74.

rejected a proposal by Erich Bollman for limiting the issue of paper money by law, on the grounds that this would create an insufficiently elastic money supply. Cardozo said that the "numerical amount of currency . . . is no criterion of excess or deficiency,"[33] since more money was needed if the velocity of money was low or a state of falling confidence prevailed. Cardozo favored extending banking capital and currency to the degree justified by actual or expected economic circumstances.[34] A credit system should have sufficient elasticity in the paper money supply to allow its "expanding gradually with the legitimate demands for credit."[35]

A basic problem that neither Cardozo nor any other early or later American writers succeeded in answering was that of defining "legitimate" demands for credit and excess credit. The clearest, albeit inadequate, statement of Cardozo's is that "a loan of credit that substitutes for coin, more paper than would have filled its place if coin had been exclusively employed, is an agent that retards the increase of wealth, checks production and leaves society poorer."[36] Cardozo referred to elasticity as "that peculiar property which is the source of its excellence and its defects."[37] He maintained that it provided funds for devel-

[33] *Southern Patriot,* July 10, 1819. Cardozo criticized Bollman's stand against the resumption of specie payment by the Bank of England. Bollman claimed that this resumption would bring distress to the working class and hurt commerce. He also believed that the value of paper money was more stable than specie. A fuller discussion of Bollman's views on banking may be found in Dorfman, I, 487–89.

[34] *Southern Patriot,* March 17, 1836. At this particular time Cardozo thought that the supply of currency should not be increased to correspond with the unusually high prices prevailing, particularly of raw cotton, since he doubted that demand would expand sufficiently.

[35] *Ibid.,* November 14, 1839.

[36] *Ibid.,* December 29, 1837. Cardozo added the view that "Credit is an instrument for a more perfect distribution of capital . . . and contributes to the increase of wealth . . . when it does not exceed in its representative character the amount of money which is required to circulate an increased quantity of commodities."

[37] *Ibid.,* November 19, 1839. See also *Evening News,* September 10, 1847.

opment or for lessening the impact of panic, but, when pushed to excess, it promoted instability. Cardozo believed that an exclusively specie system would upset the functioning of our commercial system if the paper system had been institutionalized.[38] In general, Cardozo was wary of tampering with firmly established institutions even though he was quite critical of their operations.

Cardozo consistently favored the repeal of all statutes against the practice of usury. He held that "The price given for the use of money [the interest rate] should be left, like every article of commerce, to be regulated by circumstances [i.e., the market forces]," and that the consequence of usury laws "is to raise the rate of interest by narrowing competition in the money market, and to repress the circulation of capital, and check the improvements of society, by throwing impediments in the way of borrowers who have genius and enterprise." [39]

Cardozo claimed that usury laws were a self-defeating measure in that they necessarily led to attempts at evasion in the form, for example, of charging premiums or of backdating a renewal note. At the beginning of the crisis of 1837, Cardozo took the exaggerated position that the usury laws were "the primary source of expansions and contractions of the paper circulation." [40] His point was that setting a maximum interest rate during a period of expansion would give a profit-motivated bank an incentive to increase the amount of its loans to compensate for the reduced interest income resulting from the setting of a maximum rate which did not coincide with the market rate of interest. Therefore, the attempt to impose a ceiling on the interest rate might precipitate an expansion of paper

[38] *Southern Patriot,* January 28, 1834.
[39] *Ibid.,* December 17, 1818. See also *Evening News,* March 3, February 23, 1849.
[40] *Southern Patriot,* June 15, 1837.

money—credit—beyond reasonable limits in the sense of furthering inflation and eventually leading to a contraction.

Cardozo viewed interest-rate manipulation as a proper bank weapon to control speculative situations resulting from an overissue of paper, but he believed that the usury laws impeded the operation of this preventive check. If the banks were able to raise the interest rate above the legally set rate, pressures in the money market might be relieved, since funds would tend to be funneled to those businessmen who were basically solvent, although temporarily short of funds.[41] The weakness implicit in this view is that it neglects the fact that speculators may be as willing to pay the advance in interest rates as more "legitimate" enterprisers.

Cardozo's nonacceptance of laissez-faire principles in dealing with banking problems during this early phase of his writings was evident in his endorsement of McVicker's idea of compelling all new banks to invest their capital in public securities, and forbidding them from issuing paper beyond the amount of their capital stock. He said, "It is pernicious . . . that the circulating medium of a state should be left to the operation of individual interest." [42]

Banks at an early date were classified as banks of discount, where bank money was exchanged for commercial paper such as bills of exchange; banks of deposit, where a receipt was given for money deposited; and banks of issue or circulation, where credit was extended in the form of bank notes. According to Miller, the idea "that banks of deposit and discount are entirely different in character

---

[41] *Ibid.*, June 21, 1837.
[42] *Ibid.*, February 9, 1828. McVicker's policy was referred to as "free-banking," in the sense that groups of people could freely incorporate as a bank if they deposited the required amount of government securities with the state authorities. See Dorfman, II, 521–22.

from banks that add the function of issuing credit in the form of circulating notes was very nearly the universal views in early British and American economic thought]." [43] This differentiation of function stemmed from a misconception of the nature of deposits. As Miller said, "The part that deposits play in causing fluctuations in the volume of the media of payments was overlooked . . . because of the failure to understand that deposits are created by the banks themselves in the process of making loans." [44] Deposits loaned out are an addition to the money supply, since they can be used by both the depositor and the borrower; thus, banks can create deposits as well as notes.

The orthodox nature of Cardozo's views on this subject during this period is obvious. He favored bank freedom to lend funds placed on deposit, including their own capital, but advocated restrictions on the power of the banks to issue their own money. In presenting his position, which on this issue followed the views of the "currency" school, Cardozo said:

We are not of the loco foco school. We are not advocates of unlimited freedom in banking. We ask . . . for a modified system of freedom. We wish banking in its legitimate meaning . . . thrown open to the freest competition. When we speak of legitimate banking, we do not mean the issue of paper money. This we would place under restriction. . . . When we speak of freedom in banking, we confine our meaning to banks of discount and deposit. [45]

Cardozo would restrict the power of issuing notes (money creation) to a few large mercantile houses, but thought

[43] Miller, p. 115. Members of the English "banking school" like Tooke, Fullarton, Wilson, and Gilbart are clearly an exception to this position.
[44] *Ibid.*, pp. 115–16.
[45] *Southern Patriot,* June 17, 1837. Cf. June 20, 27, 29, 1837; October 13, 1846. Cardozo's suggestion that the Locofoco school favored unlimited freedom in banking is not correct. They did adopt McVickar's "free-banking"

that the idle funds of the community would be put to productive use by the large number of banks of deposit and discount (money lending). The latter banks would in essence serve as intermediaries between small lenders and borrowers—an operation which Cardozo viewed as highly profitable. Although Cardozo, in common with the "currency" school, favored control over bank-note issuing, he did not support government regulation of total bank credit operations. The actions of note-issuing and deposit-discount banks would mutually check each other, because the availability of loanable funds in the latter would tend to restrain the issuing of notes by the former.

In attacking New York's free banking laws, Cardozo claimed that although banks of deposit were self-regulating, banks of issue had no self-restraining checks on their operations and therefore should not be given unrestricted liberty. He said that "the expansibility of their deposit bank credit is invariably regulated by the profits which can be made on legitimate employment of capital." [46] In other words, the expansion of deposit-discount operations is a symptom of legitimate business demands, whereas the excessive banking of the note-issuing banks promotes currency fluctuations and general instability. The technical reasoning behind Cardozo's claim that banks of issue have a greater motive to expand their circulation than deposit-discount banks is based on the unproved assumption that, although an overissue of notes can increase the loanable funds of deposit-discount banks, it necessarily lowers the interest rate and bank profits. Actually, the profit rise de-

position (see footnote 41 of this chapter); they favored repealing all usury laws and laws restraining the incorporation of banks, and were opposed to giving the banks unlimited note-issuing ability. Their position on social and political issues was, in general, more radical than Cardozo's; they were more concerned with workingmen's rights and controlling monopolies. See Dorfman, II, 652–61.

[46] Southern Patriot, October 18, 1838. Cf. Evening News, October 13, 1846.

pends on the amount of the overissue in relation to the interest rate, a ratio that is impossible to predict in advance.

On a practical level, Cardozo explained the difference between the two types of banks as follows:

Banks of deposit may unquestionably overtrade as well as banks of issue, but the distinction lies here, the former gives so little scope to speculation, that it is necessarily limited in duration and degree, while the latter nurse and extend it by constant accessions of credit.[47]

The key fault of this entire approach, which Cardozo shared with virtually all early American writers on banking subjects, lies in its attempt artificially to separate note-issuing and deposit-discount operations from one another.

1837–1847

In his following period of partial laissez-faire advocacy, Cardozo continued to favor controlling the note-issuing ability of banks but drastically altered his views on the relation of government to banking practices.

During the period of crisis of 1837, Cardozo shifted away from his early advocacy of a national bank because the political struggle attending efforts at rechartering upset the general harmony of the economic system. Complete separation of government and banking became Cardozo's new theme. In a series of articles entitled "Government and Banking," [48] he effectively pointed out that a profit-motivated national bank that had the use of public funds could and did employ them to excessively stimulate an economy and trigger off business crises. Public banks could

[47] *Southern Patriot*, November 13, 1838.
[48] *Ibid.*, July 11, 12, 13, 15, 17, 19, 21, 22, 25, 27, 31; August 3, 4, 7, 9, 11, 12, 1837.

maintain adequate control of the banking system during periods of ordinary commercial activity, but they exercised imperfect control in periods of inordinate speculative activity. Mismanagement opportunities were maximized when the national bank had access to government funds. In addition, public funds were more subject to sudden withdrawal than were private deposits, and this situation could create drastic economic consequences.

Cardozo's position appears to have been that banks inevitably extend their credit accommodation beyond safe limits, and the possibilities for this excessiveness are increased when national banks have a large supply of public funds available for their use. It is unreasonable to expect a public bank operating partly with intentions of maximizing profits always to use its regulatory power over the currency for the benefit of the public.

Cardozo suggests that public and private interests may diverge because the public may be hurt by speculative activity while banks may profit. Given this divergence, the choices would then be either to separate government and banking, a laissez-faire solution, or to operate the public bank for public welfare rather than private profit, a government-directed solution.

It is quite possible that Cardozo altered his earlier, more favorable view of the Bank of the United States when he observed the difficulty of operating it in the interest of the public. He apparently never considered the possibility of not operating a bank on a private-profit basis, although he held to the idea that if there were enough public spirited people with long-run foresight, the Bank of the United States could regulate the monetary system effectively:

To expect that banks will not make as large a profit as possible out of such circumstances [the expansion of the early 1830s] is perhaps expecting too much from human nature. To per-

mit the power of counteracting the public good for the benefit of corporate interests, by blending commercial with political functions—by uniting the duties of bankers with those
that belong to a due regulation of the circulation—is the
strangest of all anomalies in our political system. . . . The
conductors of a public bank are as dealers under the influence of irresistible sympathies of trade, and interested at all
times in its extension to increase their profits, with which the
important function of regulating the currency is generally,
if not necessarily, incompatible.[49]

Cardozo was ready to grant that a national bank provided
greater security, cheapness, and steadiness in the exchanges
in an ordinary period, but insisted that these advantages
were more than outweighed by the bank's interferences
with the foreign and domestic exchanges in a period of
speculative activity.

After the period of business crisis had passed and sufficient time had elapsed to acquire perspective, Cardozo
backtracked somewhat on these views. He indicated that
he was still favorably disposed to the concept of a national
banking institution; at the same time, he recognized an
unwillingness of the people to accept the accompanying
centralization of power. His pro-Unionist orientation
yielded in the face of popular opposition:

We are friendly to a National Bank. We like it for the very
odor of Nationality, for which it is disliked by those Ab-
stractionists who are for splitting sovereignty into insignif-
icant parts and fragments. We like it because it would give
us a currency of uniform value and afford valuable aids to
commerce. But we cannot shut our eyes to the facts of
history. . . . The people will never approve an institution
which they believe, however delusively, stands . . . connected
with the policy of centralization of power to an irresponsible
and irremovable monied aristocracy.[50]

[49] *Ibid.*, July 25, 27, 1837.
[50] *Ibid.*, August 20, 1841. Cf. November 22, 1837.

In a review of Henry Carey's *The Credit System of France, England and the United States,* Cardozo rejected the author's avowal of unrestrained competition in banking as part of a self-adjusting mechanism. Instead, he thought that this competition would lead to credit abuses and inordinate fluctuations of economic activity.[51]

Dorfman has dealt with the political and personal background events that accompanied Cardozo's shifting views on the relationship of government and banking.[52] He points out that Joel Poinsett,[53] a strong South Carolina supporter of Jackson in the nullification crisis of 1832, had become Van Buren's economic adviser during the crisis of 1837 and had used Cardozo's newspaper as his "mouthpiece" for advocating banking reform measures. Cardozo defended the separation of government and banking as well as the subtreasury scheme of the Van Buren administration. Van Buren implicitly admitted that the use of state ("pet") banks had not been an effective monetary instrument in controlling credit speculation.

There was considerable diversity of opinion in the South on this issue. In supporting the subtreasury plan, Cardozo denied that it would cause either a locking up of funds or a sudden expansion and contraction of the currency as a result of disrupting movements of specie. He thought that the frequency of gold payments to public creditors would approximately match the payments re-

[51] *Ibid.,* July 20, 1838. Cardozo said, "If the unrestricted use of credit in the form of paper money were allowed, the profits to be made by an irredeemable paper currency for only a short period would present a temptation too strong to be resisted."

[52] Dorfman, II, 854, 857, 858. Reference is made to the Poinsett-Cardozo correspondence which is at the Historical Society of Pennsylvania.

[53] Poinsett was one of the few prominent Southerners who remained pro-Union without swerving. The views of Poinsett and Cardozo on political and economic issues were quite similar until the latter moved closer to a moderate secessionist position. Both favored free trade but did not think that the existence of tariffs was sufficient reason to justify secession. Poinsett, however, was less favorably disposed to the institution of slavery. See also J. Fred Rippy, *Joel Roberts Poinsett, Versatile American.* Chapters 6,

ceived. If expenditures in one area were greater than receipts in that area, the subtreasurers would draw on the accumulated surplus of some other areas.

Although Cardozo claimed that the close relationship between government and banking tended to further the centralization of commerce and monied influence in the North, particularly in New York, he rejected the widely held Southern view that it was the original or main cause of the concentration.[54] A high tariff and the national bank diverted British capital, the main source of funds for the development of commerce, banking, and manufacture, from the South to the North, and helped to make New York into the leading commercial center of the country.[55] Whereas the South increasingly concentrated on agriculture, the North used British capital, facilitated by the Bank of the United States, for a vast scheme of internal improvements which fostered the commercial development of the North. Specifically, he approved of using British capital for internal improvements—primarily railroads —banking, manufacturing, and commerce. Because the subtreasury scheme had an "anti-consolidating tendency"[56] through keeping the public funds out of the control of New York banks, it was viewed as being conducive to the development of direct trade by the South with Europe.

Cardozo wrote, "The great and substantial principle of the sub-treasury scheme is to prevent trading on the public funds."[57] Unlike either the Bank of the United States or the system of state banking, government deposits under

10, 11, 15, 16 have useful coverage of the period covered by Cardozo's writings.

[54] *Southern Patriot,* August 17, 1838. In this article, Cardozo specifically rejected Calhoun's idea that the combination of the tariff and the Bank of the United States had caused the centralization of commerce in the North.

[55] *Ibid.,* August 17, October 11, 1838.   [56] *Ibid.,* September 27, 1837.

[57] *Ibid.,* October 14, 1837.

this plan would not form a part of banking capital, although creditors would have a claim for specie on funds paid into the government by debtors. Cardozo thought that requiring the banks to redeem their notes in specie had the salutary effect of checking the overissuing of loans.[58] If they knew that sudden payment of duties in specie might be required of them, they would not be as free in extending loans.

Cardozo believed that the subtreasury would be a better general regulator of the economy than the national bank, since the latter was unable to restrain its own activities. A subtreasury plan was introduced as a bill in 1837 but failed to become law. It was introduced again in the following year with modifications, chief of which was a provision for a gradual transition to the payment of public debts in specie. In the interim period, the notes of specie-paying banks were considered acceptable substitutes. Cardozo also accepted the modified measure,[59] but it suffered the fate of its predecessor. In July, 1840, a bill setting up an independent treasury system was passed, bringing the system of "pet banks" (many of which had failed) to an end. Cardozo approved, thinking that this system would reduce bank speculation with public funds.[60] Partial specie payments on debts to the government were allowed for a three-year period.

In the following Whig administration, the Independent

[58] *Ibid.*, November 24, 1837. In this article Cardozo differed with his fellow South Carolinian, Hugh Legaré, who thought that commerce and trade would be crippled by the specie requirement. Apparently Legaré believed that credit was a constant stimulus to productive power. For a thorough discussion of the various shades of public opinion in South Carolina on the subtreasury issue, see Van Deusen, pp. 156–63.

[59] *Southern Patriot*, June 18, September 20, 1838. A chronological description of the various banking measures can be found in Dewey, pp. 235–43.

[60] *Southern Patriot*, July 14, 1840. Dewey viewed the independent treasury system as "a protest against State banks as well as against a national bank." Dewey, p. 259.

Treasury Law was repealed, but an impasse developed between President Tyler and the Clay-led legislature on the creation of an alternative. The efforts of the latter to establish a national bank (called the Fiscal Bank of the United States) were rebuffed by Tyler on the grounds that such a bank would infringe on states rights. The bill provided for a fiscal corporation and state branch banks with the power of buying and selling bills and drafts (of which Tyler approved) as well as making loans in its operation as a bank of discount (which Tyler vetoed). Cardozo, on the whole, sympathized with the efforts of the Whigs, although he did register some objections. He opposed the provision which set a fixed limit between the amount of specie and the notes in circulation on the grounds that it would make banking operations too rigid.[61] In December, 1841, Tyler proposed his own plan for an exchequer bank, but it was rejected by the Congress. The principal features of this plan included:

(1) Setting up a board of control with agencies at key commercial centers. The board would collect, keep, disburse, and transfer public moneys. The branches were to be controlled by the states.

(2) Issuing non–interest-bearing exchequer bills with a limit set at $15 million. These could be used to pay debts to the government or for purchases by the government. The object was to furnish a credit-worthy paper currency equivalent to specie.

(3) The bank would have power to buy and sell domestic exchange (bills and drafts).

Cardozo correctly predicted the rejection of the proposal by Congress, although he personally was not opposed to it.[62] In actual operation, there was a return to the use of state banks as depositories for the public funds. In a very

[61] *Southern Patriot,* June 18, 1841.
[62] *Ibid.,* December 28, 1841.

short period, the banking system had gone through the cycle of replacing a national bank with a state bank system (i.e., Jackson's "pet" banks), of abandoning the state banks in favor of a subtreasury system, and of rejecting subsequent plans for various approximations of a national bank. This instability of the Federal financial situation was compounded by the repudiation of debt obligations by many states during the years 1837 to 1844, thus causing a considerable loss to foreign investors as well as a downgrading of American credit.[63] Cardozo saw the effects of monetary policies in the United States and England as interlinked because economic expansion and speculation in the former would be much lessened if credit from the latter was not forthcoming.[64]

Cardozo was concerned with the problem of developing preventive checks against credit abuses rather than curing their after-effects. He recognized the impossibility of exercising full control over the fluctuations of economic activity by monetary techniques, but believed that foresight could lessen its impact. He said:

All systems of paper currency have inherent defects [i.e., instability] and can never be brought within restraints that ensure constant stability and uniformity. The best devised

[63] Dewey, pp. 243–46. Cardozo stressed the importance of enforcing debt payments to maintain a good credit standing. He favored raising taxes and pressuring the banks to resume specie payments for this purpose. *Southern Patriot*, January 12, 1842.

[64] Cardozo said that "The fountain head of the evils produced in the United States by the abuse of paper money is to be sought in the British system." *Ibid.*, August 5, 1840. In this article, Cardozo dealt with an interesting British banking reform proposal of Torrens. In this plan, banks were to place in the mint an amount of gold equal to one-fourth of their average circulation of the previous year. They would receive stamped notes for the whole amount of their circulation and the issuing banks would be compelled to redeem these notes in gold. Of this scheme, Cardozo said, "The great difficulty . . . is the management of the deposits, and whether or not they should be considered as loanable capital by the banks and thence constitute a part of their circulation."

schemes present only approximations to this desirable result. . . . Bank operations influenced by outward events, arbitrary and fluctuating, can never be brought within the unbend-
ing and rigid rule of an act of Parliament.[65]

The well-being of the system required a flexible monetary
system, but not one which was fully responsive to all business demands for loans. Cardozo advocated giving power to
public commissioners, who were unconnected with either
the banks or the government, to check or enlarge the
money supply as conditions warranted. Unusually high
borrowings or importations would be a signal to tighten
the credit reins. This has similarities to the countercyclical monetary policy pursued by the present Federal
Reserve System. Cardozo favored a law placing a limit on
bank profits, directing the surplus beyond an ordinary rate
of return into the public treasury, and limiting bank loans
to an amount which would enable the banks to earn this
ordinary return.[66]

He became less favorably disposed toward the subtreasury plan, because its relative inflexibility tended to promote contraction of the currency.[67]

1847–1853

The following period, during which Cardozo embraced
laissez-faire banking principles, contains his least-known
writings. The sharpness of the change emerges in a com-

[65] *Ibid.*, September 24, 1844.

[66] *Ibid.*, November 13, 1839. The loan limitation was set at 50% of the
bank's capital actually used in banking. The idea concerning the legal limitation of banking profits can be found in Raymond. See his *Elements of
Political Economy*, II, 154–58.

[67] *Southern Patriot*, November 26, 1842. Cardozo said that the national
bank was "an engine of political power" and the subtreasury scheme "an
instrument of oppression to credit."

parison of Cardozo's early and later views on the New York system of free banking. Under the free-banking laws, incorporation procedures were very simple. Any bank could issue bank notes that were based on a deposit of approved securities. Adherents of this view, such as Henry Carey, held that the competition of numerous banks had beneficial results.

It is worth noting that free banking and laissez-faire banking are not precisely equivalent terms. The counterpart of free banking is chartered banking. The former provides for freedom of entry to all banking groups that meet certain basic prerequisites, such as purchasing a required amount of stocks or bonds, while the latter limits the number of banks to those who receive a charter. Free banking is thus an expression of laissez-faire as far as freedom of entry is concerned, although in actual operation it may tend toward laissez-faire in a wider sense. Bray Hammond declared:

Free banking was an application of *laisser faire* to the monetary function. . . . Though the law [establishing a free banking system] made any one "free" to engage in banking, tho freedom was qualified to the extent that one must have the necessary money to start and must meet certain other formalities . . . [F]ree banking meant, in effect, an indefinite and unlimited number of banks.[68]

In late 1847, Cardozo became an advocate of free banking. In marked contrast to his earlier view of the system as a promoter of speculative banking and instability, he extended high praise to the free banking system in New York. He said, "Free banking is the best system for the community as it permits the expansion and contraction of the circulation in conformity to the public wants." [69]

[68] Bray Hammond, *Banks and Politics in America from the Revolution to the Civil War*, pp. 572–73.
[69] *Evening News*, November 20, 1847. For the earlier critical view see

During this phase of his writing, Cardozo criticized British banking measures which allowed competition and self-regulation to prevail in the lending of deposits, while at the same time providing for public supervision of bank-note issuing. He favored abandoning all legal controls over the amount of note issues or the rate of interest. This was the position of the "banking" school.

Cardozo also rejected the idea that speculation was produced by overissuing of bank notes; instead, he claimed that the history of banking indicated that the injudicious use of bank deposits by the public was a more direct cause of monetary disturbances. Cardozo shifted to the view that "there is no necessary connection between bank issues and speculation," [70] and that, in fact, there was no rational explanation for speculation. Since commercial crises had occurred under all forms of banking regulations, he favored experimenting with freedom in banking. Because large speculative movements are carried on with deposits, the spontaneous action of the public, particularly the mercantile class, was viewed as the cause of monetary problems. Public demand determines the amount of bank notes that will be absorbed into circulation.

In stressing the importance of the actions of the public in influencing economic activity, Cardozo said, "It is the public which in most cases, acts on the banks, and not the banks on the public." [71] Idle bank deposits will be directed into business channels only when an optimistic public demand stimulates its employment. Speculative activity does not require the use of bank notes. The use of book credits or bills of exchange, often redrawn through many hands, makes the actions of the trading public independ-

---

Southern Patriot, October 18, November 13, 1838; *Evening News,* October 13, 1846.

[70] *Evening News,* November 18, 1847.

[71] *Ibid.,* November 16, 1848. Cf. January 5, 1849.

ent of banking or legislative measures and lessens the importance of bank notes. Cardozo stated that the proportion of a circulating medium in the form of bank notes as opposed to these other devices had become quite unimportant. He thus saw the situation with bank deposits as an important key to business cycle analysis.

Cardozo recognized the limitations to the effectiveness of monetary policy, particularly in periods of recession:

Although banks can not expand unless there exists a certain sympathy in the public that answers correspondently . . . the converse is not equally true. . . . They may restrict their discounts below the legitimate wants of business . . . [and] excessively distress the circulation. . . . When banks find in their coffers an accumulation of deposits and a limited call for discounts, they use all possible expedients to attract borrowers. The Bank of England lowers the rate of interest, often ineffectually. It cannot at times overcome the *vis inertiae*. It cannot when stagnation has settled over every branch of business, enlarge its loans.[72]

In order to provide protection against the discrediting of the currency, Cardozo at first favored requiring a deposit of public stocks as security for the money issues of the bank and a rigidly enforced scheme of specie payments. As he moved still closer to laissez-faire banking, however, he looked on public control over specie convertibility of bank notes as ineffectual, and therefore favored giving the public free rein. The possibility of discredit following excessive note-issuance or use of deposits would be the only restraining instrument. Cardozo said, "The fear of discredit, which is sure to follow non-convertibility, is the internal check on the managers of a paper currency, as the public demand for coin is the true external security against bank notes becoming excessive." [73] He thought that profit-

[72] *Ibid.*, November 16, 1848; November 19, 1847.
[73] *Ibid.*, October 14, 1848. Cardozo added that business crises were as

motivated managers were able to set up their own controls, including those convertibility requirements which experience indicated as being desirable. In this period, he regarded any effort to set up public controls over banking activities as completely futile.

He reaffirmed these ideas in a review of Henry Middleton's *The Government and the Currency*.[74] He took the position that there is no legislative regulation which can adequately control the currency and credit of the country, because periods of excess loanable funds alternate in a seemingly inevitable way with periods of shortages. The possibilities of controlling this flow appeared remote to Cardozo. He said, "The payments in and out of bank are not coincident and this no legislation will rectify or can prevent. . . . The quantity and value of bank notes are determined by the action of the public." [75] Neither limited nor unlimited liability of the banks appears to produce greater stability. It was impossible to know the best relation between specie and credit created by the bank, since this ration is bound to vary with the state of economic ativity. A prudent body of directors, rather than government regulation, was considered the only way to achieve safe regulation of the banks.

To summarize this phase of Cardozo's banking views, one can say that, in Cardozo's opinion, the surest way of obtaining a sound currency and credit system was free banking and the continued policy of separation of government and banking.

---

likely to occur with a specie standard as with a paper money system. He mentioned that the value of specie varied with certain economic-political conditions and raised the possibility of allowing banks to pay specie at current market rates rather than fixed mint prices. *Ibid.*, March 24, 1849.

[74] Cardozo, "The Government and the Currency," *Southern Quarterly Review* (September, 1850), pp. 123–32. Henry Middleton was a South Carolina economist of considerable ability, who wrote on such topics as banking, value theory, and the economics of slaveholding.

[75] *Ibid.*, p. 128.

Cardozo threw off the "currency" school errors of exaggerating the importance of regulating note issues and minimizing the role of deposits, only to embrace the "banking" school error of viewing banks as passive instruments catering to the "needs of business." Banking policy clearly affects the willingness of businessmen to borrow, which in turn affects economic activity. In addition, adherents of the "banking" principle missed the point that the banking system as a whole created overissues even though the individual bank could not permanently do so.

AFTER 1853

Another sharp change was evident in Cardozo's thinking during the year 1853. This phase represented a retreat from the laissez-faire orientation of the previous period and a reappearance of his hostility to free banking.[76]

Cardozo became reconvinced of the abuses of a paper-money system and reverted to his earlier position of favoring the restriction of banking powers to the deposit-discount functions of receiving deposits and making loans. Allowing the banks the privilege of note-issuing results in banking abuses by giving them a powerful weapon for self-enrichment. As before, Cardozo held that competition in the issuing of bank notes had a tendency to lead to a cumulative overexpansion of bank credit.

The creation of a money scarcity by the Charleston banks, and perhaps the numerous failures under the free-banking system in New York, appears to have been instrumental in altering Cardozo's laissez-faire banking approach. He claimed that these banks were sending their

[76] Cardozo's banking views in this period can be found in the following issues of the *Evening News:* February 17, 1853; May 1, 15, July 28, August 12 (the most definitive article), September 28, November 29, 1854; November 13, 1855; January 26, 1856.

bank funds to distant cities for investments of an illegiti-
mate character in an attempt to circumvent the South Carolina usury laws, which set a legal maximum of 7 percent
interest.

Cardozo's criticism was that Southern banks involved in
speculation sent specie to the North, "shaved" Southern
credits, and charged usurious rates on credit. A writer described these actions of the South Carolina banks:

[They] were buying cotton bills in the West payable in
Mobile, New Orleans, etc. and when the bills matured, these
funds were invested in bills payable in New York and Europe
and then reinvested in Southern paper.[77]

Cardozo was quite correct in pointing out that the credit
shortage in the 1850s was aggravated by the use of Southern bank credit facilities for financing out-of-state operations, which was in turn prompted by the state usury laws.

Evidence that this type of money-scarcity-creating operation was profitable is seen in Cardozo's figures that bank
dividends of the Charleston banks were 7 to 16 percent in
1853. The point, however, that the conservative banking
policies of the South Carolina banks were partially responsible for the credit shortage of the 1850s escaped Cardozo's
attention.

The South Carolina banks generally pursued a conservative policy, stressing the importance of a sound, convertible currency. This tended to hinder the development and
necessary readjustments of the South Carolina economy.
As Smith said:

The banking system worked fairly well from the standpoint
of large merchants and large planters. Its basis weakness
was that the great majority of farmers and planters and
small merchants were unable to secure either productive
credit or long-term credit. . . . The development and read-

[77] Alfred G. Smith, Jr., p. 210.

justment of the economy was seriously hindered by lack of credit. . . . The legislature deliberately followed a policy of restricting the expansion of banking and credit facilities in order to protect the profits of the State's own bank.[78]

Despite his generally sympathetic attitude toward the planting class, Cardozo held that loans to them were the most insecure type of loan, since planters were unable to repay them in a short period. He said, "The essential principle of all safe and sound banking consists of advances to merchants, on short dated paper, not renewable, which enables banks to effect a rapid conversion of their assets." [79] Cardozo's prime concern was to subject the banking system to sufficient control to prevent economic and social instability. Since a loose bank policy tended to promote economic development at the high price of increased instability, Cardozo was willing to slow down the former to prevent the latter.

The general principle advocated by Cardozo in this period was that banking activities should be regulated by the legislature in order to restrain the proclivity of profit-motivated banks to produce either excesses of currency that thus aided speculation or shortages that hindered legitimate business operations. He said, "The law should define the banking to be permitted and should put its management under a systematized supervision and control." [80] The specific policy measures favored included the following:

(1) Limit the power of note-issuing to only one bank, the State Bank of South Carolina, and restrict the power of

<hr />

[78] *Ibid.*, pp. 216–17. Cardozo's approving comment on the conservativeness of the Bank of Charleston was, "Banking in the city of Charleston has always followed and rarely preceded the course and currents of business. With the expansion of trade, was the extension of banking facilities." Cardozo, *Reminiscences of Charleston,* pp. 44–47. Cited by Smith, p. 200.

[79] Cardozo, *Reminiscences of Charleston,* p. 45.

[80] *Evening News,* August 12, 1854.

all other banks to receiving deposits and making loans. It would not be necessary to control deposit-discount operations, since their effect on the volume of currency and prices was not considered significant. In direct contradiction to his earlier thinking, Cardozo said that merchants and jobbers are enabled to give extended credit to others solely because banks extend credit to them. In the previous free-banking period, Cardozo held that speculative activities could be carried on without substantial bank credit.

(2) Require rigid enforcement of specie payments and set a fixed ratio of liabilities to specie as an indirect restraint on the banks, thus putting a ceiling on their expansionary ability. In this connection Cardozo said:

The great desideratum, therefore, of banking is to devise a constantly operative check, which will preclude contraction, because preventing expansion. Nearly all the panics of our banks and commercial classes arise from fear of the future more than present pressure.[81]

Cardozo, at this time, also thought that specie should be the main currency and credit mainly supplementary.

(3) Set up legislative controls over the activities of bank directors, controls that prevent them from receiving personal bank loans or using bank credits for out-of-state operations. Cardozo, in essence, defended the right of the public to oversee the way the currency was administered.

(4) Require a large paid-up capital to provide greater security for bank funds.

Cardozo continued to believe that the spirit of rash enterprise rather than excessive bank credit was the basic cause of speculation and general instability, but in this period he emphasized that the banks can have an important subsequent causal influence by extending the ability of the business class to intensify the speculation. This provided

[81] *Ibid.*, November 13, 1855.

sufficient reason to control and delimit the sphere of legitimate credit expanding-contracting operations.

The decade following the reestablishment of the subtreasury system in 1846 was one of considerable national
prosperity. Cardozo took the position that although this
system was effective in checking a speculative situation, its
inelasticity in a period of falling confidence was a grave defect.

In two post-Civil War articles on banking, Cardozo defended a scheme of government paper money against the
national banking system [82] which had been established
during the war. Under the National Banking Act, the
member banks had to invest their capital in Federal government bonds, which served as security for their note issues. This had the tendency of producing a currency with
insufficient elasticity. Cardozo's position on currency and
credit issues was similar to the one of restricting banking
functions to deposit-discount operations that he had taken
in the immediate pre-Civil War period, but now he hoped
to achieve these ends with less legislative control. He favored a "voluntary agreement among banks to establish a
graduated rate of discount" [83] to control bank credit speculations. This would be accomplished by raising or lowering the rate of discount as the term of credit lengthened or
shortened. Cardozo favored setting up a three-man board
of currency having the sole authority to issue notes payable on demand in gold, the board's official policy being to
reduce or increase the currency when it became excessive
or short. Its issuance of notes would be limited to a certain
unstated proportion of the national revenues and would
be determined by the public demand for currency. Possi-

[82] Cardozo, "Essay on Banking and Currency," *The Bankers Magazine
and Statistical Register* (March, 1869), pp. 673–97. "Systems of Banking,"
Southern Review (April, 1870), pp. 355–401. This latter article is unsigned
but is clearly Cardozo's.

[83] Cardozo, "Essay on Banking and Currency," p. 685.

ble conflict between this necessary proportion and the demands of the public was not discussed. Cardozo indicated his partial acceptance of the "banking principle" by saying, "The quantity of the circulating medium is determined by the wants of the community. . . . [T]he public requirements . . . are the only self-regulating principles of the currency." [84]

In his advocacy of credit controls by adjustments of the interest rate and the period of the loan, Cardozo was a precursor of later banking legislation. His awareness of the aims of monetary policy are shown by his statement, "There are two evils, to be shunned in banking: too great a reduction in the rate of interest, stimulating speculation, and too great an elevation of the rate, checking enterprise." [85]

Cardozo's changing views on banking problems represent a search for a method of reconciling laissez-faire, social conservatism, and the peculiar financial position of the Southern economy. The dual dependence of the South on the North and Europe increased the vulnerability of its financial institutions. The fluctuation of Cardozo's banking views between various forms of social controls and self-regulation can only be understood against a background of rapid but unbalanced economic development with differential rates of growth in different sections, marked instability of the domestic and international market, and significant political and social change. Despite periodic business crises, the Northern economy was developing in a more rapid and diversified growth pattern than the Southern economy. Both centralized and decentralized banking ultimately proved to be incapable of making the antebellum Southern economy less economically vulnerable and dependent.

[84] *Ibid.*, p. 682.   [85] *Ibid.*, p. 696.

Cardozo's acceptance of a national bank in the early period was a partial reflection of the fact that the economic and political antagonisms between the sections had not fully matured. During the nullification crisis of 1832, for example, no other Southern state was willing actively to support the position of South Carolina, although all of them unanimously opposed the protective tariff. Although he recognized that the national bank had a more beneficial effect on the Northern commercial economy than on the Southern agrarian economy, Cardozo viewed the two sections as part of an interdependent, harmonious system. His gradual shift toward favoring the separation of government and banking coincided with a realization that a national bank system could not, or would not, effectively control the powerful forces of economic expansion, and that the opposition to the bank was too widespread to expect its effective continuance.

In the 1840s he hoped that commerce and manufacturing would take roots in the South. He gradually came to question whether or not the benefits of a Federal system were being eroded by a growing sectional conflict. Cardozo at this time believed that decentralization and a more laissez-faire operation of the banking system would facilitate this development and decrease the economic dependence of the South. As part of this process, he advocated a removal of restraints on the note-issuing ability of the banks. By the 1850s, however, Cardozo realized that the uncontrolled operation of profit-motivated Southern banks was creating a credit shortage in the South, at least in certain sections, which had the effect of restraining legitimate enterprise.

Despite his shift of focus from the national to local levels, Cardozo returned to his early advocacy of interfering with the free-market mechanism in the area of banking

operations. The realities of the Southern political economy ultimately led Cardozo to advocate public control
over the banking mechanism in an attempt to protect the
over-all economic interests of the South.

SEVEN

Business Cycles

NOWHERE is the contrast between the orthodox English school and some of the early American economists more clearly evident than in the discussion of business cycles.

One observer claimed, "In their treatment of commercial crises and business cycles our early writers were particularly stimulating. It is quite possible that a few of them had here a better understanding than any of their English contemporaries." [1] The view that business cycles were a continually recurring phenomenon was widely accepted in early American economic discussions.

Cardozo referred to a crisis as "having its origin in one of those general and irresistible changes in human affairs, which appear to follow in a cycle, alternating at periods ir-

[1] Miller, p. 187.

regular in duration, but powerful in action, in proportion as the previous period is prolonged." [2]

Alternations in the level of economic activity were inevitable in a commercial society. A credit system, moreover, increased its vulnerability to economic disorders. Cardozo said, "Whilst banks continue to be depositors of almost all the loanable capital of the community, much of it seeking investment, expansions and contractions are inevitable." [3]

The expansion and contraction phases of the business cycle did not, however, possess a definite periodicity. With reference to England, he said, "There appears to be no natural or necessary connection between the crises which appear to recur almost regularly in English history about every ten years, and the period of national prosperity and their attendant reverses." [4]

Cardozo discussed business cycles in the context of an international economy, in which fluctuations were transmitted from one country to another by its effects on trade. He believed that an isolated country would not experience business fluctuations, and that the effects would be slight if wars did not exist and changes in a country's structure took place in a gradual fashion.[5] Since rapid expansion tended to breed the conditions for reversal, Cardozo claimed,

[2] *Southern Patriot,* May 31, 1837. *Ibid.,* June 3, 1837. Cf. *Evening News,* February 8, 1851.

[3] Cardozo, "The Government and the Currency," p. 130.

[4] Cardozo, "Essay on Banking and Currency," p. 694. In this article he drew a distinction between financial and commercial crises. The former was based on speculation in securities and the latter on speculation in commodities. The crises of 1847 and 1867 were presented as examples of financial crises, and those of 1825, 1837, and 1857 as commercial crises.

[5] *Southern Patriot,* June 29, 1826. He said, "If a country were insulated from all others . . . its prosperity would not be subject to those ebbs and flows which inseparably accompany the fluctuations of foreign markets. Nor would states make those sudden starts in wealth, and be liable to consequent reactions, if wars did not, by interrupting commercial intercourse, produce in proportion to their duration and extent, ruinous gluts."

"The growth of prosperity in nations must be gradual to be durable." [6]

In common with most early American economic theorists, Cardozo stressed the importance of the relationship between crises and abuses of the credit system. His views, however, went beyond a pure monetary explanation. The interplay of money and "real" factors was strategic in Cardozo's analysis. The "electric chain of commerce" [7] transmitted the effects of extended credit from one sector to another. Cardozo's business cycle analysis is related to his changing views on banking, in that he tended to view the cycle as more than a purely monetary phenomenon during the period of his free-banking advocacy, during which he believed that public monetary control measures had limited use. At this time he held that business crises could not be prevented either by the government or combinations of the large capitalists, and that they occurred regardless of whether or not a paper-money or specie-based system was in use. In periods when he favored more legislative control over banking activities, Cardozo tended to regard properly applied monetary policy as having an ameliorative influence over the business cycle. He was certain, however, that even a properly applied policy could not arrest speculative tendencies sufficiently to prevent business cycles.

Cardozo's description of the business cycle centering on the crisis of 1837 is valuable for the insights it reveals about his analytical method. He stated that his objective in studying this crisis was to determine what part of the trouble was functionally related to government policy measures, and what part was due to "causes of general operation" [8] or endogenous to the workings of a business enter-

[6] *Evening News*, October 12, 1850. In this article, Cardozo also noted that economic prosperity in the United States was aided by the emigration of labor and capital from Europe to the United States. Cf. *Southern Patriot*, March 28, 1838.

[7] *Southern Patriot*, April 1, 1819.   [8] *Ibid.*, June 7, 1837.

prise system. It was concluded that the latter were much more important causes of the crisis than any government measures. Although government monetary policies did not originate the speculation, they might, if improperly applied, have an exacerbating effect. Cardozo said that although "the measures of government aggravated the disturbances to commerce and postponed the restoration to a more wholesome state of things, it is impossible that these measures could originate a general excitement, the sources of which must be sought in commercial events." [9]

Speculation played a key role in Cardozo's business-cycle model. Speculative buying is based on favorable expectations, which in turn are conditioned by actual economic conditions. Cardozo rejected the simplistic relationship between prices and the money supply postulated by the quantity theorists. Speculation and price increases were seen as preceding an expansion of credit, although their effects were furthered by such an expansion. Cardozo said:

When the general rise of prices took place from excessive speculation, the currency was acted upon before it acted on prices, but by enlargement still further increasing them, and giving greater and more fatal intensity to speculation. . . . An expansion of the currency is first an *effect* before it becomes a *cause* of general excitement, which has its sources in commercial events. [10]

Cardozo attempted to examine the root causes for the recurring waves of speculative activities. He emphasized

[9] *Ibid.*, May 31, 1837. Cardozo specifically mentioned the removal of government deposits from the Bank of the United States in 1833. He said, "It did not augment the mass of the currency. . . . It did produce commercial failures because those banks which had been deprived of the public deposits, losing a portion of those funds which constituted the basis of their issues, were compelled to call in part of their circulation but . . . the evil was both temporary in duration and local in its influence." See also *ibid.*, June 7, 1837.

[10] *Ibid.*, May 24, July 25, 1837. In the former article, Cardozo refers favorably to Tooke's work, *High and Low Prices,* as expressing the same view. See also *ibid.*, May 23, 30, July 22, 1837.

that certain conditions present in the trough of the cycle prepared the way for increased speculation, regardless of the monetary policies pursued by government authorities. A country in a state of prolonged recession was implicitly viewed as poised on the threshold of speculative activities. If another fellow-trading country is in a roughly similar position, the possibilities of mutual stimulation are considerably greater. Cardozo had a partial awareness of the self-generating features of a business cycle, although his analysis was weak concerning the precise factors that brought an expansionary period to an end.

Monetary conditions cited by Cardozo as favorable to a revival were low interest rates and an abundant supply of loanable funds, which exist after a long period of general stagnation. Although these factors were the preconditions for a speculative increase in demand, certain "real" factors were responsible for triggering off the expansion. Among these Cardozo included depleted inventories, low prices and profits, decline in the tariff on products where domestic demand is rising, and availability of investment-seeking domestic and foreign capital.

The starting basis of the expansion in the 1830s, according to Cardozo, was the comparative stagnation of the 1825 to 1830 period. A roughly similar situation prevailed in England.

The large holdings of government bonds by the Bank of the United States were completely liquidated by the end of 1830 as the government paid off its public debt. This repayment lent itself to overtrading as the profit-motivated banks had an incentive to use the idle funds for extending credit. Cardozo dates the start of speculation in the United States as 1831, and 1833 for England. The low prices of English export goods and their low supply in the United States resulted in a sharp increase of 40 percent in the value of United States imports in 1831, an increase from

$60 million in 1830 to the sum of $83 million in 1831.[11] He said:

It was therefore at the end of 1830 when the stocks of foreign merchandise having been reduced and capital was so abundant in the United States that an opening for speculation by a more profitable investment of it presenting itself, an enlargement of commercial transactions took place.[12]

The increased importation of foreign goods was a critical initiating element in Cardozo's business-cycle model. The causes of this increase were the depletion of foreign inventories, lowering of the tariff, and the availability of bank credit first from domestic sources and later from foreign sources. The idea presented was that increased demand for imports would be followed by an increased reciprocating demand for a country's exports, thereby intensifying the expansive influences:

The most usual source of disturbance from commercial changes is such a stimulus given to the consumption of foreign products from the accumulation of stocks and low prices, that while the rate of consumption is accelerated, the supply being the same, the market soon becomes comparatively bare. This is a never failing accompaniment of an abundance of capital and a low interest of [sic] money. . . . The commercial event which led to the late speculation in the United States was the large importation of foreign goods in 1831, the low prices and consequently increased consumption having exhausted stocks at the close of 1831 . . .

[11] Ibid., July 22, 25, 1837. Although, as Cardozo noted, imports of foreign goods fell in 1832 to $76 million from their excessive 1831 levels, they were still well above 1830 levels. Cardozo attempted to distinguish between the parts of this increase in demand which were speculative and those which were "normal," but the line of separation was vague. In the latter article, he said, "An increased amount from 10–15% would have been sufficient to have replenished the stocks, on any reasonable scale of consumption. The excess from 25–30% [made possible by bank credit] we consider artificial demand produced by speculation."

[12] Ibid., August 12, 1837.

rendering capitalists impatient for new investment that promised larger returns.[13]

These events had a twofold speculative effect on the British economy: (1) It stimulated their production of export goods, which were highly sensitive to the state of economic activity in the United States. The relative prosperity of the British export industries was considerably influenced by the state of the American market. (2) It stimulated British investments in the United States.

Although the increased American demand for loans stimulated speculation in England, the latter's economy was in a state of readiness because of low profits and large accumulations of money capital. The situation was described as follows:

The public mind in the United States . . . was in that state to fit it for the high stimulus that succeeds long stagnation or quietude in trade. . . . The impulse of speculation was excessive from the previous stagnation. . . . A similar stagnation at the same time in England led to low profits and a large accumulation of capital. The inducement to lend, by her capitalists, on an unusually large scale, from the high comparative interest rate in the United States produced the temptation in the United States to borrow, in the form of imported merchandise and money. We multiplied our debts abroad. . . . The treasure we borrowed in the form of precious metals we made the basis of new issues of paper, that added fresh materials to the stimulus.[14]

Cardozo attempted to separate chronologically the cause and effect reactions of the American and British econo-

[13] *Ibid.*, July 22, 25, 1837. Cardozo did not observe that to a minor extent the expansion of the export sector in the United States might be counterbalanced by a decline in the import-competing industries. This would not occur in England, since there was no domestic producing sector competitive with their imports from the United States.

[14] *Ibid.*, May 23, 1837. Cardozo mentioned that in 1835 the interest rate was 2–2¼% in England, and 5–10% in the United States. See also *ibid.*, May 13, 1837.

mies, a task made difficult by their close interdependence. He contended that the overexpansion of credit in 1831 by the Bank of the United States set the stage for the eventual crisis. Cardozo particularly emphasized the importance of the role played by the Bank of the United States in maintaining the excessive level of importation. Figures were presented showing that the net circulation of money rose 30 percent between January, 1831 and January, 1832, only 5 percent less than in the whole previous decade. The increased money supply sustained the excessive import level:

[This] excess arose out of a speculative demand produced by the action of the United States Bank on the issues and domestic exchange of the country which in turn operated on the consumption and price of our chief article of export in foreign countries thus giving rise in the English and American markets alternately to speculation and overtrading. . . . If the bank had not fully met the demand for money for purposes of speculation in the import trade in the 6 months from January to July 1831 . . . the speculation would have here ended and the successive action and reaction on the consumption of cotton in Great Britain . . . [and] the consumption of British fabrics in the United States leading to the catastrophe of 1836 would have been prevented.[15]

Cardozo's position is that a restraining monetary policy by the Bank of the United States in 1831–32 would have checked the self-reinforcing chain of increasing imports and increasing speculation. The sharp increase in the American demand for British cotton goods in 1831 led to an increased demand for American cotton by the following year. In effect, the increased consumption of English manufactured goods by the United States gave a mutual stimulus to both countries, a process described as "each country . . . alternately exciting the other by a reciprocal de-

[15] *Ibid.*, July 22, 31, 1837. See also *ibid.*, August 12, 1837.

mand for its products." [16] Cardozo clearly believed, how-ever, that the original impetus for this cycle started in the United States and developed cumulative reciprocal effects in England.

Cardozo insisted that objective criteria existed which showed that speculation was developing at this period:

(1) United States banks were losing gold because of a large import balance.

(2) The state of the foreign exchanges indicated that the value of the pound was rising relative to the dollar. To stem the flight of gold, the Bank of the United States drew bills on foreign countries; it paid its debt partly with bills of exchange drawn to the order of foreign exporters. According to Cardozo, this interference with the free operation of foreign exchange was the wrong course of action, since it prevented the specie flow equilibrating mechanism from operating, and thereby had the effect of extending both the range and the duration of speculative tendencies. He said:

She [the Bank of the United States] prevented by her inter-ference with the foreign exchange that necessary rectification of the disturbance produced by an over-import which should be accompanied by an exportation of specie as its natural corrector. . . . Overtrading was nourished and sus-tained by the Bank of the United States.[17]

On one hand, Cardozo appeared to be saying that if the bank had not expanded the currency in 1831 and had played the "rules of the game," the large importation and ensuing speculative expansion would not have taken place; on the other hand, he looked at the bank's credit-expand-

[16] *Ibid.*, July 22, 1837.

[17] *Ibid.*, July 31, August 7, 1837. In the former article, Cardozo stated that the proper criterion for a national bank to employ in regard to the supply of currency was to limit the amount to the "rate at which the pop-ulation and domestic exports augmented." See July 27, 1837. This is an interesting forerunner of the idea of gauging the money supply by the national income level.

ing activities as the logical and expected action of a profit-motivated institution with access to a large supply of government funds.

The policies pursued by the Bank of England also came in for considerable criticism. At the onset of the crisis Cardozo saw the "leading and original cause" [18] as stemming from the abrupt shift of the Bank of England to a restrictive credit policy, particularly with those mercantile houses dealing with the United States. Those houses had invested heavily in American securities (primarily in state internal improvement schemes) based on the credit accommodation of the Bank of England. Cardozo softened his adverse judgment of England's action as he more closely examined the actions of American business firms and banks. He recognized that tightening of credit was not the cause of the crisis, as he had earlier maintained, but rather a symptom of the previous policy of too loose credit.

The large outflow of capital from England was accompanied by an unprecedented influx of gold to the United States between 1833 and 1836; the value of gold imports was greater than the value of gold exports by $35 million. The gold movements were, however, symptomatic of disequilibrating conditions. The tremendous capital movements from England to the United States upset the normal gold balances and the monetary systems of both countries.

Cardozo soundly criticized the Bank of England's policy of increasing the supply of money at the same time that it was losing gold. The figures that he presented show a decline in their specie holdings from $50 million to $26 million between 1833 and 1836, while the money supply increased from $137 million to $152 million.[19] If the Bank of England had used the preventive check of raising inter-

[18] *Ibid.*, May 4, 1837. See also *ibid.*, April 7, 19, 28, 1837.
[19] *Ibid.*, June 2, 1837.

est rates in the early phase of speculation, it would have forestalled the need for sudden contraction:

The Bank of England lost her gold from her own imprudence. . . . If this institution had resolved on the first indication of the drain on her vaults, to contract her issues, which she could have done by simply raising the interest rate to borrowers, the present shock to commercial credit would not have been felt.[20]

Speculation in the United States was intensified by the expansion of credit based on the abnormal gold imports. America was able to maintain a large import balance during the 1834–1836 period by continued imports of capital, which were accompanied by imports of specie. This continual borrowing had the effect of aiding economic espansion in the United States, providing foreigners with high interest returns, and delaying the appearance of a business crisis. Cardozo described the 1834–1836 period:

The phenomenon was thus presented for 3 successive years of a favorable exchange and heavy imports of specie in face of a large foreign debt for imported merchandise. . . . We prevented that reflux of specie which our excessive importation would have effected in 1835 by adding to our demand on European capitalists for fresh supplies of their surplus

[20] *Ibid.,* May 5, 1837. See also *ibid.,* May 9, 1837. The rate of discount at the Bank of England from 1832 to June 1836 was 4%; from June, 1836 to August 1836 it was 4½%; after August 1836, it was 5%. Cardozo claimed that if it was raised to about 5% in 1834 when the loss of gold indicated the presence of speculative activity, the exodus of gold and credit to the United States for speculation in land and produce could have been halted. He referred favorably to an article on banking in the April, 1837 issue of the *Edinburgh Review,* which also condemned the Bank of England for not raising the rate of interest earlier than it did. Cardozo accurately guessed that this unsigned article was by McCulloch. *Ibid.,* June 23, 1837. According to recent research by Frank W. Fetter the author was McCulloch. See Frank W. Fetter, "The Authorship of Economic Articles in the *Edinburgh Review,* 1802–47," *Journal of Political Economy* (June, 1953), p. 256. The title of McCulloch's article was "State of the Currency, The Bank of England and the Country Banks."

treasure. . . . The extension of our banking system and the subsequent increases of speculation in merchandise, public lands, in property of every description, with a corresponding stimulus to prices could not have been effected in any other way except by foreign capital in the form of the precious metals borrowed from those who had treasure to lend and were induced to do it from the temptation of a high comparative rate of interest. The specie basis for enlarged issues of paper by multiplication of banks in the United States was thus founded in the large amounts borrowed abroad.[21]

In summary, this was Cardozo's position: The basic causes of the crisis were the real factors present in the previous phase of the cycle. The policy of the Bank of the United States allowed the speculative tendencies to develop. Once the opportunity for arresting this situation at an early stage had passed, the cycle became inevitable. Although foreign capital was not the cause of the speculation or business cycle, it provided the necessary fuel for its continued sustenance, and thus aggravated its effects. Recurrent periods of mercantile excitement were inherent in a system with so many potential business investment opportunities.

Cardozo suggested that the enterprising spirit of the people created a continual psychological propensity in the United States for commercial speculation. All that was needed for transfer of this propensity into effective action were propitious circumstances. The recurrent appearance of speculative tendencies was grounded in "real" economic

[21] *Southern Patriot*, May 25, 1837. Cardozo overemphasized the importance of this gold as a prerequisite for credit expansions. In a later comment on the 1837 crisis, Cardozo questioned whether the foreign exchange in the pre-crisis period actually was favorable. He said, "The nominal exchange was against, while the real exchange appeared to be in favor of the United States. . . . The negotiation of a large number of bonds in the English market produced an excess in the supply beyond the demand for bills, which afforded a profit on the export of the gold to the United States." Cardozo, "Essay on Banking and Currency," p. 676.

conditions, although banking policy may condition its timing and intensify its effects. He later gave a more precise picture of the nature of speculation and the respective roles played by domestic and foreign credit in the cyclical process:

A real or apprehended scarcity of a staple commodity takes place. Those whose business it is to watch the vicissitudes of the market and investigate sources of supply, give a sudden impulse to demand and a speculative or artificial rise occurs. If this is met by the abundance of money and the facility of procuring credit, the speculation increases, but could make only a limited progress if it were fostered exclusively by a loan of capital obtained from domestic sources. It would, however, admit of rapid extension if nourished by a loan of credit in the form of bank issues, based on borrowed capital from abroad. . . . It is in proportion to the sums that can be obtained from foreign sources that the duration and magnitude of the speculation will be determined.[22]

A recent study of this cycle by Matthews arrives at substantially the same conclusions despite some important differences in detail.[23]

Cardozo's main intellectual indebtedness in his treatment of business cycles and capital accumulation is to the anticlassical economists Lauderdale and Malthus. For purposes of illustrating their influence on Cardozo, it is useful to set off their approach from that of the classical school of

[22] *Southern Patriot*, November 9, 1839. Cardozo claimed that the crisis of 1825 was less intense than that of 1837 because the former was not nurtured by foreign capital. In a statement similar to Keynes' concept of "animal spirits" (to explain the psychological underpinnings of investment decisions), Cardozo said, "It may happen to be discovered that the general mind after a season in which it slumbers and has become apathetic, is anxious for excitement, and rushes with an impetuosity and energy proportioned to its previous indolence, into the sphere of commercial speculation." *Ibid.*, May 20, 1840.

[23] R. C. O. Matthews, *A Study in Trade Cycle History: Economic Fluctuations in Great Britain, 1833–1842.* Pp. 43–69 deal specifically with the American market. This study will be discussed in Appendix I.

Smith, Ricardo, Say, and Mill. An early American exponent of the anticlassical group whose work influenced Cardozo was Daniel Raymond.[24]

The classical school generally viewed capital accumulation as an unmitigated blessing [25] and the *sine qua non* for economic growth. The anticlassicists rejected this hypothesis, or ringed it with significant qualifications, on the grounds that rapid capital accumulation could set up imbalances in the economy which could reduce production. The classical school viewed commercial crises (i.e., business cycles) as temporary and minor deviations from a full employment norm, and was unwilling or unable to integrate a business cycle theory into its static equilibrium model. Being geared essentially to long-run rather than short-run analysis, classical thought on the whole assumed away the key problem of business cycles. Fluctuations in demand and supply could account for short-run deviations between market price and natural price, but it was thought that these deviations, which were only transitional phenomena, took place around a norm determined by the labor theory of value.

The validity of much of classical analysis rested on implicit assumptions of full employment and vigorous com-

[24] The word "influence" is perhaps an unfortunate one because of the difficulty of presenting sufficient proof. In the strictest sense "influence" exists only if it is acknowledged. Perhaps the method used is best described as showing the chain of intellectual development from Lauderdale to Raymond to Cardozo in those areas where there was an overlapping of ideas. On some issues it is likely that the influence of Lauderdale on Cardozo was direct.

[25] This is somewhat less true of J. S. Mill. He took the view that continued capital accumulation would eventually drive the rate of profit down to a minimum. However, he viewed this stationary state of capital with aversion only if the country was in a backward stage of development. See his *Principles of Political Economy* (New York, Longmans Green, 1923), Book 4, Chapters 3, 4. Ricardo cautiously admitted that in the short run "The substitution of machinery for human labor is often very injurious to the interests of the class of laborers," but this appeared to be more of a minor qualification than of the essence of his system. See his *Principles of Political Economy and Taxation*, p. 264.

petition. Although these assumptions did not impede an analysis of distribution theory and economic growth within a given social system, they were ill-fitted to deal with problems of business cycles. In terms of policy, classical theorists were concerned with the abrogation of the Corn Laws, which they considered fetters on the growth of commerce and industry. Their assumptions fitted in well with the policy they were attempting to justify and the orientation of their interests to the ascending bourgeoisie.

The business cycle analysis of Lauderdale and Malthus focused on the effects of various factors which upset the equilibrium between production and consumption and between savings and expenditure. Their analysis was better equipped to analyze short-run phenomena such as cycles, since their assumptions in rejecting Say's Law were not as confining. They stressed the social and economic short-run disequilibrating effects of repealing the Corn Laws or paying off the public debt too rapidly. Unlike the classical school, they emphasized the importance of demand in influencing the composition of output and the level of economic activity.

The parallels between Lauderdale, Malthus, and Cardozo are striking. All three viewed the landed class as the seat of higher civilization in a society where power and wealth were shifting to a commercial-manufacturing class. In terms of policy,[26] they were concerned with minimizing the strains on the social and economic institutions as a result of rapid industrialization. Controlling and channelizing the forces of social, political, and economic change were critical.

Each stressed the importance of gradual economic devel-

[26] The free-trade advocacy of Cardozo in America and pro-Corn Law position of Lauderdale and Malthus in England is explainable by the different historical conditions confronting the two economies. Protecting the interests of the landed class in the latter required the retention of the Corn Laws, while in America it demanded the abandonment or control of the protective tariff.

opment as a means of avoiding instability. Rapid capital accumulation was viewed as having a detrimental effect on the economy. This required using an analytical method which partially abandoned the frictionless, competitive, long-run equilibrating model of the classical economists.

Lauderdale, Raymond, and Cardozo shared a common skepticism of the classical views on capital accumulation; they were concerned with the question of how this accumulation developed. Lauderdale rejected Smith's notion that capital, or wealth, can only be increased in proportion to what can be saved out of the revenue. He claimed that parsimony, or savings, was not a way of increasing public wealth. Public wealth can only be increased by [27] increasing the produce of land, increasing the exertions of labor,[28] or replacing labor in the performance of work.

Lauderdale believed that capital accumulation pushed beyond a critical limit would reduce total production by reducing consumer expenditures. He thought that capital could be effective in increasing wealth only as long as it was used to replace labor in the production of items for which there was a demand. Parsimony, instead of being viewed as increasing wealth, was seen as merely changing the direction in which labor was employed. Lauderdale further maintained that in addition matters became worse because the decreased value of consumer expenditures was greater than the value of the labor or commodities involved in capital accumulation.[29]

This contention probably results from his error of overstressing the immediate effects of parsimony and in insisting that parsimony must create a decrease in the produc-

[27] Lauderdale, Chapter 4, particularly pp. 208–10.

[28] Adam Smith has a passing reference to the second method. In conformance with his general sympathy for the workers, he takes the point of view that high wages encourage diligence and industry. See *Wealth of Nations*, p. 81.

[29] Lauderdale, p. 212.

tion of consumer goods. Actually, savings could arise out of the increased profits of previous periods.

Although Lauderdale's thinking on this subject was an adumbration of the Keynesian [30] concepts of effective demand and the multiplier mechanism, it is curious that he apparently was more aware of the multiplier effects of consumer spending than of investment spending. He seemed to feel that the negative multiplier effects of decreased consumer demand are greater than the positive multiplier effects of increased investment demand:

As the increase of value and consequent encouragement given to that species of labor [in capital goods production] is occasioned by a diminution of things that would be immediately consumed, it must reduce their value by the portion of demand it abstracts from them in a greater degree than it increases the value of that labor, or of those commodities to the acquisition of which it is perverted. . . . The check given to production by the abstraction of demand [for consumer goods] has a more powerful effect in diminishing wealth, than the encouragement arising from an extension of demand [for capital goods] has in augmenting it.[31]

The most likely explanation for Lauderdale's theory is that he emphasized the short-run as opposed to the less certain long-run effects.

Raymond's views on capital accumulation were in the same anticlassical tradition as those of Lauderdale and Cardozo. Cardozo held that through making savings and investment identical, the classical economists had confused

[30] Alvin Harvey Hansen discusses the business cycle implication of Lauderdale's work in terms of Keynesian economics. See his *Business Cycles and National Income* (New York, Norton, 1950), pp. 229–40.

[31] Lauderdale, pp. 211–13. Although agreeing that rapid capital accumulation had undesirable effects, Malthus thought that "Lord Lauderdale appears to have gone as much too far in deprecating accumulation, as some other writers [e.g., Say, Mill, and Ricardo] in recommending it." See his *Principles of Political Economy*, p. 314. Malthus was less than generous in acknowledging his intellectual debt to Lauderdale.

national and individual wealth. This has a remarkable similarity to Raymond's statement that the "absurd doctrine of augmenting national wealth by accumulation proceeds from confounding national with individual wealth." [32] Whereas individual wealth can be increased by saving a part of revenue and using it to buy property and lend money, national wealth, defined as the capacity to obtain goods, is not increased by saving. Raymond and Lauderdale held the anti-Smithian view that industry, or application of effort, rather than parsimony was the key to increasing national wealth.[33]

However, Raymond's position is less rigid than Lauderdale's and somewhat closer to Cardozo's. Raymond appears to take the position that decreased consumption, equivalent to increased parsimony, does not per se increase national wealth; it may create imbalances between production and consumption and thereby affect the level of employment. Although a nation cannot directly increase its wealth by parsimony, the increased use of labor in capital goods production, referred to as effective or permanent labor, enlarges the productive capacity of the country which makes for more rapid economic growth. But it is essential that this increased output be consumed in order to maintain economic activity. Thus Raymond appears to say that capital accumulation which takes place out of increased income is more effective than that which takes place out of decreased consumption.[34]

Raymond accepts the Malthusian idea that "savings pushed to excess destroys the motive to production." He says:

It may be laid down as a universal rule, that a nation is in the greatest state of prosperity, when the annual consumption just equals the annual production, or in other words, when the pro-

[32] Raymond, I, 138.   [33] Ibid., II, 90.   [34] Ibid., I, 145–50.

duction of one year is entirely consumed in the following year.[35]

Raymond demonstrated a quite clear grasp of the workings of a capitalist system when he said:

If more goods are manufactured in one year than can be sold at a saving [profitable] price . . . he [the businessman] perhaps dismisses some of his workmen . . . and there will be less quantity manufactured the next.[36]

Cardozo looked at the relationship of capital accumulation and business cycles in a quite similar fashion. He criticized the Richardian idea that the effects of accumulating capital out of diminished consumption or increased revenue from rising profits are equivalent. Cardozo viewed the question of capital accumulation in terms of how it affected the profit incentives of the business man, and how it affected the balance between production and consumption. Lauderdale and Raymond were concerned almost exclusively with the second aspect, although Raymond was somewhat less so. In reference to the Ricardian views on capital accumulation, Cardozo said:

Profits can not continue the same in one quarter while expenditure is reduced in another, or increased in one quarter while expenditure continues the same in another, for expenditure must keep an equal progress with profit, if all classes of producers are to benefit by an interchange of their respective productions.[37]

[35] *Ibid.*, I, 122–23. In a view prophetic of the early New Deal, Raymond advocated destroying the unconsumed yearly surplus, pp. 123–24. The reference cited by Raymond is to Malthus, p. 7.
[36] *Ibid.*, I, 124–25.
[37] Cardozo, *Notes*, p. 112. Malthus' concern with the relationship of profits and capital accumulation is seen in his statement. "The natural and legitimate encouragement to the increase of capital is that increase of the power and will to save which is held out by certain and steady profits. . . . It is precisely the high profits of stock occasioned by the demand for commodities, and the consequent demand for the means of producing

Cardozo is saying that profits in one sector of the economy are affected by changes in other sectors, since expenditures by one sector are a prerequisite for making profits in other sectors. The analysis here has a mixture of static and dynamic elements.

Cardozo continues his discussion in highly modern terms:

No general or permanent increase of profit can take place unless consumption in one quarter keeps an equal progress with production in some other—unless, in short, demand, whether for the necessaries and conveniences of life, or for articles of productive investment, is equal to the supply of the whole mass of commodities of every kind.[38]

We see that Cardozo here brings together the two levels of analysis. He says that if consumption in one sector does not keep pace with production in some other sector, imbalances will develop which will prevent profits from increasing. In Keynesian terms, the point is that there cannot be a general increase in profit unless there is a demand for consumer and investment goods equal to the total supply of commodities.

He concludes by saying:

It follows that profits can not continue the same if expenditure be reduced, or raised if expenditure continue the same, without destroying the balance between produce and consumption. Commodities would cease to be produced if they were not consumed.[39]

In other words, if expenditure is reduced, profits will fall, and further capital accumulation will be halted.

Cardozo had a rudimentary version of the accelerator concept. He held that rising, rather than falling, consump-

---

them, which at once give the power and will to accumulate." Malthus, pp. 329–30.
[38] Cardozo, *Notes*, p. 112.   [39] *Ibid.*, p. 112.

tion, was an essential prerequisite for rising investment. He said:

It is the increase of productive power that adds to capital and not savings from ordinary expenditure—not reducing consumption, for it is constantly increased consumption that gives the most effective stimulus to the inventive powers and industrious efforts of producers. The actual consumption is necessary to the actual production.[40]

Cardozo also showed the relationship between expenditure analysis and the public-private wealth distinction.

In a key paragraph Cardozo said that Ricardo by "assuming that the laboring classes do not reproduce a greater value than they consume" made the same mistake as the Physiocrats:

. . . [T]aking for granted that there is the same amount of productive power with a smaller as with a larger number of producers [this follows from Ricardo's idea of the inverse wage-profit relationship and his notion that a large population does not confer an advantage on a country] it follows that production is not coextensive with consumption, and the natural balance between them is thence destroyed. It is from the same principle [that laborers reproduce a value equal to their own consumption] that saving in expenditure is made identical in its effects with an increase of productive power on the riches of society, thus confounding the increase of individual with that of general wealth.[41]

There is a danger of reading too much into these sentences. It appears that the passage can be interpreted in the

[40] *Ibid.*, pp. 119–20. He denied, however, that increased consumption by the workers, as a result of government transfer payments, could have more than a temporarily beneficial effect. He said, "No increased consumption but what is the effect or accompaniment of enlarged production can be durable or wholesome." *Evening News*, August 3, 1847. Cardozo felt that this kind of rising consumption was artificial and unsustainable and therefore could not stimulate production.

[41] Cardozo, *Notes*, p. 12.

following way: If laborers reproduce a value equal to their consumption, the effects of savings and investment are the same; individual and general wealth will be increased. Cardozo is implicitly saying that this assumption is erroneous. If, however, the laborers reproduced a value greater than their own consumption, the effects of savings and investment are different. Process analysis rather than static terms must be employed for a full understanding of the issue. If the workers produce products with a greater value than those which they consume,[42] the balance between production and consumption will be upset; this amounts to saying that savings are not automatically invested. If this happens, the result will be a gain for some individual businessmen, which is not necessarily coexistent with an increase in the general wealth in the following period. In Keynesian terms, an increase of savings in any period, by virtue of reducing consumption, may cause a reduction of income which will eventually reduce the actual savings.

A complementary interpretation is that Cardozo rejected the Ricardian notion that the effects of capital accumulation out of reduced consumption and the effects of capital accumulation out of increased revenue are equivalent. In the immediate instance, both methods will have the same effect on individual wealth; the individual is consuming less than he is able at the present time for the sake of a future income. However, the results of the two meth-

[42] If the embodied labor theory of value is rejected, it would tend to follow that the value produced by labor exceeds their wages (which roughly equals the value of the commodities they consume), since the value of the product would also include the other costs of production of rent and profit. Cardozo declared that "the productive classes reproduce a greater value than they consume during their maintenance." Cardozo, *Notes*, p.84. Malthus presented a closely related point that arrives at Cardozo's results. He said, "It is in the nature of things quite impossible . . . that the labourers of any country can continue to be paid an amount of products of so high a value as the value of what they are themselves able to produce for their employers; because if they were so paid, their employers would always be losing by so employing them." Malthus, p. 106.

ods of capital accumulation are not equivalent from the point of view of general wealth. Capital accumulation which uses the savings resulting from reduced consumption may upset the balance between production and consumption, with the result that general economic activity and general wealth are adversely affected.

The writings of Cardozo and Raymond seem to represent the earliest evidence of "pre-Keynesian" thinking in American economic thought on more than a superficial level.

There is close kinship between Cardozo and Raymond concerning the relationship between savings, investment, and the public-private wealth distinction. Both were aware of the differential effects of savings as viewed from the position of the individual or the general public.

Cardozo came a shade closer to the idea that not all savings are invested; he appeared to have had a clearer picture of the relationship of consumption and investment. He wove together a more varied assortment of economic elements into his analysis than did Lauderdale or Raymond. In a rudimentary way, he showed the interdependence of capital accumulation, profits, savings, consumption, investment, and their relation to the distinction between public and private wealth. Cardozo did, however, have an important blind spot, one which indirectly points out what the writer regards as Lauderdale's most vital contribution. Lauderdale had the surprisingly advanced view that the distribution of wealth (income, in modern terminology) determined the nature and extent of demand, as well as the allocation of labor.[43] He was among the first to show the relationship between inequality and a low level of demand, and their subsequent impeding effect on the increase of public wealth.[44] This aspect was neglected by

[43] Lauderdale, pp. 312, 313, 341.   [44] *Ibid.*, p. 344.

Cardozo, possibly because of his view of America as a "natural society" in which the glaring inequalities of Europe had not yet come into existence.

A full development of Cardozo's business cycle theory was hampered by a partial acceptance of Say's law of markets as the long-run equilibrating norm of a capitalist society. He thought of war, tariffs, and the paper money credit system as creating important short-run deviations from this norm. It is in his analysis of these deviations that some of Cardozo's richest insights are found. Cardozo said:

The balance between savings and expenditure is never in ordinary times disturbed. Neither transcends its proper limits when left to the influence of the usual stimulants; but they run into alternate extremes when unusually high profits, which of course are temporary and artificial, beget a spirit of gambling adventure in all the departments of industry.[45]

Transitions from war to peace were viewed as a cause of alternations of prosperity and distress. Cardozo held that

The wealth of a country may increase too rapidly for its prosperity [i.e., unusually stimulating conditions tend to breed excesses which bring about a reversal]. . . . Those countries which have had their powers of production excited in the greatest degree, will have to endure, when the reaction occurs, the longest period of suffering.[46]

He later added, "The tendency of all overaction in trade and mercantile dealing is to recoil when the stimulus is withdrawn in which it had its origin." [47]

Periods of wartime prosperity created inducements for

[45] *Southern Patriot,* March 17, 1821.

[46] *Ibid.,* April 11, 1821, Cardozo, *Notes,* p. 48. With reference to the cotton industry, Cardozo said that after supply had been increased under the stimulus of high prices, "A reaction will take place which will tend to decrease prices much below the point to which they would have fallen if the advance had not been so sudden." *Southern Patriot,* May 31, 1825.

[47] *Evening News,* May 15, 1851.

excessive borrowing based on high profit anticipations and spending. In the changed postwar period, imbalances developed between supply and demand. Cardozo suggested that the high spending pattern during the war reduced the purchasing power for hiring labor in the postwar period. He stressed the importance of adequate demand in maintaining economic activity via maintaining consumer purchasing power and business profits. Although Cardozo was sure that eventually equilibrium between supply and demand would be restored, "convulsion and distress" were seen as necessary features of the equilibrating process.

Cardozo held that the decrease in foreign demand as countries converted to peacetime production in the postwar period had the cumulative effect of diminishing domestic consumption by reducing the income with which countries could buy each other's products. With reference to England in the recession following the Napoleonic Wars, Cardozo said:

Her immense manufacturing power (which is composed of . . . her population and machinery) has been built up . . . by a corresponding foreign demand. . . . An impulse once received continues at the same rate for some time after the momentum which imparted the movement [i.e., foreign demand] ceases to act in the same direction. The powers of science continued to be applied in England to the improvement of machinery after the demand for its results had diminished. . . . [This] has left the prodigious powers of production without adequate powers of consumption. . . . The excess and the deficiency coexist. . . . Production can not be excessive unless consumption be diminished, as the one is a measure and limit to the other. . . . The production of all in this post-war period are in excess because the consumption of all is diminished.[48]

[48] *Southern Patriot,* June 17, 1826; May 8, 1821. In the second article, Cardozo referred to an English debate on the overproduction theory of the Earl of Liverpool and the underconsumption theory of the Marquis of Landsdowne. The remedy proposed by the former was "time and patience"

Cardozo recognized in a rudimentary way how the turning point of a business cycle takes place, and the possibility of a temporary general glut if technological developments proceeded too rapidly to be effectively employed by society. In a later discussion of European economic conditions, Cardozo pointed to the lack of effective demand as the basic cause of general stagnation. He said:

In Europe invention and discovery have outrun either the desire or ability to consume . . . the products of industry. . . . Absence of demand . . . is the source of general stagnation in all departments of business and industry.[49]

Cardozo rejected the idea that a rising population necessarily sustained the level of demand. He said:

Mankind enlarge or contract the scale of their comforts and enjoyments as they are well or ill rewarded for their labor, and a smaller population may excite a more active demand for food and clothing under a powerful stimulus to their industry than a greater population with a lesser stimulus.[50]

He held that the rise in population during the stimulating economic conditions of wartime intensified the economic distress of the postwar period. He claimed that the disequilibrating demand-supply conditions in the commodity markets were more readily correctable than those in the labor market.

---

while the latter favored a "removal of commercial restrictions and diminished taxation." Cardozo in essence argued that a business recession necessarily involves both overproduction and underconsumption. He said that free trade was the key remedy for economic stagnation. By creating new wants, it helped to restore the balance between expanding production and lagging consumption. *Ibid.*, May 30, 1829.

[49] Cardozo, "Essay on Banking and Currency," p. 694. He added that "The plethora of capital in England renders any tendency to a more rapid capital accumulation inevitable as contributory to those periods of speculation accompanied by reaction and revulsion." *Ibid.*, pp. 683–84. Cardozo is clearly an exception to Miller's statement that "The notion of general overproduction or glutting of the market, in explanation of commercial crises and cycles played little part in American discussion." Miller, p. 203.

[50] *Southern Patriot*, May 23, 1821.

Cardozo favored a gradual rather than a rapid reduction of the public debt so as not to "clog the wheels of commerce, by withdrawing too rapidly from circulation those active funds which are its aliment." [51] He held that the effect of paying off the national debt during a period of recession was to increase the difficulty of finding profitable investment openings. Debt repayment at such a time is not necessary since there is no actual scarcity of money in a depression. He declared that:

. . . the payment of the public creditors must necessarily throw a much greater amount of capital into the money market than would have found its way there without such payment. The difficulty of finding profitable investment will assuredly increase as the public creditors are paid off, admitting that things continue in their present state of stagnation. But this shows conclusively that there is no real scarcity of money. Everyone is anxious to lend on sufficient security, but few are able to borrow on this condition.[52]

Although Cardozo believed that it was necessary to accompany public debt creation with adequate taxation for making payments on the debt, public and private debt were seen as quite different phenomena:

The latter [i.e., an individual] could liquidate his obligations with no disturbance of fiscal arrangements beyond the circle of his indebtedness. A nation has its system of taxation and debt so blended—its different branches of revenue so intermingled with its financial arrangements—that a liquidation of a large [public] debt, unless in the most gradual manner, would introduce great confusion.[53]

[51] Ibid., January 29, 1820.
[52] Ibid., June 29, 1829. Lauderdale and Raymond also recognized the potentially undesirable consequences of rapid debt repayment. Lauderdale, pp. 249–55, cited by Hansen, pp. 231–32. Raymond, II, 318, 329–30, 353.
[53] Evening News, April 4, 1849. Cardozo did not take Raymond's position that a national debt could have beneficial effects. He unequivocally said, "A national debt is a national evil; but the too sudden redemption of such debt would be an evil of scarcely less magnitude than the burden of interest however heavy."

He also rejected President Monroe's idea that increasing tariff rates during a recession would have the beneficial effect of raising revenue. He said that this would only raise the price of manufactured goods relative to the price of agricultural products, leaving the farmer with less purchasing power to buy manufactured goods, thereby impeding the restoration of equilibrium between production and consumption.[54]

During Cardozo's pro–laisez-faire banking period (roughly 1847 to 1854), he leaned closer to the view that the business cycle was less of a purely monetary phenomenon and therefore less susceptible to monetary control measures. He attempted to demonstrate that excessive fixed-capital investment such as railroads created imbalances in the economic system by upsetting the equilibrium between production and consumption. Cardozo visualized competition for the limited supply of capital between the railroad proprietors and other mercantile-manufacturing interests. The use of large amounts of bank loans and resources by the railroads diverted capital from the quick investment returns associated with trade and manufacturing to the slower returns on railroad investments. Expenditure on the latter circulates gradually, and therefore:

. . . the money employed in paying for materials and distributing wages of those employed on railroads could not return in sufficient time and adequate amounts to the original sources of supply [i.e., the banks] so as to be made available for the purpose of commerce and general industry. . . . There can be no equality between the amounts withdrawn and returned within the same period.[55]

In other words, money employed in railroad investments could not complete the money circuit rapidly enough to be

[54] Southern Patriot, March 20, 1821. Cardozo said, "That which deprives one class of producers of a part of their profits, restricts their consumption of the products of another class of producers."
[55] Ibid., November 10, 11, 1847.

used for commerce and industry and therefore economic growth would be impeded.

Heavy fixed-capital investment altered the natural, established relation between fixed and circulating capital. Cardozo followed Adam Smith's usage—the former referring to machinery, plant, and equipment involved as instruments of production, and the latter referring to provisions, work in process, and inventories of finished goods. Circulating capital provides economic services in a shorter period of time than does fixed capital. Investing in fixed capital elongates the structure of production, to use Hayek's term,[56] but ties up the country's resources for a longer period of time. The relationship between fixed and circulating capital is a close and interdependent one.

As Smith said:

Every fixed capital is both originally derived from, and requires to be continually supported by, a circulating capital. All useful machines and instruments of trade are originally derived from a circulating capital, which furnishes the materials of which they are made, and the maintenance of the workmen who make them.[57]

Circulating capital, in real terms, thus includes the raw materials required for constructing a fixed asset, as well as the necessary consumable commodities for supporting the workmen employed in its production; these commodities are referred to as the wages fund. In this sense circulating capital is necessary for the profitable functioning of fixed capital.

Different types of business enterprises require different proportions of these types of capital. The higher the ratio of fixed to circulating capital, the greater the sacrifice of present enjoyment for future profit. According to Cardozo,

[56] Friedrich A. Hayek, *Prices and Production* (London, Routledge and Kegan Paul, 1960), especially Lecture II, pp. 32–68.
[57] Adam Smith, pp. 266–67.

the large future profits resulting from the excessive investments in the railroads was accomplished by checking the
present production of manufacturing and commerce. Cardozo describes the loss as follows:

Money is not required for railroad expenditures but the instrument for obtaining materials, and for distribution as wages
to those employed on these structures. But after the expenditure is over, there is a value consumed in iron, provisions and
clothing, equivalent to the sums expended; while if the capital
is not reproduced in a form equally valuable and equally productive, as when in the shape of these consumable products,
there must be an absolute loss. . . . The values consumed [i.e.,
the circulating capital] will, it is true, be replaced by other
value [i.e., the fixed capital good], but in the conversion the
consumption has not been equally productive. The railroad
remains, but the floating capital, which is absolutely necessary
to a reproduction of a same class of commodities which have
been consumed, or their commercial equivalent, is absorbed.[58]

Circulating capital of the previous period, in the form of
provisions and fabricated commodities, comprises the
wages fund—the source of the worker's consumption—for
the current period. An increase in production of fixed capital means that fewer resources are being used in the current period to produce tangible consumable commodities
required to continue the employment of labor. Circulating
capital in the form of subsistence products and raw materials are absorbed in the process of creating fixed capital.
Cardozo fears that if a significant part of the net output of
any given year takes the form of fixed capital, future production will be impaired because the consumer goods and
raw materials, part of the circulating capital, available for
the next period will be lessened. Lavish outlays on fixed
capital, which drastically alter the relative proportion be-

[58] *Evening News*, November 11, 15, 1847.

tween fixed and circulating capital, was thus viewed as creating cyclical instability as well as reduced economic growth.

Under normal growth conditions Cardozo held that the ratio between fixed and circulating capital would be unvarying; they would grow at approximately the same rate. He declared that:

It is precisely, in the natural progress of wealth, as [money] wages fall and machinery is improved, that circulating capital increases, and in the same proportion with fixed capital. The proportions never vary, in a wholesome state of things, in any employment. . . .

It is not meant by this that these two kinds of capital are always equal in quantity in the same employment. Some employment require a larger and others a less portion of the one or of the other.[59]

The suggestion is that although the initial ratio of fixed and circulating capital varies between industries, under normal conditions both capitals will increase in each industry in such a way as to maintain the same proportionalities.

If we assume a given total capital for any given period, an increase in fixed capital clearly does imply a decline in circulating capital. In all business enterprises, a certain amount of circulating capital is needed to support the fixed capital. Therefore, under the above assumptions, it follows that an increased output of fixed capital means a decline in the output of some manufactured commodities which no longer have the requisite amount of circulating capital. Although Cardozo had a time dimension in mind, his analysis suffers from the lack of a clear-cut distinction between short-run and long-run phenomena. His model is neither fully static nor fully dynamic. By implic-

[59] Cardozo, *Notes*, pp. 54–55.

itly operating with a constant fixed capital input : output ratio, he overlooked the fact that an increased output of fixed capital could increase productivity to the point where there is an increased output of consumable goods (circulating capital) available out of an increased annual output. In his concern with the transitional period, Cardozo slighted the long-run secular forces, but his analysis did have the merit of implicitly focusing on the difficulty of maintaining a high rate of capital accumulation and economic growth. He was well aware of the impossibility of setting the proper balance between fixed and circulating capital with precision, but he rejected the notion that capital was profitably employed regardless of how it was spent.[60]

This is Cardozo's clearest statement on the danger level of fixed capital investments:

There is one principle that should never be lost sight of in constructing public works [e.g., railroads]. They can never be undertaken with safety unless by the gradual accumulation of a surplus of general wealth. If they are constructed more rapidly than in the ratio of this accumulation, it is certain that resources for this purpose must be drawn from those means which nourish the different branches of productive industry. . . . The only proper application of capital for this purpose [i.e., railroad investment] is after accumulation. . . . It is but too evident that the same amount of circulating capital can not build railroads and perform mercantile operations.[61]

In other words, if investments in fixed capital have the effect of diverting savings away from other uses, it is exces-

[60] *Evening News*, November 15, 1847. Cardozo favorably cited an article, "Financial Effects of Railway Legislation," *London Bankers Magazine* (October, 1847), for coming to the same conclusion.

[61] *Evening News*, November 2, 1848; April 7, 1849. Cardozo also claimed in the former article that the prosperity resulting from the increased consumer spending by the laborers employed on the railroads was more apparent than real. This was not explained further, except to state that "the natural relation of capital to employment is disturbed."

sive. Cardozo probably meant that fixed-capital investments should be in an amount equal to the savings which
are not used for the replacement of circulating capital.
The suggestion appears to be that the funds for these investments should come out of rising profits—to be more
exact, the part of private profits above that needed to replace the circulating capital used up in current production—rather than from reduced consumption. In modern
terms, Cardozo appears to be saying that the correct
amount of investment is the increased saving resulting
from increased output.

He believed that it was essential to attract European capital by the comparatively higher interest rate to provide
simultaneously for railroad investments and other needs of
commerce and manufacturing. But this too was seen as
having certain limitations. Cardozo said that the rate of
railroad investment was too rapid when the promoters
have "borrowed (at home and abroad) large sums . . .
more rapidly than the annual income realized could cover
the current expenses and interest on the sums they borrowed." [62] The extensive issuing of railroad bonds was
seen as overloading the stock market and intensifying pressures in the money market. It also put pressure on the balance of trade by directing productive efforts away from export products.

Cardozo thus appears (at least in this period) to be taking the position that the maldistribution of capital, accompanying the process of rapid economic growth, causes crises
through upsetting the equilibrium between production
and consumption. This business cycle theory of disproportionate investment has a close kinship to the overinvest-

[62] *Ibid.*, December 21, 1855. In this article, Cardozo rejected Henry Carey's
idea that the depreciation of railroad capital was due to free trade. Carey
reasoned that free trade led to overimportation, particularly of iron for
railroad construction. This, in turn, created an adverse balance of trade,
loss of gold, and depreciation. Cardozo attributed the depreciation to the
excessive amount of speculative investments in railroads.

ment school. They both implicitly assumed that consumption-investment (or circulating capital-fixed capital) imbalances tended to bring about crises, although their suggested "cures" were different. The overinvestment school criticized the consumers for attempting to spend too much and making less savings available for ever-abundant investment outlets, while Cardozo blamed the businessman for attempting to invest too much in fixed-capital goods.

Cardozo assumed the existence of an economic system with a high degree of responsiveness to price changes. He also viewed the restoration of a normal price level as the essential element in the recovery from a business crisis. Price changes would bring demand and supply into equilibrium:

The balance when lost between productive power and the capability to consume must be restored so soon as the additional force imparted to the former has given increased energy to the latter by cheapening products, as it is no less evident that production soon finds its limits in non-remunerating prices and markets not admitting of further extension. . . . The boundary to consumption is found in high prices and the exhaustion that attends extravagant expenditures. . . . The balances may oscillate between these extremes for a longer or shorter period from monied disturbances or the alter[n]ations of war and peace.[63]

He claimed that technological progress created very few problems of disequilibrium since falling prices (made possible by declining costs) would enlarge demand. It is likely that, under the more competitive market structure and lower per capita income prevailing at that time, Cardozo's

[63] *Southern Patriot.*, May 18, 1842. *Cf. Ibid.*, October 11, 1839; Cardozo *The Tariff*, p. 29. In the latter pamphlet, Cardozo said, "There is a limit to be found somewhere between the high prices which stimulate production and retard consumption, and the low price which stimulates consumption and retards production."

high price-elasticity assumptions were more valid than today.

With specific reference to the cotton industry, Cardozo indicated an awareness of the interaction of actual and expected economic conditions on prices:

The price of cotton when high is more generally the result of speculation than consumption. Speculation is readily checked by apprehension and consumption rapidly cut off by high prices, by contraction of debt and by economy and caution which uneasiness produces. It is the apprehension of consumption rather than the diminution itself which causes rapid and large falls in prices. . . . One decline produces another until its downward gravitation acquires an accelerated impetus.[64]

An important factor contributing to disequilibrium or instability in our system is that people make purchases on their expected incomes, made possible by a credit system. Businessmen, in particular, anticipate their income in making purchases, based on present sales and profits. In a credit-operated system, market changes taking place in the interval between sales and payment add to instability. Cardozo said:

The goods which are ordered this year may be intended to meet a demand, the result of prosperity from the previous year. If prices are remunerative and sales rapid, producers enlarge and augment their consumption. They anticipate their income. They buy more than usual, because they sell more than advantageously. But the periods of sale and payment never correspond with those who buy and consume largely on credit. When the day of liquidation arrives, the market has perhaps fallen for those products, which are the exclusive means of payment.[65]

[64] *Evening News,* January 22, 1855. In this article, Cardozo suggested that the cotton farmers forward their crop for sale rather than hold it back because of the expectations of low prices.

[65] *Ibid.,* October 12, 1854. Cardozo used the above argument to demonstrate the impracticability of adjusting a tariff to the varying circumstances which influence the purchase of imports.

Cardozo was against the use of countercyclical government spending. He held that these spending schemes would increase the difficulty of reestablishing normal relations between debtors and creditors.[66] Government spending would aggravate the effects of speculation rather than cure them. The system would eventually cure its own aberrations if left alone. The use of government funds to put the unemployed to work was seen as only temporarily beneficial because it would add to the public burden and decrease public revenue.[67]

In a perceptive description of a liquidity crisis during a period of general panic, Cardozo indicated an awareness of the need for an expansionary monetary policy:

At such periods . . . all bankers and dealers in money increase their reserves. . . . The prevalence of hoarding becomes general. The whole mass of currency becomes inadequate to the wants of the public—prices fall. . . . It is at such mercantile junctures that banks instead of contracting should enlarge their accommodation and issues.[68]

During the liquidity crisis of 1837, as temporary remedies, Cardozo suggested that the British creditors extend the time of repayment for the American borrowers, and that the American government issue a limited number of treasury notes to cover very necessary government expenditures.[69]

Despite his rejection of government spending to deal with economic crises, Cardozo recognized that an attempt to economize private expenditures during a recession could worsen conditions. Thus he wrote in 1829:

If a portion of a community or society which chooses to practice the precept of economy, limit its consumption, how can this

[66] *Southern Patriot,* May 13, 1837.   [67] *Evening News,* August 3, 1847.
[68] *Ibid.,* September 10, 1847.
[69] *Southern Patriot,* April 12, June 26, 1837.

fail to injure other portions of the same economy, who depend for their subsistence on the existing demand for their labor or the produce of that labor? If consumption is lessened generally, production which is now excessive, must become more so. The evil of gluts must become aggravated.[70]

Twenty-five years later he similarly declared:

The same undue limitation as to private expenditures would throw out of employment a large number of laborers who supply the commodities on which such expenditure is made. . . . At a period when numbers of the working population are thrown out of employment, the withdrawal of sums [via reduced private expenditure], which diffused among those who live only by their daily labor, would largely aggravate the general distress.[71]

The precise reasons for Cardozo's rejection of public spending while stressing the importance of maintaining private spending are unclear. It would appear that a basic acceptance of a market-directed economy based on the principle of consumer sovereignty lay behind this dichotomy. A "natural" balance existed between consumption and investment (or production) which would be upset through intervention by government. On an economic level, Cardozo claimed that government spending would abstract from private spending. He was aware that the amount of government spending was considerably higher on Northern projects than on Southern ones.[72] The potential instability resulting from government spending thus had sociopolitical as well as economic overtones. This may well have accounted for Cardozo's reluctance to countenance the use of a countercyclical fiscal policy while

[70] *Ibid.*, July 12, 1829.   [71] *Evening News*, December 14, 1854.
[72] Cardozo's position on internal improvements from the Southern viewpoint is discussed in Chapter Nine.

implicitly recognizing the need for one. He accepted business cycles as the price that had to be paid for economic growth because the attempt to control them may have had wider repercussions on the Southern political economy.

EIGHT

Slavery and Secession

A STUDY of Cardozo's views on slavery provides a useful frame for an examination of the diverse and changing social forces operative in the antebellum South. As an articulate and influential spokesman for the controversial view that the development of Southern manufacturing, aided by slave labor, was the key to transcending the limitations imposed by a plantation-slave system, Cardozo's writings on slavery deserve close examination. His position on the slavery issue, more than anything else in his writings, illustrates the conflict between scientific analysis and a social commitment to defend the vital socioeconomic interests and institutions of the South.

Cardozo's views on slavery reflected his historical and regional conditioning. His sympathies were with the slave system as it existed. He referred to the planters as "the great interest of the South." [1] Yet his position, in terms of

[1] *Evening News,* April 8, 1854.

the Southern environment, was moderate rather than extreme.

A brief sketch of the historical background provides a useful frame against which to examine Cardozo's thought. In the period before the invention of the cotton gin, slavery was regarded generally as a gradually decaying institution,[2] although it was relatively profitable in the coastal plain region of the South that grew rice, tobacco, and indigo. Whitney's invention coincided with the development of the factory system in Europe. As a result of the subsequent enormous increase in the world demand for cotton, the widespread cultivation of that crop became highly profitable and thus strengthened the institution of slavery. The plantation [3] became the dominant economic and political unit, while the political economy of slavery and cotton fused.

The justification for the use of the term "political economy" with reference to slavery instead of a substitute such as "the economics of slaveholding" is that the economics of slavery were inseparable from the political conditions of early nineteenth-century America. The continued profitability of slavery and cotton production depended on the political situation.

The profitability of cotton-producing and slavery tended to vary together. The cotton plantation system,

[2] The value of slaves generally declined after the first quarter of the eighteenth century due to their large supply relative to the demand existing at that time. In this early period, many colonies attempted to put restrictions on the importation of slaves. The foreign slave trade was prohibited in 1808 by an earlier Act of Congress, effective January 1, 1808. All of the states of the United States, except South Carolina, prohibited it earlier.

[3] Although evidence indicates that cotton could be almost as profitably grown on a small area as on a large one, the size of the plantation increased in the antebellum period. This was the result of the westward migration to more fertile lands, and the buying up of smaller farms in depression periods. Large-scale production was crucially important in the cultivation of rice and sugar cane. See William B. Hesseltine, *A History of the South (1607–1936)*, pp. 320–21.

based on slave labor, was precariously dependent on the foreign market; the overwhelming portion of the crop was sold on a fluctuating foreign market. Cyclical swings in the level of economic activity in England had quick repercussions in the Southern cotton economy.

The geographical distribution of slave population reflected the pattern of cotton production. As cotton production spread from the less fertile coastal areas to the Southwest in response to the increased demand, the economic importance of the former declined, necessitating a painful readjustment.[4] Although the plantation system was predominant only in the "black belt," where the concentration of slaves was the greatest, "the institution of slavery came to be regarded as absolutely essential to Southern prosperity."[5]

Slaves were unequally distributed among owners in the antebellum South. In 1860, slaves comprised about one-third of the total Southern population[6]—3,953,696 out of 12,315,374. Only 384,753 were slaveholders. Of this amount, 174,503 owned less than five each, and 7,929 owned more than fifty each; a trifle more than two percent of the slaveowners owned fifty or more slaves. Thus, only a small minority in the South had any slaves at all, and of this group, almost half owned fewer than five slaves each. Slave ownership, however, was more widespread in the

[4] An example of the problems faced by these older states is covered by Alfred G. Smith Jr. in his *Economic Readjustment of an Old Cotton State: South Carolina, 1820–1860.* He mentions that the share of the total cotton output produced by South Carolina declined from 50% in 1811 to less than 30% in 1821. After 1820, there was a net exodus of slaves from South Carolina, and the volume of foreign trade handled by Charleston declined in the 1820s. *Ibid.,* pp. 7–8.

[5] Russel, p. 11. He further said, "The people of the farming districts had an interest in slavery in that they found markets for their surplus products chiefly in the planting regions."

[6] These figures were cited by Emory Hawk, *Economic History of the South,* p. 221. The percentage of slaves in the total Southern population declined steadily, but slightly, between 1830 and 1860 from 34.3% to 32.1%. Approximately 60% of the slaves worked in cotton production.

deep South than in the border states; in South Carolina, for example, almost fifty percent of the white families were slaveowners although only a small fraction had significant holdings.[7]

Despite the relatively small number of slaveholders, slavery occupied a position of pivotal importance in the Southern economic process because of the occupational concentration of the slaves in the production of export crops. Slaves were thus the main source of labor for the most valuable economic sector.[8] Since profits in this sector were the most important source of a surplus for capital accumulation, slavery obviously played a crucial role in directly determining the rate of economic growth in the antebellum South and in indirectly influencing it in other sections.

Cardozo viewed the economic and social well-being of the South as dependent on the cotton plantation system and slavery. He consequently saw abolitionist agitation as a "conspiracy against property," [9] which tampered with the life lines of the Southern economy. He advocated the drastic measure of giving the postmasters discretionary authority to inspect the mails in order to screen out abolitionist tracts ("incendiary publications") [10]: Northern

[7] David D. Wallace, p. 434.

[8] Precise proof of this point is unavailable, although it was generally assumed to be true by writers of the pre-Civil War period. One writer in *DeBow's Review* stated that "The value of the product of slave labor exports nearly quadruples that of free labor exports." Mann Butler, "Cotton is King," *DeBow's Review*, September, 1855, p. 314. Also see E. Deloney, "The South Demands More Negro Labor," *DeBow's Review*, November, 1858. He estimated that Negro field laborers of 8 cotton states accounted for practically all of the output of 3.1 million bales.

[9] *Southern Patriot*, July 31, 1835. Cardozo's usual moderate tone was absent in his discussion of abolitionist activities. He denounced their press as "an engine of destruction and death" which aimed to "break up the order and succession of property."

[10] *Ibid.*, July 30, 1835. Cardozo justified this measure on the grounds of "the laws of social comity as between commonwealths united under one form of general policy" and "the instinct of self-interest."

agitators were held responsible for the Vesey slave revolt in the Charleston area in 1822.[11] Cardozo stressed the common interest of Southern and Northern property owners in suppressing agitation, as it threatened the social orders of both societies.[12] He claimed, "It is the genius of slavery which has built up Northern manufacturing . . . [and] invigorated the whole commercial system of the country." [13] Cardozo's views in this respect were a reflection of the Southern intellectual's general position.

Cardozo felt that the security of slavery depended primarily on the vigorous growth in the wealth, power, and influence of the South, but this, in turn, depended on the diversified development of commerce, manufacturing, and agriculture, which he correctly viewed as a prerequisite for achieving economic independence for the South. Slavery and free trade supported each other in the sense that free trade, based on comparative advantage, made it mutually profitable for the South to concentrate on slave-produced cotton and for England to serve as the manufacturing nation. The complementarity of the English industrial economy and the Southern agrarian economy thus tended to reinforce Southern cotton cultivation based on slave labor, and was unconducive to the growth of Southern manufacturing.[14] In this sense, free trade tended to reinforce the Southern slave economy.

Cardozo would not have accepted the idea that the evolution of a diversified economy was retarded by slavery. To him, free trade, the development of Southern manufacturing, and the retention of the slave system were possible and

[11] *Ibid.*, August 5, 21, 1822. After the insurrection was put down, Cardozo advocated setting up a committee of notable public servants to investigate the slave conditions and make recommendations for bettering the security of the city. There was no mention, however, of slave conditions per se, nor of the kind and degree of restraints he favored.

[12] *Ibid.*, August 7, 1835. February 9, 1838.

[13] *Ibid.*, January 28, 1837. [14] Taussig, p. 73.

desirable, rather than incompatible. Cardozo championed the idea of developing Southern manufacturing as a potential way of making its social system more viable. Although he believed that the tariff was not the basic cause of the economic woes of the South, he took the view that the tariff, by oppressively taxing the economic system of the South, was attacking its social system of organization based on slavery:

The tariff . . . falls most heavily and directly on the export productive industry, and this in large part is Southern. . . . In affecting her products it strikes at the very root of her domestic institutions and slave labor.[15]

The position of South Carolina and her politicians toward manufacturing altered considerably. In the post-Revolutionary War period the State gave considerable encouragement to establish new industry, particularly cotton mills. Aid was extended in the form of loans or profits from lotteries. By the 1830s, however, attitudes shifted against manufacturing, although occasional calls for the development of Southern manufacturing were made in the newspapers.

A new movement for encouraging diversification of agriculture and the growth of manufacturing grew out of the extended agricultural depression in the 1840s. Whereas many, perhaps most, Southerners attributed this depressed state to the tariff (there was an increase in tariff rates between 1842 and 1846), Cardozo said that the distress in the cotton industry and the general economic decline of the South relative to the North was due primarily to overproduction, lack of agricultural diversification, and an absence of manufacturing activity in the South. Cardozo's series of essays entitled "Domestic Industry,"

[15] *Evening News,* October 31, 1855.

starting February 23, 1842,[16] appeared to be the first systematic effort advocating the development of Southern manufacturing.[17]

There was considerable sentiment in the South against establishing manufacturing, and, in particular, against employing slave labor in it. Some of these reasons were given: [18]

(1) It would encourage protariff sentiment in the South.

(2) It would increase Northern opposition to slavery by increasing the competition with wage labor.

(3) The idea was widely held that slaves were more profitably employed in agriculture than elsewhere.

(4) There was fear that class consciousness would develop among the poor whites or Negro slaves who worked in manufacturing.

[16] In a much earlier article, Cardozo had praised a Colonel Duane for pointing out the desirability for the development of manufacturing in the South. *Southern Patriot*, November 21, 1818. At a somewhat later date, Cardozo expressed doubts as to whether the South could develop a cotton manufacturing system able to compete effectively with the Northern manufacturing system, where the accumulated backlog of capital was much greater. True to his Federalist rather than sectional leanings at this time, he said that the South stood in relation to the North as the North did to England. *Ibid.*, July 30, 1828. The 1842 series was favorably referred to in *Niles Register*, LXII, 71. This was cited by Alfred Smith, Jr., p. 116, and Russel, p. 36.

[17] A similar, but more elaborate, series was published by William Gregg in the Charleston *Courier*, September 20, 1844, et. seq. They were reprinted in pamphlet form, *Essays on Domestic Industry, or an Enquiry into the Expediency of Establishing Cotton Manufacturers in South Carolina*. Like Cardozo, he did not resent the growth of commerce and manufacturing in the North; he stressed the possibility of employing large numbers of nonproductive, underemployed Southern white laborers through the introduction of manufacturing. *Ibid.*, pp. 33, 112. Gregg invested his own capital in a manufacturing concern, which showed a considerable profit. It was conducted along semiphilanthropic lines, reminiscent of Robert Owen.

[18] This section draws from Chauncey S. Boucher, "The Ante-Bellum Attitude of South Carolina Towards Manufacturing and Agriculture," *Washington University Humanistic Studies*, III, Part 2, No. 2 (April, 1916), pp. 243–70; Van Deusen, pp. 266, 279, 280; and Russel, pp. 55–57.

(5) There was fear that the immigrants who would
come to the South to work in manufacturing pursuits
would not be proslavery.

There was, in other words, a fear that agricultural diversification and the growth of a mercantile-manufacturing
economy would be a potential threat to the institution of
slavery and would tend to undermine the existing social
order, it which planters constituted the dominant socioeconomic class. As a general rule, those favoring secession
were less in favor of efforts to develop Southern manufacturing.[19] Cardozo implicitly rejected the validity of the
above objections.

Cardozo said that South Carolina had reached the stage
of development when its cotton production could no
longer compete with the more productive virginal territory of the Western states. He believed that reliance on a
one-crop economy had the disadvantageous effect of making an economy more vulnerable to business fluctuations.
Therefore, he took the position that South Carolina
should gradually establish cotton manufacturing and diversified production. Only a moderate revenue tariff
would be required to develop Southern manufacturing.[20]
Cardozo felt that this could be accomplished without external capital. He appeared to have envisioned a shifting of
resources from agriculture to manufacturing, as well as the
fuller utilization of underemployed resources. The end result would be the more complete utilization of existing
resources in more productive combinations.

[19] Russel, pp. 154–55.

[20] *Southern Patriot,* March 3, 1842; *Evening News,* March 11, 1846. In
the *Essays* Gregg agreed, but he later advocated a protective tariff to encourage the growth of an iron and coal industry in the South. Gregg to
Governor Seabrook, May 10, 1850 cited by Van Deusen, p. 281. Duff Green
was another active promoter of schemes for developing a comprehensive
network of Southern railroads and mining. See Fletcher M. Green, "Duff
Green—Industrial Promoter," *Journal of Southern History,* February, 1936,
pp. 29–42.

According to Cardozo, the older Southern states like South Carolina had a sizeable surplus of slaves and unemployed whites that could be advantageously shifted to manufacturing. He reasoned that the sale of surplus slaves would yield enough income to buy machinery and establish cotton factories; he regarded that portion of the slave property that did not create value in excess of the expense of maintaining it as unproductive capital, because the cost of maintaining the capital good—slaves—was greater than the revenue derived from the sale of their products. Cardozo also said that this surplus labor did not "reproduce an annual value equal to the ordinary interest of money." [21] He believed that Southern manufacturing would make possible the conversion of the unproductive part of slave and wage labor into productive capital, which in turn would tend to raise the rate of profit.

Cardozo appears to have had two complementary courses of action in mind:

(1) Selling part of the slaves and using the funds to set up manufacturing enterprises employing cheap white wage-laborers.[22]

(2) Shifting some of the slaves from farming to higher productivity manufacturing operations.[23]

[21] *Southern Patriot*, February 26, 1842. Also see *Evening News*, December 15, 1848.

[22] Gregg focused attention on the existence of a large group of illiterate, poor whites (perhaps $\frac{1}{3}$ of the total white population) whose poverty, he felt, was reinforced by the lack of diversification. Gregg, pp. 48–50, 106, 107. Another writer said, "Many thoughtful Southerners regretted that so much of the capital, enterprise and intelligence in the South was employed in directing slave labor to the almost complete neglect of a large part of the white population." Russel, p. 53.

[23] An indication of this dual approach is evident in a theoretical model of Cardozo's. He reasoned that if 76,000 slaves (representing the excess of slave population over whites in South Carolina) were sold at $300 each, it would yield enough money to establish 100 factories, each with 5000 spindles. He estimated that this would convert the equivalent of 100,000 bales of cotton into manufactured goods. Cardozo estimated the labor requirements at about 40,000, of which he arbitrarily supposed that half

Cardozo viewed the spending of productive workers as having a general expansionary effect through a chain-like stimulation of other branches of economic activity such as retail trade:

The measure of that benefit [from the development of manufacturing involving the use of slave or cheap white labor] is mainly to be determined by the increased expenditure necessary for maintaining productive instead of unproductive labor. . . . The money employed for slave maintenance . . . has very narrow limits. That which rewards skilled industry has no boundary to its capacity for enlargement. Each accession of numbers possesses a self-multiplying power as to wealth and population.[24]

The difficulty of interpreting these statements springs from the fact that productive slaves involved in manufacturing did not receive any more wages than did unproductive slaves,[25] defined as those who do not reproduce the expenses of their maintenance, involved in agriculture. Cardozo probably felt that the low cost of supplying subsistence for the slaves would enable Southern factories employing slave labor to overcome some of the cumulative advantages of Northern manufacturing firms. These new factories, however, would also open up employment opportunities for the poor white wage-earners. Cardozo maintained that the spendings of this latter group would tend to spread their beneficial effects to other sectors of the

---

would come from the unemployed white group and half would be slaves shifted from growing cotton to manufacturing. *Southern Patriot,* February 26, 1842.

[24] *Evening News,* December 15, 1848.

[25] An interesting exception has been noted by Clement Eaton, "Slave Hiring in the Upper South: A Step Toward Freedom," *Mississippi Valley Historical Review,* March, 1960, pp. 663–78. He shows that a slave-hiring system with free market aspects developed in the upper South in the 1840s and 1850s. Slaves who were leased out by their masters as factory or domestic workers were often paid a wage over the amount paid to the owner, and a few skilled slaves hired themselves out and paid their owners part of the wages they received.

economy. He appears to have taken the position that the increased production of manufactured goods, stimulated by the cost advantages of slave labor, would also benefit the underemployed white worker, and via the latter, would diffuse its effects to all sectors. Within the agricultural sector, Cardozo claimed that some of the unproductive slave labor should be directed to growing food products to feed the emerging manufacturing class. He said that this course would result in steadier income and employment as well as increased profits. In addition to the South's having abundant and cheap raw materials and water power, low transportation costs, and a favorable climate, Cardozo believed that the significant advantage for developing manufactures in the South was the lower cost of slave labor compared to white.[26] He stressed the point that the minimal cost of feeding and clothing a slave worker enabled Southern firms to have approximately the same cost of manufacturing as typical Northern concerns. Another advantage that Cardozo attributed to the development of Southern manufacturing was that manufacturing industries would revive sooner from commercial crises than agriculture, partly because Southern prosperity would be less tied to the state of economic activity in the British mills. Cardozo said that

[26] *Southern Patriot*, February 28; March 3, 10, 1842. Cardozo said, "Our slave institutions are in fact admirably adapted to it [domestic industry]." *Ibid.*, March 2, 1842. Gregg took a somewhat extreme position of claiming that Negroes were superior in factory performance to the whites in that they were more easily controlled, and the owner received the advantage of their uninterrupted services. Gregg, pp. 47, 48, 78.

At an earlier date, Cardozo had chided a Northern writer, whom he believed was Matthew Carey, for suggesting that it would be profitable to employ the slaves in cotton manufacturing. *Southern Patriot*, October 11, 1827. Although Cardozo continued to adhere to the position that slaves could be advantageously employed in manufacturing, he later expressed some misgivings about mixing them with poor white workers. *Evening News*, May 31, 1849.

Gregg expressed the same views in a letter to the *Evening News*, March 29, 1849. It might be added that the cost of transportation in the South was *not* cheap, except down navigable rivers.

the impediments to the growth of manufacturing were much greater in the North than in the South, due to the benefits that the latter would derive from accumulated technological developments and the greater ease of acquiring capital and skilled labor.[27] He believed that the fundamental reason for the slow economic growth of the South was the misdirection of its capital.

Reversing his earlier position, Cardozo in the 1840s held that investments in manufacturing were more profitable than in agriculture. He maintained, "A given sum invested in an establishment for this purpose [domestic industry] will yield a far greater percentage than the same sum invested in land and Negroes." [28] This reversed his earlier view that capital in South Carolina was more profitably directed into agriculture than into commercial activities.[29] The advantages of diversified economic development including manufacturing that Cardozo saw can be summarized as follows:

(1) It would provide increased productive employment for a large group of unproductive consumers.

(2) It would tend to stabilize income.

(3) It would provide greater protection against the business cycle.

(4) It would benefit other sectors of the economy, such as agriculture and retailing.

(5) It would increase the productivity of capital by investing it in manufacturing, where the yield on an invest-

[27] *Southern Patriot*, March 8, 1842. Gregg later adopted this same position. Gregg, p. 44. An interesting variant of Cardozo's viewpoint may be found in Thorstein Veblen, *Imperial Germany and the Industrial Revolution* (New York, Viking, 1954), Chapter 4. He said that Germany, through starting her process of industrialization at a later period than England, received the benefit of starting new industry at the highest attained level of technological development. England, however, was "paying the penalty for having been thrown into the lead." *Ibid.*, p. 132. Veblen's point appears to be borne out by the recent development of manufacturing in the South.

[28] *Southern Patriot*, March 2, 1842.   [29] *Ibid.*, October 18, 1823.

ment would be highest. Since slaves were the main form of Southern capital, shifting them from agriculture to manufacturing was necessary. This was particularly true in areas where the soil was relatively less fertile than the newer lands in the Southwest.

(6) It would increase the economic independence of the South.

(7) It would strengthen the institutions of the South by arresting its economic decline.

It is interesting to examine Cardozo's rejection of Henry Carey's idea that the gradual emancipation of the slave was conducive to the economic growth of the South. Carey's scheme appeared as a letter in Skinner's *The Plough, the Loom and the Anvil*. Carey believed that an increase in the value of slave-grown products was conducive to the growth of freedom. In response, Cardozo said, "The principle is undeniable as a general theorem that the increase of wealth promotes the increase of freedom, subject to this limitation, provided wealth is not too unequally distributed." [30]

The process of gradual emancipation envisioned by Carey was tied up with the diversification of the Southern economy. In the first stage, he thought that the diversification of the Southern economy would yield a surplus, part of which would go to the slave, who thus would become to some degree a wage receiver. In the next stage, the slave would be allowed to cultivate a portion of his land and to sell his produce. Cardozo said that this was a general practice throughout the South. The slave in this stage became a payer of rent.

Carey was trying to show that the elevation of the slave to freedom in gradual stages, involving the selling of labor time for wages, was beneficial to the slaveowners. Cardozo believed that the underlying error of Carey's gradualistic

[30] *Ibid.*, January 11, 1849.

approach arose from confusing serfdom in Europe with slavery in the United States:

> [These] opposite conditions of society [are] produced by differences of race. What is called serfdom in Europe admits of the gradation suggested by him [Carey], for the elevation of the serf does no violence to known principles of human nature any more than the drafting into the mass of the community of liberated slaves in the ancient commonwealth offered any violation of those principles. . . . How is it possible, after the slaves have become comparatively enriched, to prevent conflicts between the two races? This scheme therefore, of elevating the slave is one that has no warrant in history or in the knowledge of human nature.[31]

Cardozo concluded this review with a statement of his belief that an increase in the value of the products of slave labor would enable the owner to increase the comforts, but not the freedom, of his slaves.

Although the development of industry in the South lagged far behind that in the North, there was nevertheless a significant amount of industrial development in the slaveholding South. The census of 1860 indicates that in that year there were 20,000 manufacturing establishments in the South employing over 110,000 workers, comprising a capital investment of $96 million. Although the antebellum South was predominantly an agrarian society, there were several Southern cities with a considerable number of working people. White wage workers in those cities sometimes felt the competitive pressure of slave labor. The threat of using slave labor, sometimes latent, other times exercised, was an effective weapon against agitation by white workers for shorter hours or higher wages. Negro labor had been successfully employed in a variety of industrial pursuits in the antebellum South.[32]

[31] *Ibid.*

[32] Van Deusen, p. 267; Alfred G. Smith, Jr., p. 126. A contrary view was implied by Russel, p. 55. He said, "Many Southerners were interested in

There is early evidence of white wage workers protesting the use of Negroes in certain crafts. Typical was a complaint by a white carpenter from antebellum Georgia that the contractor's "predilection for giving employment in your line of business to ebony workers have either so cheapened the white man's labor or expatriated hence, with but a few solitary exceptions, all the white masons and carpenters of this town." [33] Baltimore whites went so far as to present a petition to the State House of Delegates in 1808; they complained that slave competition caused loss of employment to whites.[34]

Some members of the South Carolina aristocrary reacted with alarm to these labor protests; their reaction came not from a strong desire to encourage the development of manufacturing or to aid the Negro workers but from a concern with the possibility of white workers' attaining the power to exclude Negroes from employment in manufacturing or skilled trades.

C. G. Memminger, later Secretary of the Treasury in the Confederacy, expressed this viewpoint:

Drive out Negro mechanics and all sorts of operatives from our cities, and who must take their places? The same men who

---

manufacturing only so long as it appeared possible to conduct them with slave labor; when experience finally demonstrated the superiority of white labor, their interest declined." It is difficult to ascertain the extent to which slave labor was used in manufacturing. Phillips, in "The Economics of Slave Labor in the South," said, "The employment of slave labor in factory work was relatively slight . . . partly because their labor at market rates usually prevailing for slaves was too dear for the purpose." Phillips, p. 123.

[33] *Southern Banner* (Athens, Georgia), January 13, 1838. Quoted by Julia A. Flisch, "The Common People of the Old South," *American Historical Association Report*, I (1908), 139. Also see Yates Snowden, *Notes on Labor Organizations in South Carolina, 1742–1861*, No. 38, Part 4.

[34] Flisch, p. 139. The author sympathetically describes the social organization of the South as "a flexible aristocracy, modified and changed, and constantly influenced by the democratic principle. . . . The lower class . . . accepted the leadership of the men to whom circumstance had given the higher social position, but it was not a blind acceptance of hereditary rank. . . . The superior must prove his . . . ability to govern in conformity with the prejudices or predilections of the inferior." *Ibid.*, p. 135. It

make the cry in the Northern cities against the tyranny of Capital—and there as here would drive before them all who would interfere with them—and would soon raise here the cry against the Negro—and be hot Abolitionists. And every one of these men would have a vote.[35]

Was this fear grounded in reality? That the non-slaveholder [36] had justified economic and political grievances against the planters and were at least partly aware of them is quite clear. Although Ulrich Phillips is undoubtedly correct in his observation that slave labor had the effect of worsening the economic position of the white laborers by decreasing their employment opportunities,[37] a thorough analysis of the relationship between slaveholder, non-slaveholder, and slave is complex rather than simple, strained rather than stable. A conflict raged on three levels simultaneously—class, race, and section.

Cardozo and other Southern sympathizers denied the existence of class conflict within the South:

There is no hostility, latent or open, in the Southern states between the proprietors and nonproprietors of slaves, for the obvious reason that there is industrial unity in the scheme of Southern labor, while on the contrary there is industrial diver-

<hr/>

is necessary to add that these "prejudices or predilections" were at least influenced if not cultivated by the leadership.

[35] Quoted by Boucher, "The Ante-Bellum Attitude of South Carolina Towards Manufacturing and Agriculture," p. 256.

[36] The non-slaveholders were not a totally homogeneous group. They included small farmers, lower ranks of mechanics, clerks, laborers, and many small shopkeepers. Their income status probably ranged from desperate poverty to modest standards.

[37] Phillips, "The Economics of Slave Labor in the South," *The South in the Building of the Nation*, V, 124. Alse see Paul H. Buck, "The Poor Whites of the Ante-Bellum South," *American Historical Review*, October, 1925, pp. 41–54. He states, "The plantation system by virtually monopolizing industry rendered superfluous the potential labor contribution of the poor white, consigning him to a life of uselessness so far as productive society was concerned. . . . Southern society as it was organized before the Civil War provided no position that the poor white could fill that was not already being satisfactorily filled by others." *Ibid.*, pp. 47, 49.

sity in the Northern. The almost sole and paramount interest of the South is connected with the great staple cotton
. . . [which] depends on slave culture and the integrity of the slave property. . . . The organism of slave labor is so interwoven with the whole industrial, social and domestic relations of all classes at the South, that it not only doesn't interfere with the employments and sources of support of this class [white workers] but permeates through all their affinities and interests.[38]

Unlike a competitive labor market in which capital is created by labor, slavery had the beneficial effect, according to Cardozo, of transforming the laborer into capital:

Capital owns labor, classes are not in extremes in the struggles of life, and therefore the material of radicalism being comparatively limited, accord and consistency more largely prevail. The institution of slavery is a harmonizing bond of union and sympathy.[39]

This stress on the harmonious elements in the Southern system led Cardozo to overlook elements of friction between slave labor and wage workers on the one hand and wage workers or independent farmers and slaveowners on the other. Differentials of wealth and power were extreme in the antebellum South. One writer noted that per capita income in 1860 in the Mississippi Black Belt, in which the plantation was dominant, was ten to fifteen times greater than in East Mississippi, home of the poor whites.[40] The

[38] *Evening News*, August 7, 20, 1856.
[39] *Ibid.*, August 31, 1854. In this article he added, "The radicalism of anti-slavery seeks a universal fusion of humanity in the crucible of an unnatural levelism." Cardozo described the position of the Southern Negro as "independent dependence." *Ibid.*, December 20, 1850. Thomas Dew presented the idea, accepted by Cardozo, that slavery prevented a conflict of interest between capital and labor by making labor and capital one and the same. "Southern Literary Messenger II," p. 277, cited by William E. Dodd in "Contributions of the South to Economic Thought and Writing to 1865," *The South in the Building of the Nation*, V, 571. Gregg had approximately the same idea. He said, "Labor is capital." Gregg, p. 107.
[40] Buck, p. 42.

upcountry people throughout the South resented the disproportionate power wielded by the plantation class, power made possible by the under-representation of the upcountry districts. B. F. Perry, editor of the upcountry Greenville *Southern Patriot* and a strong Unionist, voiced the fear of the non-slaveholder that the plantation class was precipitating a war:

Tell the barons of the low country that if they involve the State [of South Carolina] in war they may defend themselves as well as they can.[41]

The upcountry people also objected to a tax system which discriminated against them:

The planter-controlled legislature exempted all buildings on rural land, though they might rank as palaces, while the cottage of the town mechanic paid its share.[42]

Although Hinton Helper in his famous book, *The Impending Crisis of the South and How to Meet It,* undoubtedly went further than most non-slaveholders in viewing slavery as the enemy of the white masses and appealing to them to abolish it by excluding slaveholders from office, he is symptomatic of an incipient class consciousness.

The poor white was a victim of the South's dilemma. As long as slavery existed, his employment opportunities were limited. The planters preferred not using a mixed labor force, because labor discipline could not be rigidly maintained. Few employment opportunities were created

---

[41] Quoted by Wallace, p. 515. Wallace described the sectional alignments within South Carolina: "The black plantation districts were for the extremists while Charleston and the white up-country were moderate." *Ibid.,* p. 513. It is interesting to note that in the early tariff debates in South Carolina, the black plantation districts were the most moderate, perhaps because they did not yet view the institution of slavery under attack and had a large residue of nationalistic feelings. See John L. Conger, "South Carolina and the Early Tariffs," p. 431.

[42] Wallace, p. 425.

outside of the plantation proper, since many of the prerequisites for industrial development did not exist. The minority of Negroes that were not in agriculture—slaves and free men of color—competed with the poor whites and therefore were resented by them. The latter probably feared that this competition would increase if the slaves were freed, and therefore favored their exclusion from competing occupational lines. Although they did at times resist the political control of the planting class, with few exceptions they were not actively hostile to the institution of slavery. Their class consciousness took the deflected form of promoting their immediate self-interest by opposing the group that threatened their status. Incipient opposition by the poor whites to the institution of slavery thus never matured. Ultimately the race conflict was decisive, and the non-slaveholders sided with the planters in the sectional conflict with the North to defend an institution in which they were almost as much victimized as were the slaves.[43] "The two South Carolinas [the non-slaveholding mass and the planter-based aristocracy] were moving toward their inevitable conflict when a far greater conflict postponed their trial of strength." [44]

The sections of the South in which opposition to secession was greatest were invariably areas of high white-low slave population,[45] a condition most prevalent in the border areas. Perhaps the basic reason for the lack of unity

[43] Buck says: "In their radical attachment to the institution of slavery they were expressing a groping class consciousness based upon instinctive self interest." He also noted that the non-slaveholder group "rested on a congeries of complex interests which prevented the development of a class consciousness that could be directed against the institution of slavery." Buck, pp. 41, 54.

[44] Wallace, p. 515.

[45] A similar situation prevailed in the South Carolina nullification crisis of 1832. The pro-nullification group was strongest in those countries where the plantation slave-labor system was most strongly entrenched. See Chauncey S. Boucher, *The Nullification Controversy in South Carolina*, p. 107.

in the Democratic Party was that it included both the independent farmer and the planter, with the former desiring a liberal land policy and the latter fearful that such a policy would weaken slavery by altering the political balance of power.

The period of most rapid growth of Southern manufacturing was in the agricultural depression of the 1840s, particularly between 1845 and 1850. The recovery in the 1850s tended to make agriculture more profitable and to lessen the drive for the development of manufacturing. "Throughout the antebellum period the South oscillated between diversification and concentration on money crops." [46] This oscillation appeared to be partly a response to the relative profitability of agriculture and manufacturing. During the depressed 1840s, manufacturing profits were high relative to those earned by the planters. Apparently profits of 15–20 percent in the factories were not uncommon.[47] Active agitation for agricultural diversification and development of manufacturing, however, died down by approximately 1850. The increased profitability of cotton cultivation in the fifties weakened the socioeconomic underpinnings of the argument for diversification. In addition, a large number of failures in Southern factories in the early fifties helped further to dampen Southern interest in manufacturing.[48]

[46] Ralph W. Haskins, "The Cotton Factor, 1800–1860: A Study in Southern Economic and Social History" (unpublished doctoral dissertation, University of California, 1950), p. 111.

[47] Based on notices appearing in Southern journals and newspapers in the 1840s, Russel said, "Statements were frequently made and rarely contradicted that mills already in operation were earning 15–20%." Russel, p. 45. Although it is impossible to judge the exact validity of these figures, it would appear that the severe depression in Southern agriculture in the 1840s—average cotton prices for 1830–1840 were 12.6¢ and fell to 8¢ for 1840–1850 (5¢ in 1845)—made profits in manufacturing higher in a relative sense.

[48] The most complete analysis of the attempt to diversify industry in a Southern state and the causes of its relative failure is found in Van Deusen, pp. 262–303.

Cardozo's wavering position in this period was probably in response to the changing political conditions. On one hand, he continued, albeit infrequently, to urge diversification of the Southern economy, mainly on the grounds of the necessity for increasing the economic independence of the South and of accelerating its rate of economic growth. He also thought it was wise for the South to develop manufacturing, since she would not permanently be in the Union.[49]

On the other hand, Cardozo was aware of the benefits of Southern specialization in agriculture and the possible economic dangers of redirecting capital away from agriculture. He said that redistributing capital away from agriculture would affect Southern exports, which would entail increasing taxes to maintain revenue, thus having the deleterious effect of causing an extensive exodus of capital.[50]

Cardozo attacked a pamphlet by Rutledge, who tried to demonstrate that the Southern economy was annually weakened to add to Northern wealth. Cardozo indicated that he still believed that both the North and the South benefited from Southern production of cotton and Northern concentration on commerce and manufacturing:

Without Northern capital and labor largely employed in manufacturing for the South, the South would have been compelled to divert her capital and industry from the soil for these purposes. She has, in freeing her resources from a less to a more productive use of them, enlarged her capacity to produce, although limited to a narrow range of production.[51]

If secession occurred, the South would have to shift its capital to manufacturing and commerce, thus decreasing the value of its exports.

[49] *Evening News*, October 26, 1850; May 20, 1854. By the early 1850s several Southern conservatives like Cardozo anticipated the South's eventual secession from the Union.

[50] *Ibid.*, August 26, 1851.   [51] *Ibid.*, September 25, 1851.

Cardozo, however, was aware that agricultural specialization resulted in a narrowed range of output, which pre-
sumably increased the vulnerability of the South through
becoming part of an interdependent system. Cardozo said
that Northern capital received only the fair interest return
on its investments to which it was entitled.[52] This denial
of significant economic exploitation of the South by Northern capital implies that the major grounds on which
Cardozo favored eventual secession were that the North
threatened the continued existence of the slave-property
system. This is partly confirmed by his statement, "It is
vain to disguise it; the great issue of our day in this country is, slavery or not slavery.[53]

Cardozo urged the South to combine precisely because
he was aware that the settling of the territories was shifting
political power to the non-slaveholding states,[54] thereby
threatening the social structure of the Southern economy
as well as their "way of life." Cardozo believed that it
would be extremely difficult for South Carolina to increase
its output of manufactured goods for domestic consumption and agricultural export products simultaneously by
redirecting her capital and labor. He said that this would
require "an inconceivable elasticity of capital and physical
effort." [55] This is certainly not fully compatible with his
earlier idea of utilizing unemployed or unproductive
whites, since such labor does provide elasticity for production purposes. He may have had in mind the temporary
grinding of gears which occurs when an economy switches
its resources from one sector to another.

On the whole, Cardozo continued to believe in the importance of economic diversification but became increasingly concerned with political problems as the Civil War
approached. It is reasonable to infer that Cardozo took the

[52] *Ibid.*, August 19, September 25, 1851.　　[53] *Ibid.*, March 23, 1854.
[54] *Ibid.*, August 23, 1848.　　[55] *Ibid.*, June 12, 1851.

position that the beneficial economic effects of Southern specialization within the Union were gradually being over-balanced by the growing political weakness of the South, which in part resulted from that specialization.

Cardozo's views on the relative efficiency of slave and wage labor underwent a considerable change. In the early period, he held that the latter was two to three times as effective as the former, which justified the efforts of the profit-seeking planter at reducing the standard of living of the slaves. His social commitment to defend slavery is revealed by his defense of the increasing exploitation of the slave:

The higher profit they [the Southern states] derive from agri-cultural investment . . . can originate in nothing but the same cause that compels us to reduce the standard of comfort for our slaves from their comparative ineffectiveness, that we may receive a fair remuneration of living profit on our capital.[56]

Since the low slave productivity was partly a result of their low living standards, the statement is not wholly correct. Low slave productivity resulted from low living standards, as much as it created them.

In the later period, however, he held that Southern slave labor in cotton was more efficient than voluntary labor elsewhere, since slavery ensured the availability of a large, continuous supply of labor—although he claimed that part of this higher efficiency was due to the higher motivation of the proprietor.[57] Cardozo consistently adhered to the view that slave labor was employed inefficiently when utilized predominantly in agriculture. The malallocation of Southern capital was viewed as impeding its economic growth:

[56] Cardozo, *The Tariff*, p. 39.
[57] Cardozo, "Supply and Consumption of Cotton: Present and Prospec-tive," *De Bow's Review*, XXII (April, 1857), 344.

All the surplus capital among us, in our cities, if there is any surplus, is absorbed in banking, while in the interior it assumes the shape of land and negroes. It is this exclusive direction of our active means into a limited channel, that impedes the industrial progress of the South—that locks up her wealth in a narrow field.[58]

It would appear from these somewhat contradictory remarks that Cardozo took the position that the higher exploitability of slave labor in the form of lower living standards and longer hours of work made it less costly than wage labor, although when exclusively directed into cotton production the efficiency of slave labor was lessened.

The economic growth of America was accompanied by the furthering of both nationalism and sectionalism. As the former grew weaker, the latter became stronger. Cardozo's thought paralleled this development. His early pro-Unionist tendencies were gradually replaced by sectional leanings, as the process of economic growth strengthened the elements of discord in the American social system. He came to view the slavery issue not only as a question of property rights, but as part of the broader question of the relative political power of the sections.[59] He condemned any move to exclude slavery from future territories added to the Union on the grounds that this "would give a fatal preponderance to the Northern states in the Councils of the Union (i.e., the Senate)." [60] Cardozo regarded slavery essentially as a "practical question." [61]

[58] *Evening News*, January 30, 1856. Cardozo appeared to be aware that little diversification was actually taking place. See also *ibid.*, November 6, 1850.
[59] *Ibid.*, August 18, 1847.   [60] *Southern Patriot*, August 19, 1835.
[61] *Evening News*, November 4, 1845. Cardozo further said in this article that "Labor is the ordinance of society—the law of our being. This ordinance brings into social approximation countries however modified by climate, by habits, by forms of government. Labor, necessity, dependence is the great leveller of the human race. The predial slave of South Carolina and the free English laborer are approximated to that condition which es-

With an obvious sense of frustration, Cardozo recognized that the pendulum of political power was shifting away from the slaveholding states,[62] and that world sentiment was essentially antislavery.[63] He opposed the provision in the Kansas-Nebraska Act which gave the people in the territories the right to decide whether or not to exclude slavery, on the grounds that Congress had no right to give the people the right to exclude slavery through majority vote. Fearing squatter sovereignty, Cardozo denied the right of the squatters to exclude slavery and denounced the Kansas-Nebraska Act as "another miserable subterfuge of non-intervention." [64]

He gradually began to doubt the ability of the South effectively to protect its interests through a national party, since political issues had become more sectional.[65] He felt that the South could not consistently align itself with the

---

tablishes the principle of equality between them, in fact, whatever it may be in fine spun theories of human rights and abstract speculations on social equality."

[62] *Ibid.,* August 23, 1848. Cardozo also foresaw the weakening of the ties between the South and the West because of the slavery issue. This coalition through the Democratic Party had won all but two presidential elections between 1828 and 1858. The political alliances forged out of diverse sectional economic interests proved to be fluid rather than enduring. As the Western economy became more interlinked with the Northeast, her political ties with the South weakened. *Ibid.,* August 10, 1850.

[63] *Ibid.,* June 7, 1851. Cardozo felt that the political sentiment of the British trading and manufacturing classes were basically antislavery despite Britain's commercial connections with the South.

[64] *Ibid.,* February 22, 1854. This Act repealed the Missouri Compromise of 1820, under which slavery was prohibited north of Missouri's southern boundary. Since most of the Southerners favored this bill as potentially opening the territories to slavery, Cardozo said, "We must perforce look passively on the passage of the measure." Like Cardozo, the Republicans also vigorously opposed the Kansas-Nebraska Act, but their objection stemmed from the view that slavery should not be permitted in the territories. A period of considerable bloodshed in Kansas followed as the proslavery and antislavery factions struggled for control.

[65] *Ibid.,* August 31, 1854. Cardozo was more optimistic in 1852–1853 as he thought that Pierce was carrying out a policy in a "spirit of legislative compromise." *Ibid.,* June 18, 1853.

Democratic Party because they had "temporized with anti-slavery and compromised with Southern rights." [66] He stressed that the South must achieve unity within its territory in order to protect its own interests.

The main political struggle within Cardozo's state of South Carolina in the decade prior to the Civil War was between the separate-actionists (disunionists per se) who favored immediate secession even if the rest of the South did not follow, and the cooperationists who held that secession was inevitable but felt that the South must be united before it broke away from the Union. [67] The former group was a small minority at the start of the decade, but increased considerably in strength by the latter half. Cardozo was in the cooperationist camp. By 1851 he believed that the states were no longer a well-knit group but rather a loose aggregation which was impossible to hold together permanently:

The public sentiment, North and South, has no assimilating properties. When the Union was formed their manner and opinions had a certain social approximation. Although not homogeneous they were not so repugnant as to preclude political affiliation. This cohesive property no longer exists. To hold such communities together in political bonds is impossible. . . . Parchment will not bind when education weakens. . . . A new Union then seems to be forced on us, is inevitable and

[66] *Ibid.*, September 6, 1859. Cardozo added that the South should display firmness in defending "the integrity, safety and expansion of Southern institutions."

[67] There also was a small group of Unionists, including Poinsett, Pettigru, Perry, and Yeadon, who were more strongly antiseccessionist than the cooperationists. They favored accepting the compromise of 1850 under which California was admitted as a free state, the slave trade was abolished in Washington, D.C., a more effective fugitive slave law was enacted, and no position was taken on the status of slavery in the Mexican territory. As a tactical maneuver to delay the trend to secession, they joined with the cooperationists against the disunionists, and stressed the need for the South to develop a diversified economy. At times, Cardozo's position was close to that of the Unionist group.

this must be the result of Disunion—Union between the South, Disunion with the North.[68]

Cardozo stressed the extreme economic difficulties that separate secession would entail: [69]

(1) The cost of importing would increase and the yield on South Carolina exports would fall, because British merchants and manufacturers would not take the risk of running the blockade that he anticipated would be placed against South Carolina by the Federal government.

(2) If the separate government of South Carolina put a duty on Northern goods, the Northern states in which these goods were produced would retaliate and the value of Southern exports would decline.

(3) The decrease in public revenue as a result of declining exports would force the South Carolina government to increase taxes on slaves, whom Cardozo regarded as "the only real fiscal resource in South Carolina."

(4) The inevitable disturbance of established business arrangements would put an insupportable burden on the small Southern planter. Cardozo thought that the restricted trade and increased taxation would wipe out the middle class, leaving large proprietors and laborers.

(5) The public credit of the banks would be adversely affected.

Cardozo affirmed the right of secession but claimed that expediency put off its use until some future date.[70]

He described the cooperation party as aware of the advantages of a national union while simultaneously fearing that the price might be too high. He held that the North's manipulation of the government violated the spirit of the Constitution. The critical factor stressed by Cardozo was the belief of the cooperationists that

[68] *Evening News,* May 27, 1851.
[69] *Ibid.,* May 30, June 2, 3, 4, 7, 9, 12, 18, 21, 25, 1851.
[70] *Ibid.,* June 8, 1851.

. . . no party arrangements can stay the progress of Northern opinion adverse to slavery. . . . [T]here is sufficient cause for present secession. . . . The cooperation party are necessarily forced to believe that with the increased sectional majority in Congress there can not exist equality and independence in the Union. They look to the near future for its dissolution. But they wish to take security in a more limited, that they cannot find in the less limited confederacy.[71]

In other words, when the South united, it would secede as a group.

It appears to be clear that Cardozo weighed the allaying of economic discontent in the 1850s that stemmed from the relative prosperity of agriculture in the South, against the rising social discontent generated by the potential threat to the continued existence of the Southern social structure of slavery. The waning of Southern political power made the threat more and more pressing.

Symptomatic of the struggle against the forces undermining the system was the revival of agitation for reopening the slave trade. Southern cotton prosperity in the 1850s had caused an increased demand for slaves, particularly in the areas of cotton and sugar plantations, which drove up the price of slaves to the highest level. This in turn was an element in further raising the price of cotton. Although the slave trade was prohibited after 1808, approximately 270,000 slaves were smuggled into the United States between that date and 1860.[72] There was a considerable movement of slaves within the South, particularly from the Old South and the border areas to the fertile lands of the Southwest.

As agricultural profits declined in the upper South, it

[71] *Ibid.*, September 4, 1851. Cardozo later rejected a disunion plea of the Charleston *Mercury* as impractical at that time. *Ibid.*, July 28, 1855.

[72] Hawk, p. 237. The illicit importation for the last pre-Civil War decade was estimated at 70,000.

proved profitable for the planters to engage in the systematic sale of surplus slaves to the other areas. It was estimated that over 200,000 slaves were transferred from selling to buying states in the decade between 1850 and 1860.[73] The disunionist group were strong supporters of the effort to revive the slave trade, which they viewed as necessary for the preservation of the plantation-slave system.[74]

Cardozo was against the reopening of the slave trade, but none of his available writings explains his stand.[75] The prevailing arguments at that time against the reopening the the slave trade included the following:

(1) Even if the increased importation of slaves could reduce the costs of producing cotton, an unlikely possibility because of the inefficiency of African labor, the benefits of cheaper cotton would be reaped by British and Northern manufacturers.

(2) It would lower the wages of poor white workers who had to compete with slave labor in certain jobs.

[73] Russel, p. 211. There was also a significant emigration of whites from the Old South to the Southwest. Alfred G. Smith, Jr. estimates that approximately 200,000 whites emigrated from South Carolina from 1820 to 1860. Smith, p. 22.

[74] Six out of seven members of a special South Carolina State legislative committee endorsed Governor J. H. Adams' proposal for reopening trade. It was hoped that this would somehow prevent the stagnation of the South Carolina economy. Smith, pp. 41–43. James D. B. DeBow, editor of the influential DeBow's Review, was a strong adherent of reopening the slave trade, mainly on the grounds that it would extend the basis of slavery by making more members of the white community into slave owners. DeBow was also an ardent spokesman for American expansionism. See Robert F. Durden, "J. D. B. DeBow: Convolutions of a Slavery Expansionist," Journal of Southern History, November 1951, pp. 441–61.

[75] In the January 3, 1859, issue of the Charleston Evening News, Cardozo said that he was starting a series against the reopening of the African slave trade. Unfortunately, however, there are no copies of these succeeding issues available. In a much earlier article, Cardozo said that he favored continuing a State law prohibiting the importation of slaves into South Carolina from other states on the grounds that the repeal of this law would further the "Operations of the mercenary and unfeeling slave trader." Southern Patriot, December 8, 1818.

(3) It might slow down the development of Southern manufacturing and reinforce the production of agricultural products.

(4) It might weaken the institution of slavery by lowering the price of slaves.

(5) Politically the revival of the slave trade might result in furthering disunity among the Southern states, since few had a strong interest in reviving the trade.

One scholar [76] of the period thought that the opposition of the North to the reopening of the slave trade was the straw that broke the camel's back and led to secession. It had the effect of cutting off the supply of Southern labor while extensive immigration from Europe was leading to rapid economic expansion in the North.

Cardozo's writings in the immediate postwar period indicated that he remained sympathetic to the slave system.[77] He mourned the passing of the low-country planting class, and nostalgically characterized the relationship between slave and master as a "reciprocity of protection and obedience beneficial to both." He referred to the indignities suffered by the former slaveowners, who after the Civil War had to "submit to the most degrading types of employment. . . . There is something unnatural in this reverse of position—something revolting to our sense of propriety in this social degradation." To Cardozo, slavery was at the core of the social, political, and economic conflict between the sections.

The slave system was intricately intertwined with the functioning of the Southern economy, since it provided the predominant part of the labor supply involved in the

[76] Van Deusen, Chapter 8, pp. 304–27, contains a discussion of the arguments in favor and against the revival of the slave trade in Cardozo's home state of South Carolina, during the latter part of the 1850s.

[77] The following references are to his *Reminiscences of Charleston*, pp. 8, 10.

production of cotton, the dominant form of economic activity in the antebellum South. Cardozo regarded the defense of this institution and its accompanying way of life as the main justification for secession, and its passage a cause for lamentation. His strong advocacy of industrial diversification of the Southern agrarian economy represented an attempt to effect a reconciliation between a capitalistic commercial-manufacturing system and a noncapitalistic labor market. The irony, however, was that the existence of a noncapitalistic labor market had the tendency to prevent the full evolution of a capitalistic commercial-manufacturing system. Here were the roots of the malaise of the South's economy, and its eventual denouement.

Cardozo's view that the development of manufacturing with slave labor and underemployed whites would have resulted in a net increase in Southern wealth through a more productive use of its resources misses the central issue. The economic growth potentials of a slaveholding system are closely related to the social and political strengths and frailties of that system.[78] Cardozo examined the narrow scope of the problem; he was concerned with ways of developing manufacturing without considering the nature of the social system in a wide sense, and this examination, penetrating though it was, was related to his social commitment to defend the social institution of slavery. Because of this commitment, the level of high scientific detachment that Cardozo usually employed to study value, distribution, banking, and business-cycle theory was partially sacrificed.

[78] This point will be expanded in Appendix II, as part of an analysis of a recent article with similar shortcomings.

NINE

Social Philosophy

LAISSEZ-FAIRE, free trade, and private property were the basic tenets of Cardozo's social philosophy. His vision of society was one in which mild reforms, which would not adversely affect the institution of private property, could take place in an evolutionary manner. When the exigencies of the Southern political economy required compromises with these positions, Cardozo proved to be quite adjustable.

In Cardozo's concept of the "natural order," the scope of government activities was limited to the protection of private property, enforcement of business contracts, conducting of foreign affairs, and aiding with internal improvements under certain conditions. A competitive market structure was viewed as an essential prerequisite for the creation of a natural society. He looked on America as a natural society whose institutions gave the "utmost expansion to the desires and capacities of man . . . [in which] the prizes that wait on enterprize were within the grasp of all." [1]

Cardozo's Smithian approach can be seen in his statements that "the free and voluntary pursuit of individual advantage is the sure means of promoting national wealth . . . [and] the interest of individuals will overleap any artificial barrier erected by legislators." [2] Attempts of the legislature to interfere with the laws of free commerce would necessarily prove abortive. He said, "There are some changes in society which no interference of law can arrest." [3] Among these were "revolutions of property" or changes in property ownership, a decline in the demand for labor, and postwar production shifts.

Cardozo espoused stringent bankruptcy laws to inculcate respect for property and the sanctity of business contracts. He took the view that debtor-biased insolvency laws had the pernicious effect of destroying the confidence on which commerce was based and of injuring our commercial trading relations. Since extensive British aid was instrumental in accelerating our rate of economic development, he viewed the maintenance of a good credit status as being of critical importance.[4] He called for a repeal of all usury laws [5] on the grounds that they were generally ineffective.

Cardozo's position on the Poor Laws was strikingly similar to that of Malthus, Lauderdale, and Ricardo. He de-

---

[1] *Southern Patriot*, June 27, 1818; July 15, 1819.

[2] *Ibid.*, May 26, June 3, 1819. Also December 22, 1818. In the later period of threatened secession, Cordozo said that a change in the political relations between sections or countries alters the ordinary principles regulating commercial interchanges. *Evening News*, June 9, 1851.

[3] *Southern Patriot*, February 3, 1820.

[4] *Ibid.*, October 8, 1819; March 30, 1820. A detailed study of Cardozo's Bankruptcy Plan can be found in the following issues: December 6, 10, 11, 13, 14, 18-21, 1821.

[5] *Ibid.*, December 17, 1818; February 27, 1821; June 21, 1837. *Evening News*, November 27, December 2, 1848; February 23, 1849; June 28, 1854.

scribed a process of "action and reaction" [6] resulting from the operation of the Poor Laws in England. These laws were viewed as providing a stimulus to population which increased the labor supply, especially of agricultural workers, relative to the demand. The consequent decrease in money wages provided a temporary benefit to the employers and more work for the employees. The high level of employment provided a temporary respite from poor rate payments, but eventually wages would fall enough so that poor relief was needed again. Cardozo believed that only habits of thrift and industry could prevent this circular effect and make poor relief unnecessary or of marginal importance.

In his early writings, Cardozo favored a complete repeal of the Poor Laws on the grounds that they violated the sound principles of political economy by destroying a sense of pride and independence in the working class, and by reducing the ability and incentive of the proprietor to cultivate the land. He characterized the Poor Laws:

[They are a] mischievous device to turn the streams of public charity into false channels—to destroy all the best and most efficient springs of action in the minds of the laboring class and to strip it of all pride, morality and sense of independence. . . . The Poor Rates of England starve the sources of that income by which they are fed, and convert the soil into a sterile waste, inducing its abandonment in many instances, by its proprietors, from the weight of the assessment. . . .

As long as we persist in supporting institutions which profess to relieve, at the public charge, the poorer classes, we are in effect giving a bounty to pauperism, we are nurturing habits of idleness. . . . We ought speedily in short to abolish those institutions . . . which will eventually nourish and perpetuate a race of drones and paupers.[7]

[6] *Southern Patriot,* February 8, 1831.
[7] *Ibid.,* March 23, August 26, 1818; see also *ibid.,* September 16, 1819.

Public charity, except for voluntary contributions, was viewed as having a debasing effect. Cardozo's position later became milder in that he felt that public relief to some persons, after rigid scrutiny, was acceptable, if labor of some sort was required from the inmates of the Poor Houses. Whereas earlier he had rejected the Poor Laws per se, his later position placed the fault in the application rather than the principle of these laws. Cardozo said:

Some system of Poor Rates is necessary even for new countries on certain spots where the population has a tendency to become crowded. . . . Either some fund must be provided for those who can not work, or the worst forms of vagrancy must shock the eye and harrow the feelings.[8]

Although, on balance, Cardozo advocated a policy of laissez-faire, he compromised with these principles in several strategic cases, usually under the pressure of economic events. On one hand, he rejected the notion of direct state aid to debtors in periods of economic distress on the grounds that this involved the taxing of one portion of the community to pay another. On the other hand, after a continued period of falling prices, depressed economic conditions, and debtor-class suffering, Cardozo came out for a reduction of the interest charge, so that the creditor would receive a value equivalent to that existing at the time the contract was made.[9] In the early period of the 1837 Crisis,

[8] *Ibid.*, December 1, 1827; see also *ibid.*, September 9, 1826. Cardozo feared that the large number of immigrants working on internal improvement projects would become a burden on the cities when their employment ended. He suggested that the city of Charleston work out some scheme for charging ship captains a certain amount to defray expenses to the city if these immigrants became indigent. *Ibid.*, July 30, 1836.

[9] *Ibid.*, July 26, 1820; July 3, 1821. In the latter, Cardozo said that the creditor was entitled to the benefits of a rise in the market value of a currency if the contract was not made when money was at the stage of greatest depreciation. The suggestion is that contracts are valid if made at a time of relatively stable value for the currency, even though its value subsequently alters. Expediency quite obviously took precedence over

he held that "the interference of government frequently postpones the cure [for commercial crises] if it does not aggravate the evil," and, in addition, suggested that we "leave matters to adjust themselves by the self-interest of parties with as little interference by Legislative or Executive power as possible." [10] During the crisis in the cotton market, Cardozo favored temporary government intervention to lessen the effects of rapidly declining cotton prices on the grounds that this was a defensive maneuver against the wielding of formidable commercial power by the Bank of England.[11]

Although Cardozo was not a strict constructionist regarding government aid for internal improvements, he was more favorably disposed toward the use of state rather than Federal aid. He urged liberal appropriations by the state legislature for internal improvements [12] such as railroads, canals, swamp, and drainage as a way of facilitating commercial connections between different parts of the state, stimulating new business ventures, and linking the Southern and Western economies. The fact, however, that Europe remained the main outlet for Southern staples inhibited the incentive of Southern states for developing a

principle in this case in that the pure operations of the market were interfered with.

[10] *Ibid.*, May 13, 1837.

[11] *Ibid.*, June 11, 13, 19, 1839. The relief for the cotton grower, proposed by Cardozo, was for the banks to pay the cotton producers the difference between the advance price, given by Biddle's United States Bank of Pennsylvania, and the cost of production.

[12] *Ibid.*, November 25, 1818; December 5–8, 1820; *Evening News,* October 2, December 19, 1845; May 15, 1851. Cardozo was also in favor of inviting Congress to buy stock in the South Carolina Canal and Railroad Co., holding that this did not infringe on state sovereignty. *Southern Patriot,* January 21, 1830. He urged the Southern States to make use of British capital for a vast scheme of internal improvements which fostered their commercial development. *Ibid.*, August 17, 1838. A student of South Carolina history noted that "The State [of South Carolina] aided almost every railroad built before 1860." This aid took the form of buying stock and guaranteeing bonds. Wallace, p. 377.

widespread transportation network. Unlike most Southern statesmen, Cardozo said that it was unwise for Southern states to refuse Federal government grants for internal improvements as long as they remained in the Union. He labeled the Southern anti-Federal aid position as the "merest infatuation to constitutional principles." [13] Many Southerners objected to the distribution to the states of proceeds from the sale of public lands, because they thought it was a device for keeping up tariffs. Cardozo, however, viewed these problems as quite separable.

Another case in which Cardozo deviated from the laissez-faire model concerns the magnetic telegraph. He feared that this invention might fall into the hands of a few powerful capitalists, since its high cost of operation made its use by average-size newspapers quite prohibitive. This would give them an unfair competitive advantage. Therefore, Cardozo felt that either the telegraph rate should be made cheaper or that "it should be placed under the control of government to be used only for public purposes." [14]

Perhaps a major practical issue on which Cardozo's views wavered between laissez-faire and government intervention was in the area of banking.[15] Cardozo regarded departures from nonintervention as strategic and exceptional expedients. In general, the government intervention or aid that he favored was of an indirect rather than a direct variety, temporary rather than permanent. His later writings reveal a greater willingness to condone government interference.

Although sympathetic to European reformist movements involving some shifting of power from the landed class to the bourgeoisie, Cardozo was strongly antagonistic to working-class movements. Although he was in favor of the change from feudalism, and sympathetic to the liberal

[13] *Evening News*, November 1, 1856.   [14] *Ibid.*, November 19, 1845.
[15] A fuller discussion of this point is found above, in Chapter Six.

forces operating against the arbitrary European monarchies, he thought that the rapidity and extremeness of the French Revolution had undesirable consequences because it "excessively reduced" the power of the landlords and ushered in mob rule. He expressed the judgment that "the change of property ought to be gradual." [16] Sound statesmanship should be concerned with controlling the process of social change.

Cardozo praised the attempt of Canning, the British Tory Prime Minister, gradually to reduce the influence of the wealthy landed aristocracy while refraining from yielding to the "rash spirit of Parliamentary reform." [17] He was aware of the historical shifting of power from the landed class to the bourgeoisie, which included a replacement of the landed aristocracy by a monied aristocracy:

An aristocracy of money has supplanted the more natural one which formerly had land for its basis. The seat and source of power is the stock exchange; the real ministers of state are the money lenders and stock jobbers.[18]

In the period of agitation for voting reform in England, Cardozo said:

The question of parliamentary reform is only indicative of much deeper changes in the structure of the British parliament. . . . Development of power in the middle ranks comprising manufacturing and commercial classes has been steadily progressing for the last thirty years.[19]

[16] *Southern Patriot*, May 21, 1821. Cardozo said that "until the feudal privileges are in substance destroyed there can be no real power and independence for the people . . . but a change in opinion must precede this reduction of the property and power [of the landed nobility and priesthood]." He claimed that "There must always exist a certain harmony between the principles of government, whatever they are, and the sentiments, habits, and prepossessions of the governed." *Ibid.*, April 14, 1821.

[17] *Ibid.*, July 31, September 20, 22, 1826. Cardozo said that the overrepresentation of the landed aristocracy was a defect of the British House of Commons.

[18] *Ibid.*, September 21, 1822.

[19] *Ibid.*, April 23, 1831; see also *Ibid.*, January 13, 1831.

Cardozo approved of the 1832 Reform Bill in England
which reduced the preponderant power of the agricultural
classes in favor of the rising manufacturing classes. He believed, however, that although the extension and better
distribution of the franchise was desirable, the Chartist
aim of universal suffrage was too far-reaching.

Cardozo emphasized the dangers that would arise for society when property qualifications for suffrage were abandoned:

The whole current of history shows that there are two leading
principles, which in every period of history, are more or less
antagonistical—namely, that of property combined with sound
intelligence, and of numbers, united with imperfect knowledge.
On the due balance of these opposing impulses rests social order and prosperity.[20]

Cardozo's views on this issue became more conservative
in the late antebellum period. He thought that the House
of Commons deteriorated in the period following the Reform Bill of 1832 as the representation from the cities increased. He claimed that the middle classes held the balance of power in England between the oligarchy who
controlled the rural areas and the masses who were dominant in the cities.[21]

The most tolerable reformist measures were those which
were "under the guidance of leaders who have some stake
in society" [22] rather than the unpropertied masses. Cardozo thought of himself as a "friend of national liberty" [23]
in the sense that he was moderately sympathetic to revolutions for which there was general support by the better

[20] *Ibid.*, February 9, 1838; see also *Evening News*, May 19, 1848.
[21] *Ibid.*, April 15, 1859.
[22] *Southern Patriot*, October 21, 1819. Cardozo feared the power of dema-
gogic orators over the uneducated classes because "it is so easy to kindle the
passions of an ignorant multitude and so difficult to restrain or govern
them. . . . When mobs have sway, the empire of law is at an end." *Ibid.*,
October 5, 1819.
[23] *Ibid.*, April 19, 1821.

educated, property-owner class. He held that the extension
of general suffrage, by increasing the power of the masses,
had the effect of endangering the private property system.
Cardozo reacted strongly against working-class agitation,
and viewed unions as a "conspiracy against property," [24]
interfering with the effective operation of our business society, and precipitating hostility against property. He declared:

Our workmen have entered into extensive combinations to
overcome their employers, and a hostility has been engendered
against property and its wholesome influences. . . . Our people will, we fear, proceed step by step, from the exercise of one
act of unlawful power to another until a raging and unchecked
democracy shall overspread the land.[25]

He claimed that foreigners contaminated our workers
with radical ideas which undermined the social fabric of
the system:

Unless this spirit [of popular agitation of strikes] is checked,
it is impossible that the business of a large commercial society
like ours can be carried on. If on every imaginary supposition
that they are defrauded of the fair rewards of their labor, the
great body of our artisans are prompted to suspend their employments and strike for higher wages, a speedy disruption of
the whole fabric of our extensive commercial society must follow. . . . Property is employed in the form of capital in almost
every section of our land to set laborers and artisans to work
and to keep them at active employment, which shows the fatu-
ity with which the working classes are seized in thus interrupting the course of regular industry and striking at the very
source of their property and comfort. . . . Where is there room
therefore for this unreasonable jealousy of wealth—this warfare of the poor against the rich—this array of working classes
against those who are compelled to give them employment, at

[24] *Ibid.*, August 19, 1836.   [25] *Ibid.*

the current rate of remuneration, if they would not voluntarily starve themselves. . . . Strikes arrest the accumulation of capital—the growth of the fund that pays labour.[26]

Cardozo's philosophical views were closer to Smith's harmony of interest position than to the conflict of interest views of the Ricardian classical school. He stressed the harmony of interests between the various sectors and classes in the American society. He thought that there was a natural balance between agriculture, manufacturing, and commerce which would increase national wealth if not disturbed by tariffs, monopolies, or wars. Free commerce, by creating an interdependent mutually beneficial system, was regarded by Cardozo as a powerful means of civilizing countries, and a great leveler of distinctions and economic advantages between classes as well as nations. Cardozo viewed desire for luxuries as an important work stimulus. He said that commerce, by spreading luxuries, "has introduced a principle of mutual dependence that has equalized the advantages of the different classes of men. The poor are now as necessary to the rich as the rich is [sic] to the poor. . . . Wealth in one country is the parent of wealth in another." [27]

Cardozo thought of wealth and luxury as a gradual product of commerce and the industrious habits of the people. He said that the luxury of modern times was:

. . . pretty equally diffused through the various channels, provided by commerce, to the industrious and laboring classes of society. . . . It binds all parts of the modern social system in one beautiful and harmonious scheme of general wants. . . . The appetite for luxury or the love of expense is . . . one of the wisest provisions in the constitution of the modern social order. It prevents too great an inequality—it makes that grada-

[26] *Ibid.*, June 26, 1835. *Evening News*, March 16, 1854.
[27] *Southern Patriot*, August 6, December 31, 1825. See also *ibid.*, April 22, 1818.

tion of riches which is the peculiarity of . . . the commercial period. . . . The luxury of the few is even a benefit to these [masses].[28]

Cardozo believed that the normal operations of a competitive private-enterprise economy would produce a distribution of income which was not unreasonably inequitable. Although Cardozo held that real liberty could not exist as long as there was an extremely unequal division of the land, and attributed the high level of liberty in the United States to "the originally equal division of lands," he championed a "moderate concentration of wealth." [29] His attitude is evident in a Thanksgiving Day toast to "a fair distribution of property without inordinate wealth or abject poverty." [30] Cardozo's opposition to several Federal government measures like tariffs and banking was based in part on his belief that they tended to heighten the amount of natural inequality. Cardozo favored American inheritance laws providing for an equal distribution of land among the children (of intestates) as opposed to primogeniture, the dominant legal form in Europe. He held that the American legal system "forces the people of the United States into paths of strenuous activity in the pursuit of wealth," [31] and although culture and refinements were somewhat sacrificed, the oligarchic system of Europe was avoided.

Cardozo claimed that the private property system was more compatible with Southern than with Northern institutions. He said, "The increasing spirit of leveling equality is now a striking feature of Northern society. We are con-

[28] *Ibid.*, August 15, 1818.
[29] *Ibid.*, May 21, 1821. February 24, 1838. In the latter article Cardozo said, "All liberal culture, all refinement, all steady and sure increases of prosperity are the fruits of a moderate concentration of wealth and numbers."
[30] *Evening News*, November 5, 1845.
[31] *Southern Patriot*, August 20, 1836.

tent at the South to allow property its legitimate privileges and natural influences, and surround it with the
sanctities and safeguards of regular government." [32] Cardozo held that the South was more homogeneous in interest and sentiment than the North. He described the
political structure of the South:

The Southern states in form of government are democratical
—in internal organization they are oligarchial. . . . Were population at the South wholly or nearly unmixed, as to color and
caste, it might furnish more abundant elements of material
wealth, or perhaps, a wider range of general prosperity, but it
is scarcely questionable whether it would embrace as perfect
constituents of stability, order and repose. . . . The effect of
this is that we have no mobs . . . no large popular risings, no
agrarianism, no open contempt of law, no violence to those
who administer it. . . . All the tendencies of Northern society
are destructive.[33]

Cardozo's early reaction against an oligarchic structure appears to have been tempered by his later realization that
the oligarchic features of Southern society had the effect of
promoting social and political stability, albeit at the price
of a slackened growth rate.

Cardozo's reactions to the socialistic proposals of the
early nineteenth century ranged from polite disapproval to
caustic rejection, depending primarily on the immediacy
of their threat to the private-profit system. Since the principle of individual interest was the cornerstone of Cardozo's social philosophy, he found the Utopian socialist
emphasis on cooperation irrational and naïve. He labeled
Robert Owen a "system monger . . . [having] no concep-
tion of the simple harmony of the social machine. . . .
The rich would be rendered poor and the poor, poorer [in
Owen's scheme]." [34] Cardozo rejected Owen's notion that

[32] *Ibid.*, August 22, 1835. [33] *Evening News*, October 1, 1845.
[34] *Southern Patriot*, June 26, 1821.

the effects of the machine can be damaging to the laboring classes; he erroneously believed that Owen wanted to abolish the division of labor.

He also rejected Owen's idea that economic distress was caused when production exceeded consumption as a result of technological development. Cardozo accepted Say's Law as a long-run equilibrium model, although he acknowledged that production can exceed consumption in a short period. In rejecting Owen's overproduction thesis, Cardozo said, "Consumption is always the measure and limit of production and production of consumption." [35] Continued demand was necessary to induce the business man to maintain a certain production level. A rational capitalist would shift his capital from a low to a higher profitability sector. Although by philosophical inclination Cardozo was a classicist, his occupation as a journalist compelled him to deal with day-to-day events in which deviations from a balanced production-consumption model were the rule. This tended to impart to his analysis a wider range than the classicists employed (i.e., a short-run as well as long-run approach).

The nonrevolutionary character of Owen's Utopianism induced mild disapproval from Cardozo, while he predicted (correctly) that the New Harmony experiment would fail. He said:

To us it seems clear that his schemes are incompatible with the present state of society—its wants, its resources, its general improvement, its complicated interests, especially . . . the greatest triumph of civilization and commerce—the division of labor.[36]

Although Cardozo vigorously attacked working-class activity when directed against private property, he said that

_____
[35] *Ibid.,* July 21, 1820, also October 12, 13, 1819. This concept was discussed above, in Chapter Seven on business cycles.
[36] *Ibid.,* May 20, 1825.

the nonrevolutionary Utopian trade unions in England that attempted to put the unemployed to work by opening shops were a misguided but not a dangerous group.[37] Their ineffectualness was indicated by their repudiation of revolutionary methods and strikes for higher wages. Cardozo claimed that a plan for an equal sharing of profits by the workers and capitalists advocated by a Utopian socialist convention ("Industrial Convention") would equalize poverty rather than wealth.

The Industrial Convention . . . is a sworn foe to all employers. It advocates the cause of the laborer, but it denounces the class who give the laborer employment. . . . This opposition to employers is founded on the most mistaken view of the principle of equality and justice. . . . Is the capitalist entitled to no remuneration for this capital invested—for his risk of losses and ruin—for the energy and enterprise which he displays. . . . The world is governed by a system of compensation. . . . Let each be contented with his allotted station.[38]

At an earlier date, Cardozo had praised the establishment of Mechanics' Institutes for the Poor in England as a way of teaching the poor the folly of radical change and the necessity for accepting their status in the social system. They would be "taught to submit to temporary

[37] Cardozo said, "Their principles of association are too loose to produce results of any magnitude or importance. . . . They are guided by no systematic or well-defined plan of action. They can only be successful by convulsing the whole social order. But for this they want . . . organization . . . unity of design . . . leaders of ability . . . means of offensive operation." He claimed that the Utopian trade unionists confused capital and the circulating medium and did not understand that the organizing ability of the capitalist and some abstinence on his part are necessary for capital accumulation and profit-making. *Ibid.*, May 31, 1834.

[38] *Evening News*, October 28, 1845. The "Industrial Congress" was a fusion of two main (at times overlapping) groups: (1) Agrarians, such as George Evans, who agitated for a more liberal public lands policy (Western lands were seen as a refuge for the urban workers); (2) the Associationists, such as Parke Godwin, Arthur Brisbane, and William Channing, who were concerned with establishing a communistic commonwealth along Fourieristic lines.

privation of employment as the law of our social custom." [39]

During the revolutions of 1848 Cardozo feared that revolution for political rights would extend to a struggle over property rights. He considered the plan of the provisional government in France for regulation of industry as "an interference with the laws of the nature." He also thought of the laws of social relations between employers and employees as akin to fixed physical laws "beyond the pale of legislation," and believed that laws establishing wages, hours, and conditions of work would "undermine the whole fabric of industry reared by the spontaneous action of individuals . . . [and] terminates in the warfare of labor against capital." [40]

Cardozo held that enlightened self-interest was the key to progress, and that changes in the existing social and industrial arrangement of society would result in sacrificing the benefits of science and civilization. He attacked communism as a "universal leveller," [41] and extolled the virtues of the aggressive risk-taking entrepreneur operating in a competitive system. A society based on communism would achieve social equality at the price of increased poverty. In a discussion of Fourier, St. Simon, and Marshall Bugeaud, Cardozo said:

No social love can overcome the human motives that repel individuals from association on equal terms. The capitalist will not throw his riches into a common fund if his dividend does not, in promise at least, bear a just proportion to his contribution.[42]

[39] *Southern Patriot*, July 2, 1825. Cardozo also approved of Building and Loan Associations which he regarded essentially as savings banks to facilitate the purchase of homes by the workers. *Evening News*, August 1, 1850; October 20, 26, 1852; December 27, 1855. Cf. Cardozo, "Building and Loan Associations," *Southern Quarterly Review* (October, 1852), pp. 489–504.
[40] *Evening News*, April 4, 1848.   [41] *Ibid.*, April 6, 1848.
[42] *Ibid.*, April 20, 1848.

Cardozo was moderately sympathetic to St. Simon's scheme, as he thought that it combined cooperation and competition and rewarded the industrious and skillful person at a higher rate than the indolent and less skillful:

The distribution of the produce was to be in proportion to the capital, skill, industry, talent, and knowledge of the various contributors to the common fund. It is evident that this theory of communism makes the nearest approach to the present system of society. It combines association with competition. . . . It takes from man his great social right to employ his talent, his industry and his means in those modes which, according to individual judgment, will lead to the most advantageous results, but it still does not place the industrious and the slothful, the ignorant and the intelligent, the awkward and the skillful on the same level in the distribution of the fruits of common labor.[43]

Cardozo suggested colonization of the excess population in less crowded countries to relieve the economic distress of the European working classes. The alternative remedy of redistributing property would upset the "pre-existing social harmony." [44]

Cardozo drew a distinction between different types of strikes—those in which the workers are attempting to adjust the price of labor to the price of commodities, and those representing discontent with existing social arrangements. He was somewhat sympathetic to the former and wholly opposed to the latter.[45]

In an article indicating his ability often to transcend strictly sectional issues, Cardozo said, "The great social problem of the age is the true relation of capital to la-

[43] Ibid.   [44] Ibid., August 14, 1848.
[45] Ibid., March 1, 1853. Cardozo said that strikes (on one level) "are the symptoms of a struggle between capital and labor to adjust the remuneration of the latter in conformity with changes in the value of money."

bor." [46] He rejected strikes, cooperative schemes,[47] and government interference as remedies for obtaining adequate rewards for labor. The only acceptable method for labor to employ in order to obtain an adequate reward when prices were rising, according to Cardozo, was to appeal to the businessman's sense of justice.

The employers of labor must be brought into more intimate sympathy than at present with the employed. As the laborer is taught that strikes and combinations are finally injurious to his interests, so must the capitalist be impressed with the lesson, while his gains are permanently increasing from large additions to the currency, that it is his duty to remunerate labor correspondingly.[48]

The naïve optimism of Cardozo's suggested policy is in marked contrast with his insight that part of the worker's problem stems from the fact that "the market for labor is rarely understocked." [49]

The concept of gradualism is vital to an understanding of Cardozo's thought. He believed that statesmanship and patriotism should be concerned with controlling attempts to introduce rapid changes and with preventing disruptions of the social system. He said:

All sudden social transitions are ruinous. All solid and permanent improvement is made by slow changes. . . . We occupy an era that will not bear any large or sudden rupture of social and economic relations. Gradual changes preserve a kind of equilibrium in social arrangements. . . . Progressive amelioration . . . is the law of true social progress.[50]

[46] *Ibid.*, March 16, 1854.
[47] Cardozo rejected a proposal by a Southern newspaper to encourage the promotion of direct foreign trade to Europe through the cooperation of the merchant, planter, and farm classes. "The accumulation of capital, the formation of mercantile habits, the division of employment in conducting commercial operations, cannot be acquired by a combination of classes or individuals." *Ibid.*, February 26, 1852.
[48] *Ibid.*, March 16, 1854.
[49] *Ibid.* This idea, unfortunately, was not developed.
[50] *Ibid.*, April 23, 1853. Cardozo viewed the large-scale emigration to the California gold fields as socially disrupting. *Ibid.*, October 14, 1845.

Cardozo minimized the transitional problems caused by the increased use of machinery, and optimistically thought that increased capital accumulation would ameliorate the condition of the working class. He thought that technological improvements would create more employment and increase real wages. Cardozo adopted the Ricardian view that the relative scarcity of labor vis à vis land in the United States provided a strong incentive to the profit-maximizing capitalist to substitute machinery for high-priced labor, accounting thereby for the high level of American ingenuity in the mechanical arts.[51] He rejected Say's plan of setting up public works projects for the technologically displaced, on the grounds that such projects would reduce private employment.

The transition to mechanization, he felt, would be so gradual that any immediate loss would be minimal or nonexistent.[52] He took the view that the increased use of machinery would not upset the balance between production and consumption, except possibly for a brief period, because the increased output at lower cost (and price) would raise the demand for the product, while the increased derived demand for labor would stimulate population. Cardozo's faith in the cumulative growth potential of a "natural" society like America led him to the conclusion that both profits and wages would boundlessly advance in the process of American economic development.

The classical concept of diminishing returns and the stationary state were almost completely rejected. Cardozo claimed that "improvements in science and skill are constantly progressive."[53] The dismal conclusions postulated

[51] *Ibid.*, June 10, 1846.

[52] Cardozo, *Notes*, pp. 58–62. The same optimistic note can be found in Henry Carey's writings. He said, "The improvements in the production of commodities of all descriptions are of the same gradual and beautiful character, by which every member of the community is benefited, while none experience inconvenience." Carey, I, 208.

[53] *Southern Patriot*, August 9, 1819.

by Malthus in his theory of population were seen not as a
law of nature but rather the "result of an imperfect social
organization." [54] He stated:

[I]f the institution of primogeniture were abolished wherever
it prevails, with every species of monopoly, supposing the
security of person and property complete [a critical assumption in Cardozo's system], and the public burthens moderate,
the rate of increase in the production of food might greatly
augment, whilst the more ample leisure for instruction permitted to the laboring classes . . . might give much greater
room than at present for the action of the check entitled by
Mr. Malthus, *moral restraint.*[55]

Cardozo was in favor of as much economic growth as was
compatible with social stability. A liberal land policy
which fostered the rapid growth of the West was held in
disfavor by Cardozo because of its disruptive social influence.[56] He viewed the rapid emigration as upsetting family and community stability as well as destroying industrious habits and enterprising activities. Cardozo appeared to
have implicitly linked emigration with speculation, which
he considered a pernicious influence. Although his line of
demarcation was imprecise, Cardozo seemed to have been
concerned with differentiating between this type of "speculation" and legitimate enterprise, of which he was a
strong advocate.

He held that the rapid settlement of Western lands with

[54] Cardozo, *Notes*, pp. 123–24. The same notion can be found in an earlier
article by George Tucker, "On Density of Population," *The Portfolio*,
August, 1815, p. 172. Tucker later switched to a more pro-Malthusian position. The most thorough treatment of the reaction of early Southern economists to Malthusian population doctrines is Joseph J. Spengler, "Population Theory in the Ante-Bellum South," *Journal of Southern History*,
August, 1936, pp. 360–89. He presents the view that Malthusian population theory was used by Southern writers to justify their system of slavery.
[55] Cardozo, *Notes*, pp. 124–25.
[56] *Southern Patriot*, March 10, 30, 1819; January 15, 1820; *Evening News*,
February 7, 1850.

the use of cheap credit created a false prosperity which benefited the speculator rather than the independent farmer. He therefore favored selling public lands in relatively small plots to be cultivated by the buyer, requiring cash payments to discourage undue land speculation:

These lands should be offered for sale at longer intervals and no company or association of individuals should be allowed to purchase for the purpose of selling it out again; but a condition of every purchase should be that the purchaser himself cultivate and improve the territory he buys.[57]

Cardozo also rejected the Turner "escape-valve" theory that the existence of the moving Western frontier aided the urban masses:

[T]here is great doubt, if land were obtained without price or effort, whether the beneficiaries will be found in our overcrowded cities. The rural districts will, in all probability . . . furnish almost the whole of the emigrants to the new land. . . . The squalid masses steeped in poverty and crime will remain on the spots they now occupy.[58]

In the early period, Cardozo was vitally concerned with the natural evolutionary development of the powerful economic potential of the entire country, in which the agricultural system of the South would blend harmoniously with the commercial-manufacturing system of the North. He tried to demonstrate that the interests of both sections would be hurt by the tariff, and that only a small group would benefit from the misallocation of the nation's resources created by the tariff. Cardozo's approach on the tariff issue was more moderate and national than that of most of the Southern leaders. He thought that the benefits of a national Union indicated that the tariff ought to be a

[57] *Southern Patriot*, April 15, 1836. See also *ibid.*, March 18, July 22, 1820; January 5, 1828.
[58] *Evening News*, April 16, 1852.

compromisable issue for the South. In this early period, his leanings toward the policy of the national government are shown in this statement: "If the State governments are annihilated at once (although we should be sorry to see such a result) our liberties would be as safe then as they are now . . . by the continuance." [59] At this time Cardozo took an organismic view of society, similar to that of the Northern "American School," which included Raymond, Carey, and Phillips. Compromise and mutual adjustments were required to obtain the benefits of a Union:

There are various and even conflicting interests to be adjusted, to which end there are concessions and sacrifices frequently made from one part of the country to the other in that spirit of compromise which is the conservative policy of our Union.[60]

He was more favorably inclined toward the Supreme Court than were many Southerners who viewed the institution as attempting to overthrow the system of states' rights. He spoke of the Court as an instrument of "harmony and peace, and not of usurpation or aristocracy . . . [which maintains] the powers of the general and state government in that save balance and harmony which is so difficult in the reciprocal exercise of co-ordinate authority." [61]

Cardozo was a staunch unionist in the 1832 South Carolina nullification movement. Despite his opposition to the protective tariff, Cardozo vigorously reacted against this movement, thereby arousing the enmity of Calhoun and McDuffie. The Charleston press was split: The *Mercury* was the voice of the nullifiers, while Cardozo's *Southern Patriot* and the *Courier* backed the Union group. Car-

[59] *Southern Patriot*, October 30, 1821. Cardozo noted in this editorial that the *Richmond Enquirer* had accused him of being an "ultra-federalist."
[60] *Ibid.*, January 11, 1822.
[61] *Ibid.*, April 3, 29, 1819. See also *ibid.*, March 25, 27, 1819; April 7, 1821.

dozo's was a voice of moderation in a situation of potential violence.

In a series of well-written, moderate, legal-sounding editorials,[62] Cardozo urged the citizens of Charleston to reject the nullifiers' position. He critically discussed and dismissed Calhoun's view that the Constitution was a compact between states, which, as distinct political entities, therefore had the right to determine the extent of their obligations. Cardozo claimed that "An act which creates an obligation [e.g., the formation of a federal union of many states under a constitution] is entirely dissimilar to that which determines its extent." [63] If the states assumed the power of determining the extent of their obligations under the Constitution, it would be similar to "assuming the right to sit as judges in their own case." [64] He denounced the doctrines of the nullifiers as unconstitutional, "vile metaphysics," [65] and a nonpeaceful remedy.

Although the ostensible cause of nullification appeared to be the tariff issue, it is quite possible that the deteriorating economic position of the South lay behind the shift of South-Carolina politics from an early nationalist orientation to a nullificationist attitude. As historian Frederick J. Turner stated:

With cotton at 30 cents South Carolina was nationalistic in 1816; with it at 20 cents in 1820 she found the tariff a grievance; with it at 14¾ cents in 1824 she found the tariff unconstitutional; and with it at 9 cents in 1827 she prepared to nullify.[66]

The growing sectionalism of Cardozo's views reflected the inability of the Industrial Revolution to take root in

[62] *Ibid.*, September 7, 22, 25, 28; October 6, 11, 19, 1832.
[63] *Ibid.*, September 28, 1832. [64] *Ibid.* [65] *Ibid.*, October 6, 1832.
[66] Cited by Wallace, p. 402.

the South. He was a stronger advocate of free trade than of a general policy of laissez-faire, because the economic well-being of the Southern plantation economy was more dependent on the former than on the latter. In the early period of his writings, Cardozo's Federalist leanings were accompanied by an extolling of the virtues of a competitive, laissez-faire economy. By the 1850s his sectional leanings were accompanied by a willingness to accept considerable legislative interference with the working of the economy. He increasingly viewed the spread of Northern democracy as a threat to Southern security. He began to consider competition as more of a problem than monopoly. Cardozo appeared to favor as much monopoly as was needed to effectively combine capital, with restraints imposed by the public through legislation. He viewed the competitive struggle to establish railroad lines, banks, and insurance companies as producing disequilibrium and waste in the economy. Competition would lead to a faster rate of capital accumulation, but he feared that this would tend to create business crises. Monopolistic conditions would result in greater stability and a more gradual rate of development:

[T]he great social problem . . . [is] to open industrial pursuits of every kind to the desire for profit—to remove the fetters placed by monopoly on enterprise—without giving to such desire for profit and enterprise, action too boundless and unrestrained. . . . The line of division is so indistinct between too much and too little freedom in human pursuits, that where regulation and restraint should begin and where end is a question of great nicety. . . . We think the over-balance of evil in our day is with excessive competition. . . . The practical conclusion is that legislators must assume the trust and responsibility of enlarging monopoly and checking competition, in each case, according to circumstances. . . . If there are charters presented which profess to combine capital in sufficiently large aggregates to effect some scheme professedly of public utility, is it not within the function of legislation to limit them in number as well as to provide safeguards against fraud in management.[67]

This view—that legislators have the responsibility of controlling the mixture of monopoly and competition—represents a considerable movement away from Cardozo's earlier and purer laissez-faire philosophy. It is important, however, not to overemphasize the importance of this change. It is indicative of his willingness to enlarge the area of exceptions to laissez-faire rather than to abandon it.

When it appeared to be necessary to choose between growth and stability, Cardozo chose stability. This in essence was Cardozo's conservative vision of life, influenced to a large degree by the realities of the Southern political economy.

[67] *Evening News,* October 9, 1856.

TEN

===

Summary and Evaluation

CARDOZO'S sensitive position as a journalist enabled him to help shape Southern thought and political alignments on many of the important issues of the day—the tariff, slavery, public lands policy, banking, nullification, internal improvements, the union movement, and socialism. His writings reveal a blending of practical and theoretical aspects of the political economy. His "front-line" occupation provided a continual inducement for relating economic theory to the historical process; he examined problems in their nineteenth-century setting, whose predominant characteristic was the agrarian nature of the Southern plantation-slave economy and the growing commercialism of the Northern economy. Cardozo's cogent commentary on these practical problems, as well as more theoretical aspects of economic doctrine, reveals Southern intellectual thought at its highest level.

Cardozo's writings embrace a period characterized by a rapid but unbalanced rate of development, an unequal distribution of the fruits of development, an unprecedented increase of population, a gradual but eventually critical intensification of sectional conflict, and the settling of an immense and rich country. To focus on Cardozo is to see this period of critical and thoroughgoing change from the viewpoint of a highly articulate representative of the Southern antebellum *Weltanschauung.*

He made a valiant effort to raise himself above the din of partisan politics; yet his emancipation was partial rather than complete, more of form than of essence. He desired to search for the truths of the political economy as well as to advance the political and social interests of a section whose agrarian economy continued to lag behind the diversified, commercial-manufacturing economy of the North. His perspective ultimately was national only to the extent that nationalism was compatible with the interests of the South. The slave issue, unlike the tariff question, was viewed as uncompromisable, and secession was preferable to allowing interference with such essential Southern private property. Cardozo's "national approach" to the tariff was in at least partial contradiction with his sectional ideological commitment to defend slavery.

He championed the rise of private enterprise and diversified development in a society in which slavery was the dominant form of socioeconomic organization. The advancement of capitalism and slavery were seen as compatible aims. Cardozo's main contribution on the slavery question was his view—a minority one—that surplus slaves and unemployed whites could be profitably used in the development of Southern manufacturing. He thought that this diversification would strengthen the structure of the Southern social system. The less moderate Southerners, disunionists per se who favored immediate secession, were generally against this practice. Cardozo claimed that the development of manufacturing would be easier for the South than for the North, since the benefits of accumulated technology would be available to the South. He also held that the cost of labor and raw materials would be lower in the South.

Cardozo rejected the contention of many fellow Southerners that the economic distress of the South was primarily due to Northern exploitation through a protective tariff. He saw the economic difficulties of the South as a more complicated phenomenon, including the misdirection of capital caused by excessive investments in land and slaves, the exodus of capital and labor to the West and Southwest, and absenteeism.

He was in accord with the English classical economists' policy of laissez-faire and free trade. Free trade, in particular, was beneficial to the Southern economy. Interestingly, the English political economy implicitly justified a policy aimed at reducing the power of the landed classes. On a theoretical level it therefore posed a threat to the Southern plantation economy by suggesting that the specific interest of the planter was not in harmony with the general interest. His attack on Ricardian rent theory had the social effect of justifying the position of the Southern landed interests.

Cardozo desired a society in which agriculture would not be subordinated to commerce and manufacturing— hence the need for gradual, balanced development. His partial rejection of Say's Law and his theory that business cycles may be caused by a disproportionate rate of investment in fixed capital fitted his conservative societal perspective. The intellectual and social content of ideas tended to blend.

was expressed in modern terms: An increase of the money supply results in price rises only if there is a demand for the use of the money. Cardozo held that currency generally adjusted to the demands of commerce, rather than vice versa. He was among the first to point out the advantages and defects of an elastic money supply. It provided funds for development or for lessening the impact of a panic, but when pushed to excess it promoted instability. He anticipated some of the ideas associated with the Federal Reserve System. He advocated giving power to independent public commissioners to expand or contract the money supply as conditions warranted—a power quite similar to that exercised by the Board of Governors in today's Federal Reserve System.

Cardozo was one of the few people in pre-Civil War America whose economic ideas were presented with the same high level of subtlety, precision, and technical competence that characterized Ricardian and Malthusian analysis. Like adherents of these schools, he was influenced by his environment. The quality of his thinking on economic topics, however, deserves close attention in its own right. He was an economic scientist as well as a partisan of Southern interests.

This study suggests the critical importance of examining the intellectual content of ideas in conjunction with the social forces which helped to shape them.

Cardozo's writings, in common with most early American writers on political economy, are in marked contrast to the pessimistic character of English classical economic thought. The latter is based on an acceptance of the following: (1) the law of diminishing returns; (2) the Ricardian rent theory, in which the landlord reaps the benefit of producing more food at higher cost to feed a rising population; (3) the Malthusian population theory; (4) an inverse wage-profit relationship, in which in the long run equilibrium wages tend toward subsistence and profits toward a minimum; and (5) some version of the labor theory of value.

Like most of the early American economists, Cardozo reveals a more optimistic temper. Conditioned by the dynamic environment around him, he rejected the classical theories.

Cardozo saw the American scene as one with unlimited investment opportunities. Malthusian population theory and the law of diminishing returns were rejected as not applicable to conditions in America. He thought that technology—the key strategic factor in his growth model—and the abundance of fertile land would bring about increasing returns, so that labor and capital would both benefit from rising output. The basic conflict over distributive shares, postulated by Ricardo, did not exist in Cardozo's expansionary model of the American economic system. The returns to labor and capital need not vary inversely in a "natural" society like America. Cardozo was the first to present the view that, in the course of economic development, wages rise relatively and absolutely while profits increase absolutely.

Cardozo also was the first American economist systematically to attack Ricardian differential rent theory. While the latter was based on the labor theory of value, Cardozo's rent analysis was presented in terms of supply and demand. Unlike Ricardo, Cardozo attributed the rise in rent to monopolistic elements which restrict supply, technological improvements that lower production costs, and increases in the demand for the commodity. Monopoly rent in Cardozo's scheme is due to society's institutional arrangements rather than a law of nature (as in Ricardo's analysis). He viewed rent as the interest return on capital invested in land.

The prospect of profits was the strategic variable for Cardozo in determining whether or not certain land would be cultivated. If prices and profits are high, it makes the additional expense of cultivating inferior lands worth while. This reversed Ricardian analysis; for Ricardo, the causal arrow ran from the increased expense of cultivating inferior land to the increased price of agricultural commodities. There are several dynamic elements in Cardozo's rent presentation. He was aware that the relative expenditure, in relation to the time period of recoupment, was an important factor in deciding whether or not to cultivate a certain piece of land. His analysis, like that of the modern day, stressed the crucial role of supply and demand in both the commodity and factor markets.

Another of Cardozo's important contributions to economic thought was his treatment of business cycles. Although he accepted Say's Law as a "norm," Cardozo presented rich insights in his descriptions of the deviations of the actual economy from the theoretical, classical, long-run equilibrium model. In marked contrast to the classical economists, he emphasized the economically disruptive effects involved in the shift from a war to a postwar economy. The increase in the productive forces during the stimulating wartime period outstripped consumption in the postwar period. A lack of effective demand was seen as

the cause of a general business depression. A credit sy in which businessmen make purchases in anticipatic increased sales heightens the instability.

Cardozo understood that rising consumption, r than increased savings, had an expansive effect o economy. He saw capital accumulation resulting reduced consumption as having a less beneficial effec when it takes place out of rising revenue, becaus former may upset the balance between productio consumption. Attempts to economize expenditures a recession were seen as worsening conditions. He nized the limited effectiveness of monetary policy in ing about a recovery. He stressed the interconnected different sectors of the economy and the need for taining their gradual, proportional development. ings by one sector are a prerequisite for profit-maki where. Cardozo's thinking in this area clearly fores much of later thought.

In the continual debate between controlled and faire banking, Cardozo tended to favor the forr though his views on the proper relationship of gove and banking underwent several critical change banking in the United States was characterized by expansion of credit based on slim reserves. This c aided the over-all process of economic developm aggravated the instability of the system. Except fo period when he favored free banking, Cardozo fe: the excessive use of paper money resulting from f petition in banking violated the principles c money and banking. It fostered overexpansion a speculation, which tended to bring about extrem business cycle. Cardozo therefore favored some so lic control over the banks' money-creation ability.

Cardozo's treatment of the quantity theory

APPENDIX I

Causes of the 1837 Crisis

A RECENT study by R. C. O. Matthews of the business cycle centering on the crisis of 1837 [1] (viewed from the British side) offers an interesting comparison with Cardozo's analysis, written at the time of the crisis. Matthews' focus is Great Britain, but the interdependence of the British and American economies led to an examination of the nature of their interaction. [2]

Matthews held that internal developments specific to the United States—particularly the speculative land boom, loose banking, and rising cotton prices—were the main initiating cause of the 1837 crisis, although subsequent

[1] R. C. O. Matthews, *A Study in Trade Cycle History: Economic Fluctuations in Great Britain, 1833–1842.*

[2] Matthews said that "The state of the American market was therefore the most important single factor in bringing prosperity or depression to British export industries." The value of their exports to the United States were about 15% of their total exports. The American economy was likewise sensitive to changes in the state of economic activity in England.

reactions by England aggravated the effects. While foreign capital was of significant importance in financing internal improvements, it was not as critical as American bank capital, according to Matthews. He said:

The initial propelling force lay in internal developments in the United States itself. Our conclusion is then, that although the American boom was encouraged and influenced in its character by events in Britain, in the most important respects and especially in its timing, it was an independent development.[3]

As for the proximate cause of the crisis, Matthews said:

What brought about the crash was the increasing difficulty of obtaining funds to support a speculative movement which up to that time had been feeding on itself. This credit stringency was due partly to the change in the policy of the administration represented by the Specie Circular [requiring cash payments on the sales of public land] and the Deposit Act [distributing surplus revenue to the states] and partly to an adverse movement of the balance of payments resulting from high imports and diminishing willingness on the part of foreigners to fill the gap by lending.[4]

Although Cardozo agreed that the 1837 crisis started in the United States and reacted on England, he considered the events prior to 1833 (the starting year in Matthews' analysis) as containing the early roots of the later crisis. The depleted inventories, low interest rates, low prices, large accumulations of loanable funds, lowering of the tariff, were the factors which led to an increase in the speculative purchases of foreign imports, which sparked the upturn. Cardozo considered loose banking as a symptom and aggravator of a speculative situation, but not its originator. He said that "increased issues of paper money are never the origin of a speculative rise of prices. . . . This rise has its source in commercial events which lead to a de-

[3] *Ibid.*, p. 55.   [4] *Ibid.*, p. 60.

mand for more credit." [5] The United States demand for loans stimulated speculation in England, but the latter's economy was ready for such a stimulus because of the low profits, prices, and rate of interest that prevailed in the previous period of general stagnation.

Unlike Matthews, Cardozo regarded the rising price of raw cotton in 1833 as a result of the prior increase in the American demand for British manufactured cotton goods, rather than a trigger of the expansion.

Matthews' conclusions that the boom originated in the United States and spread to England would have been strengthened by a consideration of the factors taken into account by Cardozo. Cardozo certainly would have seconded Matthew's statement that "The slump was the logical consequence of the boom." [6]

[5] *Southern Patriot,* May 30, 1837. Cardozo noted in this article that credit expansion based on the gold inflow gave a "fresh stimulus to speculation in merchandise, public lands," etc.

[6] Matthews, p. 217.

APPENDIX II

Slavery and Economic Growth

A QUESTION has appeared in recent discussions over whether the use of slaves in agriculture in the antebellum period was the most profitable use of Southern capital. Some students contend that Southern agriculture remained undiversified, and slaves were used only sparingly in manufacturing, because higher profits could be made by concentrating on the production of cotton. In the prosperous fifties, in particular, these students held that the employment of slaves in agriculture was a more profitable use of this type of capital (i.e. slave labor) than any alternative economic activity in which an owner could have employed his capital.[1]

The Conrad-Meyer study attempted to compare the

[1] Alfred H. Conrad and John R. Meyer, "Economics of Slavery in the Ante-Bellum South," *Journal of Political Economy*, April, 1958, pp. 95–130. See also Robert Evans, Jr., "The Economics of American Negro Slavery, 1830–1860" (unpublished doctoral dissertation, University of Chicago, 1960).

productivity of capital in the form of slaves (as used in cotton production) with the productivity of capital in other forms as evidenced by the annual average returns on prime commercial paper (bonds and stocks in manufacturing and public utility concerns). Their study does not deal with two closely allied and important questions: (1) the relative profitability of slave labor in agriculture and manufacturing; and (2) the relative efficiency of slave labor as opposed to free white labor.

Conrad and Meyer stressed the importance of a system of regional specialization in the antebellum South, in which slaves were bred and exported from depleted, low-yield soil areas to higher yielding land areas. This allocation system provided an adequate labor supply for cotton producing sections, as well as capital gains to the slave-exporting states. They claimed that "the rising trend of slave prices coupled with a growing slave population is in and of itself strong evidence of the profitability of slavery." [2] The argument that slavery resulted in a loss of capital that might have gone into industrialization and diversification was rejected, and it was further claimed that Southerners specialized in cotton rather than diversification because of the high profits obtainable from cotton specialization.

In analyzing this position, it is well to keep in mind that the profitability of cotton production, on which the profitability of slavery hinged, was a cyclical phenomenon which depended primarily on foreign demand. Before the crisis year of 1819, cotton prices were at extremely profitable levels. Their course was generally downward from 1819 to 1832, except for a short-lived recovery in 1823, followed by a rise from 1832 to the crisis of 1837. From 1838 to 1848 the general price trend was downward, except for a rise in 1845–1846. A sharp rise occurred in 1849, and although

[2] Conrad and Meyer, "Economics of Slavery in the Ante-Bellum South," p. 119.

dropping considerably in 1851, prices rose fairly steadily thereafter until 1860.

Generally speaking, the periods from 1819 to 1832 and from 1838 to 1848 were ones of considerable distress for the Southern planters. Profits were made, but at considerably reduced levels, particularly on the depleted soils of the Old South.[3] Prices reflected to a large degree the cyclical swings in the foreign market. Since the average costs of cotton cultivation under slave labor were only slightly less than they were under free wage labor, the type of labor system was a minor direct determinant of the profitability of cotton production.[4]

The effects of the fluctuating profitability of cotton production were reinforced by the existence of high fixed-costs in the cotton slave-plantation economy. The supply of slaves to the individual plantation owner was more or less inelastic in the short run. Although profits were not sufficiently high to earn much of an excess over costs in periods of low prices, the high fixed-cost burden tended to reduce the mobility of capital, despite the existence of considerable profit differentials between agriculture and manufacturing.

Under capitalism, high-cost labor tends to lead to the introduction of labor-saving technology; under slavery, this

[3] James Hammond, a prominent antebellum South Carolinian statesman, noted the extreme regional variation in profits from agricultural operations. When the average price of cotton was $.08 per pound, he claimed it would result in a meager profit of only $61 per hand in South Carolina compared with $110 to $140 per hand on the richer lands. Referred to by Chauncey S. Boucher, "The Ante-Bellum Attitude of South Carolina Towards Manufacturing and Agriculture," *Washington University Humanistic Studies*, III, Part 2, No. 2 (April, 1916), p. 265.

[4] It is possible that the advantages of the plantation unit may be somewhat understated. Genovese claims, "Planters siphoned off much of the yeoman's cotton profits by charges for ginning and other services and through a cotton market that operated to give big producers higher prices than small producers." Eugene Genovese, *The Political Economy of Slavery* (New York, Pantheon, 1966), p. 283.

did not occur since labor was merely another form of capital, and a highly nonliquid form at that. The period of the 1840s, in which supply increased faster than demand, is a case in point. If one assumes a fairly stable market demand, the mobility of labor is less necessary for the proper functioning of capitalism. A slave-labor system under these conditions would be relatively compatible with capitalism. But a stable market demand was precisely the condition which did not prevail in the cotton market.

It is quite possible that the rigidity of structure of the Southern economy may have aggravated its economic problems. The relatively inflexible production structure accentuated the severity of price fluctuations by the tendency to maintain production even in periods of falling demand.[5] Cotton was still the main crop in South Carolina in 1860, despite its diminished profitability over a long period. The lack of mobility of Southern capital from agriculture to manufacturing in certain period was not due to high profits in agriculture, but to cultural and institutional rigidities. A shift of resources from agriculture to manufacturing in periods when there appeared to be "overproduction" would have had a favorable effect on economic growth in a double sense: (1) If Negro slaves were used, it might have made agriculture more profitable by decreasing supply and increasing prices. (2) If underemployed whites were used, any increase of production would have meant a net increase in society's wealth. The existence of a high rate of disguised unemployment among the poor whites because of the restricted opportunities in a plantation-slave labor economy is an example of the high social cost of that system.

[5] Historically this argument also appears to apply to agriculture in a free-labor market, but to a considerably less degree. Certainly the exodus from agriculture to other sectors in periods of adversity has been more pronounced under capitalism than under slavery. This makes for a relatively more flexible operation in the former than in the latter system.

A major fault of the Conrad-Meyer article is that it tended to examine slavery as an economic institution divorced from its accompanying status as a social institution. Manufacturing and capitalism did not take root in the South, because of economic and social reasons. On a social level, the omnipotence of the plantation system discouraged the application of entrepreneural talent as well as the use of slaves or poor whites in nonagricultural pursuits. On an economic level the growth of a diversified economy was hindered by the lack of a sufficient market for manufactured products in the South. Slavery reinforced the agrarian nature of the Southern economy and created a maldistribution of wealth.

In rebuttal of the Conrad-Meyer study, Dowd claimed that slavery "was a deterrent to economic growth despite the fact of its profitability." [6] He said that the slave system prevented the evolution of the kind of rationality associated with industrial capitalism. In discussions of the relative profitability of slavery, it is necessary to distinquish between the private and social aspects of the question. The beneficiaries of the plantation-slave system constituted a very small proportion of the Southern population. Although this group found the cultivation of cotton based on slave labor profitable in the 1850s when world demand was at a high level, the restricted opportunities of the masses indicated that the social cost of the slave-labor system was also high. According to Dowd, the plantation system squeezed out the small farmer, and in effect stunted the growth of a middle class. [7]

The existence of a large depressed income group—slaves and poor whites—prevented balanced growth. Although a

[6] Douglas Dowd, "Communication," *Journal of Political Economy*, October, 1958, p. 444.
[7] Douglas Dowd, "A Comparative Analysis of Economic Development in the American West and South," *Journal of Economic History*, XVI, December, 1956, p. 565.

surplus was earned from cotton plantation operations, it had little effect on economic development. As a short-run picture, Conrad and Meyer's model has considerable validity (from the point of view of the slave owner). A critical difficulty arises, however, in ascertaining the degree of profitability of slavery. The question of the economies of scale becomes interwoven with that of the relative efficiency of slave and free labor. It is quite possible that slaved-based agricultural production was profitable only because the economies of large-scale production—particularly in sugar and rice, and to a lesser degree in cotton— overcame the relative inefficiency of slave labor. Large-scale production based on free labor would undoubtedly have been considerably more profitable. Even if we grant, however, that Conrad and Meyer have adequately established their case that the use of slaves in agriculture was profitable to the plantation owner, their treatment is nevertheless inadequate because of their neglect of the accompanying social costs or the question of economic growth. By abstracting from the ability of a diversified economy to create external economies, they are prevented from dealing with the cumulative nature of development in a diversified economy, and the cumulative reinforcement of poverty in an undiversified economy. The great underutilization of resources of the Southern plantation economy, particularly the labor of a poor white class, made it inefficient from the aspect of growth, even though it may have been efficient on the level of profitability to some of the individual holders of slave capital.

The analytical tool employed by Conrad and Meyer was neoclassical equilibrium analysis. Because of its static frame of reference, it is ill-equipped for examining socio-economic long-run problems of growth. They have structured a paper of considerable worth and validity for a universe of limited applicability.

Bibliography

BOOKS AND PAMPHLETS

Boucher, Chauncey S. *The Nullification Controversy in South Carolina*. Chicago, University of Chicago Press, 1916.

Cardozo, Jacob N. *Notes on Political Economy*. Charleston, A. E. Miller, 1826. Reprint, New York, Kelley, 1960.

————. *An Oration on the Literary Character, Delivered on the Anniversary of the Methulogic Society, 1st October, 1811*. Charleston, Franklin Head, 1811.

————. *A Plan of Financial Relief*. Addressed to the Legislature of Georgia and Confederate States Congress. Atlanta, J. H. Seals, 1863.

————. *Reminiscences of Charleston*. Charleston, J. Walker, 1866.

————. *The Tariff: Its True Character and Effects Practically Illustrated*. Charleston, A. E. Miller, 1830.

Carey, Henry. *Principles of Political Economy*. Philadelphia, Carey, Lea and Blanchard, 1838.

Clark, Washington, A. *The History of the Banking Institutions Organized in South Carolina Prior to 1860*. Columbia, The Historical Commission of South Carolina, 1922.

Cooper, Thomas. *Lectures on the Elements of Political Economy*. Columbia, D. E. Sweeny, 1826.

Dewey, Davis R. *Financial History of the United States*, 6th ed. New York, Longmans Green, 1918.

Dorfman, Joseph. *The Economic Mind in American Civilization*. Vols. I, II, III. New York, Viking, 1946.

Gregg, William. *Essays on Domestic Industry*. Charleston, Burges and James, 1845.

Hammond, Bray. *Banks and Politics in America from the Revolution to the Civil War.* Princeton, Princeton University Press, 1957.

Hawk, Emory. *Economic History of the South.* New York, Prentice-Hall, 1936.

Hesseltine, William B. *A History of the South (1607–1936).* New York, Prentice-Hall, 1936.

King, William L. *The Newspaper Press of Charleston.* Charleston, Edward Perry Book Press, 1872.

Lauderdale, Earl of. *An Inquiry into the Nature and Origin of Public Wealth and into the Means and Causes of Its Increase,* 2nd ed. Edinburgh, Archibald Constable, 1819.

Malthus, Thomas. *Principles of Political Economy.* Reprint, 2nd ed. New York, Kelley, 1951.

Matthews, R. C. O. *A Study in Trade-Cycle History: Economic Fluctuatons in Great Britain, 1833–1842.* Cambridge, Cambridge University Press, 1954.

Miller, Harry E. *Banking Theories in the United States Before 1860.* Cambridge, Harvard University Press, 1927.

Mints, Lloyd W. *A History of Banking Theory in Great Britain and the United States.* Chicago, University of Chicago Press, 1945.

O'Connor, Michael J. L. *Origins of Academic Economics in the United States.* New York, Columbia University Press, 1944.

Paglin, Morton. *Malthus and Lauderdale: The Anti-Ricardian Tradition.* New York, Kelley, 1961.

Raymond, Daniel. *Elements of Poltical Economy.* Baltimore, Fielding Lucas Jr., 1823.

Ricardo, David. *Principles of Political Economy and Taxation.* New York, Dutton, 1957.

Rippy, J. Fred. *Joel Roberts Poinsett, Versatile American.* Durham, Duke University Press, 1935.

Rothbard, Murray N. *The Panic of 1819: Reactions and Policies.* New York, Columbia University Press, 1962.

Russel, Robert R. *Economic Aspects of Southern Sectionalism, 1840–1861.* Urbana, University of Illinois Press, 1924.

Schultz, Harold L. *Nationalism and Sectionalism in South Carolina, 1852–1860.* Durham, Duke University Press, 1950.

Smith, Adam. *An Inquiry into the Nature and Causes of the Wealth of Nations.* New York, Modern Library, 1937.

Smith, Alfred G., Jr. *Economic Readjustment of an Old Cotton State: South Carolina, 1820–1860.* Columbia, University of South Carolina Press, 1958.

Snowden, Yates. *Notes on Labor Organization in South Carolina, 1742–1861.* Columbia, Bulletin of the University of South Carolina, 1914.

Taussig, Frank W. *The Tariff History of the United States,* 8th ed. New York, Putnam, 1931.

Teilhac, Ernest. *Pioneers of American Economic Thought in the Nineteenth Century.* Translated by E. A. J. Johnson. New York, Macmillan, 1936.

Tucker, George. *The Law of Wages, Profits, and Rent Investigated.* Philadelphia, E. L. Carey and A. Hart, 1837.

Turner, John R. *The Ricardian Rent Theory in Early American Economics.* New York, New York University Press, 1921.

Van Deusen, John G. *Economic Bases of Disunion in South Carolina.* New York, Columbia University Press, 1928.

Viner, Jacob. *Studies in the Theory of International Trade.* New York, Harper, 1937.

Wallace, David D. *South Carolina: A Short History, 1520–1948.* Chapel Hill, University of North Carolina Press, 1951.

ARTICLES AND PERIODICALS

Boucher, Chauncey S. "The Ante-Bellum Attitude of South Carolina Towards Manufacturing and Agriculture," *Washington University Humanistic Studies,* III, Part 2, No. 2 (April, 1916).

Brody, Alexander. "J. N. Cardozo—American Economist," *Historia Judaica,* Part 2 (October, 1953).

Buck, Paul H. "The Poor Whites of the Ante-Bellum South," *American Historical Review* (October, 1925).

Callender, Guy S. "The Early Transportation and Banking Enterprises of the States in Relation to the Growth of Corporations," *Quarterly Journal of Economics*, XVII (1903). Reprinted by Joseph T. Lambie and Richard Clemence in *Economic Change in America*. Harrisburg, Stackpole, 1954.

Cardozo, Jacob N. "Ancient and Modern Oratory," *The Southern Review* (May, 1830).

————. "Building and Loan Association," *The Southern Quarterly Review* (October, 1852).

————. (Ed.) *Evening News* (Charleston). 1845–1856.

————. "Essay on Banking and Currency," *Bankers' Magazine and Statistical Register* (March, 1869).

————. "The Government and the Currency," *The Southern Quarterly Review* (September, 1850).

————. "Growth and Consumption of Cotton," *DeBow's Review* (August, 1856).

————. "The Growth and Consumption of Cotton," *Charleston Courier* (May 31, 1845).

————. "The Memorial of the Chamber of Commerce and the Citizens of Charleston, Against the Tariff on Woolen Goods," Proposed at the Second Session of the 19th Congress, Charleston, South Carolina (1827).

————. "Political Economy—Rent," *Southern Review* (February, 1828).

————. (Ed.) *Southern Confederacy* (Atlanta). January–April, 1863.

————. (Ed.) *Southern Patriot* (Charleston). 1818–1845.

————. "Supply and Consumption of Cotton, with Tables Annexed of the Supply and Consumption for the Last Thirty Years," *DeBow's Review* (May, 1858).

————. "Supply and Consumption of Cotton, Present Perspective," *DeBow's Review* (April, 1857).

————. "Systems of Banking," *The Southern Review* (April, 1870).

Conger, John L. "South Carolina and the Early Tariffs," *Mississippi Valley Historical Review* (March, 1919).

Conrad, Alfred H., Meyer, John R. "The Economics of Slavery in the Ante-Bellum South," *Journal of Political Economy* (April, 1958).

Dodd, William E. "Contributions of the South to Economic Thought and Writing to 1865," *The South in the Building of the Nation*, V. Richmond, The Southern Historical Publication Society, 1909.

Dowd, Douglas. "A Comparative Analysis of Economic Development in the American West and the South," *Journal of Economic History* (December, 1956).

———. "Communication," *Journal of Political Economy* (October, 1958).

Dunbar, Charles. "Economic Science in America, 1776–1876," *North American Review* (January, 1876).

Durden, Robert F. "J. D. B. De Bow. Convolutions of a Slavery Expansionist," *Journal of Southern History* (November, 1951).

Eaton, Clement. "Slave Hiring in the Upper South; A Step Towards Freedom," *Mississippi Valley Historical Review* (March, 1960).

Fetter, Frank. "Early History of Political Economy in the United States," *American Philosophical Society Proceedings* (July, 1943).

Fleming, Walter. "The Slave Labor System in the Ante-Bellum South," *The South in the Building of the Nation*, V. Richmond, The Southern Historical Publication Society, 1909.

Flisch, Julia A. "The Common People of the Old South," *American Historical Association Report*, I (1908).

Govan, Thomas P. "Was Plantation Slavery Profitable?" *Journal of Southern History* (November, 1942).

Korn, Bertram W. "Jews and Negro Slavery in the Old South, 1789–1865," *Publication of the American Jewish Historical Society* (March, 1961).

Leslie, T. E. Cliff. "Political Economy in the United States," *Fortnightly Review* (October, 1880). Reprinted in the author's *Essays in Political and Moral Philosophy*, 2nd ed. London, Longmans Green, 1888.

Mitchell, Broadus. "Jacob Cardozo," *Encyclopedia of the Social Sciences,* III, 223–24.

Phillips, Ulrich. "The Economics of Slave Labor in the South," *The South in the Building of the Nation,* V. Richmond, The Southern Historical Publication Society, 1909.

———. "Financial Crises in the Ante-Bellum South," *The South in the Building of the Nation,* V. Richmond, The Southern Historical Publication Society, 1909.

Porter, Jonathan. "Cardozo's 'Notes on Political Economy,'" *North American Review* (January, 1827).

Remini, Robert V. "Martin Van Buren and the Tariff of Abominations," *American Historical Review* (July, 1958).

Russel, Robert R. "The General Effects of Slavery upon Southern Economic Progress," *Journal of Southern History* (February, 1938).

Seligman, Edwin R. A. "The Development of Economic Thought in America," *Economic Forum,* I, No. 4 (Fall, 1933).

Simms, William G. "Early Writers of South Carolina," *XIX Century Magazine* (February, 1870).

Spengler, Joseph J. "Population Doctrines in the Ante-Bellum South," *Journal of Southern History* (August, 1936).

Stigler, George J. "Ricardo and the 93% Labor Theory of Value," *American Economic Review* (June, 1958).

Tucker, George. "On the Future Density of the United States," *The Portfolio* (October, 1814).

———. "On Density of Population," *The Portfolio* (August, 1815).

UNPUBLISHED MATERIAL

Bearden, Elizabeth. "The Southern Review." Unpublished master's thesis, Columbia University, 1925.

Ecke, Melvin W. "The Fiscal Aspects of the Panic of 1857." Unpublished doctoral dissertation, Princeton University, 1951.

Evans, Robert, Jr. "The Economics of American Negro Slavery, 1830–1860." Unpublished doctoral dissertation, University of Chicago, 1959–1960.

Fletcher, Hugh M. "History of Economic Theory in the United States, 1820 to 1866." Unpublished doctoral dissertation, University of Illinois, 1926.

Flora, Abram C., Jr. "Jacob N. Cardozo, 1786–1873: South Carolina Economist." Unpublished master's thesis, University of South Carolina, 1949.

Genovese, Eugene. "Limits of Agrarian Reform in the South." Unpublished doctoral dissertation, Columbia University, 1960.

Grampp, William D. "Mercantalism and Laissez Faire in American Political Discussion, 1787–1829." Unpublished doctoral dissertation, University of Chicago, 1944.

Haskins, Ralph W. "The Cotton Factor, 1800–1860: A Study in Southern Economic and Social History." Unpublished doctoral dissertation, University of California, 1950.

Sorrell, Vernon G. "American Economic Writers from Raymond to Carey." Unpublished doctoral dissertation, University of California, 1929.

Todd, Richard C. "A History of Confederate Finance." Unpublished doctoral dissertation, Duke University, 1950.

Index